D1714001

The U.S.–Mexican War

The U.S.–Mexican War

A COMPLETE CHRONOLOGY

Bud Hannings

McFarland & Company, Inc., Publishers
Jefferson, North Carolina

Library of Congress Cataloguing-in-Publication Data

Hannings, Bud.
    The U.S.-Mexican War : a complete chronology /
Bud Hannings.
        p.   cm.
    Includes bibliographical references and index.

    ISBN 978-0-7864-7648-0
    softcover : acid free paper ∞

    1. Mexican War, 1846–1848—Chronology.   I. Title.
    E404.H36 2014
    973.6'2—dc23   2013043759

British Library cataloguing data are available

On the cover: Adolphe Jean-Baptiste Bayot, *Bombardment of
Vera Cruz*, color lithograph, 16¾" × 10¾", 1851

Manufactured in the United States of America

*McFarland & Company, Inc., Publishers
    Box 611, Jefferson, North Carolina 28640
    www.mcfarlandpub.com*

Contents

v

Preface

The U.S.–Mexican War, also known as the Mexican-American War and the Mexican War, took place from 1846 to 1848, and was mainly about control of Texas, though as with most other wars there were also other factors in play. Mexico claimed this territory despite Texas having declared itself a republic years earlier, while the U.S. wished to annex Texas and make it the 28th state.

The U.S.–Mexican War was fought with no allies and was the first offensive war for the United States. The Treaty of Guadalupe Hidalgo that ended the war ceded California, Texas and vast portions of Arizona, New Mexico, Colorado and Wyoming to the United States. Utah and Nevada were also ceded. In return, the United States paid Mexico $18.25 million.

This chronology focuses on the military actions of the war and covers the U.S. annexation of Texas as well as the many Indian incursions before the war. The various campaigns, sieges and skirmishes in both the United States and Mexico, on both land and sea, are covered. The book also deals with the future states of California and New Mexico, but it does not deal with the politics behind the conflict.

Some of the heroes of this war went on to serve in the War of 1812. Many who participated in the U.S.–Mexican War rose to high military office during the Civil War. Many joined the military during the Mexican conflict as enlisted men or as officers. These included such men as Joseph Farmer Knipe (later a Union general), who served as a sergeant with the 2nd Artillery, and U.S. Grant and Robert E. Lee, who went on to lead their respective armies a scant fifteen years later in the war that almost ripped the United States to pieces. The contributions of the individuals who later became generals during the Civil War are also highlighted here. The list of these men is not all-inclusive and it's hard to say if it ever will be.

I have researched the military of the United States from the French and Indian War through the Civil War. Many of the early conflicts were difficult to research, so I am relieved that it has become easier to meet the challenges and overcome the obstacles that I encountered in earlier studies. The records of the U.S.–Mexican War are much better than their predecessors, making the research much easier.

Introduction

Following the American Revolution, Great Britain found that its colonies in America had cast it aside. Many of us, to be candid, take this republic of ours for granted; we're too busy to acknowledge that our present-day existence is the work of colonists who gave or risked their lives to create this place we call home.

Our precious foundations, written on a few small pieces of paper — the Declaration of Independence, the Constitution and the Bill of Rights — have been defended by that distinguished long blue line of Americans, starting at Lexington and Concord, through Bunker Hill, Valley Forge, Tripoli, the Alamo and Gettysburg; changing otherwise common places into hallowed ground.

Their line continued to Belleau Wood, the Meuse-Argonne and Château-Thierry. With relentless fury, they proved to be a unique assembly of the finest people this world could produce. On that infamous day, December 7, 1941, the line was tested again. In those dark moments when the world was stunned and our country was facing insurmountable odds, Americans held firm and pressed forward to ensure our liberty. They proceeded through ominous war clouds over the vast Pacific to Wake Island, Guam, Guadalcanal, and the Philippines.

Who can ever forget the unsung heroes of Iwo Jima or those sacred crosses left behind in Normandy? They answered the call once more in Korea, and again in the jungles of Vietnam, the Middle East and other locales around the globe, brave men and women who cared for more than just themselves.

Refresh your memory, travel through Virginia, the Carolinas, Pennsylvania and Massachusetts. Hear the Patriots speak boldly. Listen to the bell proclaim freedom and follow Old Glory from its birth in 1776 to its present state. Recall "One giant step for mankind" as gallant Americans placed the American flag on the moon. Where will Old Glory fly tomorrow? It is up to you, you are Old Glory. Your dreams are her dreams.

During the 18th century settlement of the New World, the French and Indian War (1754) determined who would dominate America. Great Britain, which fared badly at the onset of the war, would turn events in its favor after 1757. France, sensing imminent disaster, hastily proceeded to Paris to sign a peace treaty with Britain. The most prominent condition of the treaty was that France would relinquish nearly all its North American territory. This made evident that Britain would now control America.

This was not to last. In Richmond, on March 23, 1775, during a stormy session of the Virginia legislature, Patrick Henry spoke boldly: "There is no retreat but in submission in slavery, our chains are formed, their clanking may be heard in the plains of Boston. The war is inevitable, and let it come ... I repeat sir, let it come.... I know not what course others may take, but for me, give me liberty or give me death."

War began in 1775. On July 4, 1776, the Continental Congress adopted the Declaration of Independence. It was signed by John Hancock, the president of the Congress, with additional signatures added gradually. Reconciliation with Britain was now impossible. The conflict continued eight years. On February 4, 1783, Great Britain officially declared an end to the war with the Treaty of Paris. The United States of America had won its independence and accepted its role as a new nation.

Conflicts between the U.S. and Great Britain again festered to the point of war in the 19th century. The War of 1812 ravaged the country for nearly four years before coming to an end with the signing of the Treaty of Ghent. Afterward the United States dealt with Indians at home and piracy. For continuity this book includes entries for this period of history. It continues until the struggles between Texas and Mexico began in the 1830s leading to the independence of Texas and its annexation as a state, which brought about the Mexican War.

The years after the War of 1812 and before the U.S. Civil War would further test the United States. Although the Treaty of Ghent had ended the conflict with Great Britain, the mother country would continue to incite the Indians to create problems as the United States expanded farther west toward the Pacific Coast.

While the United States was engaged in conflicts with the Indians, the possibility of war with England and Spain continued. In 1823, President James Monroe, sensing further encroachment of European powers, issued the Monroe Doctrine, warning Europe not to colonize North America without permission of the United States. This doctrine was especially courageous because the U.S. did not have the real means to prevent foreign colonization; however, the ultimatum worked.

New states were being admitted to the U.S., both free and slave, increasing tension between the North and the South. It seemed inevitable that clashing philosophies must finally provoke civil war. As tensions mounted even further over the fate of Texas, the Texans took matters into their own hands and demanded independence from Mexico. Santa Anna responded by leading an overwhelming army against the defenders of the Alamo. The greatly outnumbered American Texans turned back attack after attack, but on March 6, 1836, after running out of ammunition and lacking reinforcements, those brave men, which included Davey Crockett and Jim Bowie, were slaughtered. Santa Anna, after crushing the defenders, ordered their bodies soaked in oil, stacked and burned.

Another such brutal massacre occurred at Goliad, where more than 300 Texans surrendered to Santa Anna as prisoners of war, only to be lined up and shot. These events caused the Texans to rally behind Sam Houston, who defeated the Mexicans and captured Santa Anna at San Jacinto. Their inspirational battle cry was "Remember the Alamo."

The Mexican atrocities caused outrage in the United States, moved Texas closer to statehood, and put the United States on a collision course with Mexico. The United States was anticipating war in October 1842 when Commodore Thomas Catesby Jones impulsively invaded and captured Monterey, raising the Stars and Stripes, only to discover no war had started. Apologetically and quite embarrassed, the Americans lowered the flag and sailed off.

In March 1845, Mexico broke diplomatic ties with the U.S. The United States reacted by sending Zachary Taylor into Corpus Christi to protect Texas. An American cavalry unit under the command of Captain Thornton was surrounded by Mexicans. After unsuccessful attempts to break away, the Americans surrendered. Santa Anna had some of the prisoners shot. This action initiated war.

The war with Mexico proved to be a testing ground for leaders in the coming Civil War. Many like Beauregard, Lee, McClellan, Grant and Sherman all participated. This was the first war in which West Pointers offered primary contributions, yet once again showed that European battle plans would not work in America.

The American army moved swiftly. General Taylor's men decisively defeated a Mexican army three times larger than their own at Palo Alto and on the following day at Resaca de la Palma.

On another front, Colonel Stephen Kearny moved from Fort Leavenworth with 1,500 frontiersmen heading for Santa Fe, capturing Las Vegas and San Miguel along the way. On August 17, 1846, Colonel Kearny entered Santa Fe unopposed and raised the American flag.

During June 1846, California proclaimed its independence from Mexico. On July 7, 1846, Commodore John Sloat arrived in Monterey to claim California for the United States; however, Mexican rebels subsequently revolted and took control of southern California from Los Angeles to San Diego, holding it until January 1847, when Colonel Kearny retook Los Angeles to end rebel opposition.

As these campaigns were being fought, General Winfield Scott was fast approaching Mexico City. On March 7, 1847, General Scott launched America's first large amphibious attack with 10,000 men, landing unopposed three miles outside of Vera Cruz. The siege of Vera Cruz succeeded with the capture of the fortress on March 29. General Scott's troops thrust forward, winning additional battles at Cerro Gordo, Jalapa and Puebla.

American troops continued their victorious march toward Mexico City, capturing Contreras and Churubusco. American artillery and infantry had proven themselves on the battlefield and their morale was escalating. General Zachary Taylor was continuing his victories, including the capture of Monterrey, Mexico, with the fall of its near-invincible citadel included.

On August 24, 1847, Santa Anna and General Scott agreed to an armistice, but on September 6, Santa Anna rejected the United States' demand for settlement. Scott wasted no time, positioning his troops for an attack on Mexico City.

On September 8, 1847, the Americans twice attacked the Mexican stronghold of Molino del Rey, but it held. Finally, Scott's artillery leveled the fortress, allowing the American cavalry to successfully charge and break through the Mexican defenses. This attack was followed by the successful assault of Chapultepec ("Halls of Montezuma") that brought the United States to the gates of the city. It was on September 14, 1847, that General Winfield Scott triumphantly marched into Mexico City. The United States and Mexico formally signed the Treaty of Guadalupe Hidalgo, ending the Mexican War on February 2, 1848.

This conflict was fought with no allies and was the first offensive war for the United States. The treaty signed purely ceded California, Texas, vast portions of Arizona, New Mexico, Colorado and Wyoming to the United States. Utah and Nevada were also ceded. In return, the United States paid Mexico $18.25 million.

THE CHRONOLOGY

1816

March 4   James Monroe is inaugurated as the fifth president of the United States. He is remembered best for his policy against foreign colonization of the United States, the Monroe Doctrine.

April 24   Thomas Jefferson writes to DuPont de Nemours: "Enlighten the people generally and tyranny and oppression of body and mind will vanish like evil spirits at the dawn of day."

July 27   The United States sends a detachment of troops to destroy Fort Apalachicola in Florida, which is harboring runaway slaves and hostile Indians.

August 27   In Mexico, there are no present hostilities between the United States and Spain, but Spanish guns from an armada off the coast of Vera Cruz commence firing on the American vessel *Firebrand* as it sails past the Spanish fleet.

September   The cadets at West Point receive gray uniforms to honor the regulars who had worn gray at the battles of Chippewa and Lundy's Lane. West Point still wears this color uniform and its cadets are referred to as "The Long Gray Line."

December 11   Indiana is admitted to the Union as the 19th state.

1817

February 9   Andrew Jackson arrives at Fort Hawkins, Georgia.

March 3   The Mississippi Territory is subdivided, part forming a new territory, the Alabama Territory.

March 16   Jackson halts his march at the mouth of the Apalachicola River. He orders the Corps of Engineers under Lieutenant James Gadsden to construct a fort, to become known as Fort Gadsden.

April 7   Jackson's troops capture the Spanish Fort at St. Marks. Jackson imprisons a man named Alexander Arbuthnot for inciting Indians against the United States. Arbuthnot, a British citizen, is tried and executed.

September 27   The United States

9

signs a treaty with the Ohio Indians. The Indians cede four million acres to the United States.

November Seminole Indians raid settlements on the Florida-Georgia border, retaliating against the destruction of Fort Apalachicola. They massacre 34 of 40 men, women and children on an Army keel boat.

December 10 Mississippi is admitted to the Union as the 20th state. The Mississippi Territory is divided, with the western portion becoming a state and the eastern section designated by Congress as the Territory of Alabama.

December 23 A combined operation including the Army, Navy and Marines tightens the noose on the pirates holding Amelia Island, Florida. The operation, which includes the contingents of six naval vessels, compels the pirates to surrender the facility.

December 26 General Andrew Jackson takes command of the expeditionary force in Florida.

1818

April 4 In Washington, D.C., Congress designates the American flag to remain 13-striped, with the addition only of stars for newly acquired states. President James Monroe signs the bill this day. The man most widely known for his persistence in getting this bill passed was Peter Wendover, a New York congressman. The man who suggested the change was Captain Samuel Reid of the U.S. Navy, commander of the *General Armstrong* in the War of 1812. The law read: "An Act to Establish the Flag of the United States: Section I. Be it enacted, etc; that from and after the 4th Day of July next, the Flag of the United States be 13 horizontal stripes, alternate red and white; that the Union have 20 stars, white in a blue field. Section II. Be it further enacted, that on the admission of every new state into the Union, one star be added to the Union of the Flag, and that such addition shall take effect on the fourth of July next succeeding such admission."

May 24 General Andrew Jackson's forces capture the Spanish garrison at Pensacola, Florida, to end the Seminole Wars. Jackson deports the Spaniards to Havana.

August 19 In Oregon Territory, the United States, in an effort to bolster the position of its claim on territory, has a conspicuous flag raising ceremony. It is attended by many, including the crew of the USS *Ontario*, which pulls to the dock on the Columbia River at the ceremonial location.

October 19 The Chickasaw Indians sign a peace treaty with the United States ceding their land between the Mississippi River and the Northern Tennessee River area.

December 3 Illinois is admitted to the Union as the 21st state.

1819

The War of 1812 has been over since the formal signing of the Treaty of Ghent, but in the aftermath of the conflict, piracy has become popular in certain areas of the United States. Pirates, including Lafitte, who had aided Andrew Jackson, return to the old ways. The Caribbean is infested with vessels flying the skull and crossbones. The United States, armed with information that Venezuela is giving many of these ships papers claiming registration in that country, dispatches the U.S. Navy to verify the information. Out of the visit comes a treaty with Venezuela. The treaty is obtained by the efforts of Captain Oliver Hazard Perry, who makes the voyage in bad health. The deadly "yellow fever" strikes him and he succumbs before arriving back in the United States.

February   **In Florida,** captured forts are returned to the Spanish and negotiations lead to Florida being ceded to the United States. This is accomplished by the Adams-Onis Treaty.

March 2   Arkansas is formed as a U.S. territory.

August 23   Commodore Oliver H. Perry (the hero of Lake Erie) dies on his birthday.

December 14   Alabama is admitted to the Union as the 22nd state.

1820

Archibald Henderson, at age 38, becomes the youngest ever commandant of the Marine Corps. Henderson is known for a phrase he coined: "Take care to be right, and then they are powerless." Legend has it when Commandant Henderson was departing with two battalions of Marines to fight the Indians in 1836, he left this message on his office door: "Gone to fight the Indians. Will be back when the war is over."

March 15   Maine is admitted to the Union as the 23rd state.

April   The USS *Cyane,* a corvette, captures seven slave runner ships in the waters of the west coast of Africa.

October   The United States deploys three ships to waters off the South American coast to be in position to protect American commerce during an ongoing local revolt against the Spanish rule. They remain on duty until May 1822.

1821

February 19   The treaty known as the Adams-Onis Treaty, signed during February between the United States and Spain, is ratified by the U.S. Senate.

March 5   James Monroe is inaugurated to his second term as president. He was initially inaugurated on 4 March 1817.

March 22   Stephen Decatur, U.S. Naval hero of Tripoli, dies.

July 17   The Floridas are ceded to the United States by Spain.

August 10   Missouri is admitted to the Union as the 24th state.

October   In Cuba, the United States Navy is at war with no nation at this time but is still busy because of various problems, including pirates. During October, the USS *Enterprise*, a brigantine, moves into the vicinity of Cape Antonio and seizes five pirate vessels. The *Enterprise* confiscates another vessel on December 21.

1822

January   A Dutch sloop that had been captured by pirates and is flying the skull and crossbones is overtaken and captured by the brigantine USS *Spark* after a confrontation in the West Indies. The U.S. Navy is scattered around the Caribbean attempting to expel piracy and will patrol the waters for some time. In December of 1822 the United States will fortify its efforts by creating a special squadron for that purpose.

March 30   The Territory of Florida is formed.

May 5   Captain Thomas Truxton, U.S. Navy hero of the Revolutionary War and Quasi-War, dies.

May 8   General John Stark, hero of the Battle of Bennington, dies.

September 3   The Fox and Sauk Indians agree to live on federal lands in Illinois and the Wisconsin Territory after signing a treaty.

December 22   The West Indies Squadron of the United States Navy is

established by an act of Congress in a concentrated effort to eradicate piracy from the Mediterranean Sea. Commodore James Biddle leads this aggressive armada which includes the sloops *John Adams, Cyane, Hornet* and the *Peacock.* The armada also contains the frigates *Congress* and *Macedonian* in addition to many smaller armed vessels.

The ships venture into the Caribbean and begin to clear the sea lanes, and the pirates flee to the shallow waters out of harm's way. The fleet is supplemented during 1823 when Captain Porter comes with an improvised fleet capable of wading the shallow waters to exterminate the pirates who have been ravaging shipping on the high seas. This campaign to end piracy becomes difficult, as the American squadron has to fight island diseases as well as buccaneers. The campaign is successful but wearisome. The Americans consistently assault the bases of the pirates and from the time of the Congressional Order until 1830, well over fifty pirate vessels are destroyed. The Americans extinguish piracy in the Caribbean permanently by the time Civil War erupts in the United States.

December 2 In Washington, D.C., President James Monroe issues the Monroe Doctrine, warning foreign nations to stay out of the Western hemisphere. There is much concern about countries of the Old World establishing colonies. Monroe issues an ultimatum forbidding colonization without permission of the United States. This is a courageous statement, as the United States is really not strong enough at this time to enforce the ultimatum, but it somehow persists. It reads, in part: "The American continents by the free and independent condition which they have assumed, are henceforth not to be considered as subject for future colonization by any European power."

1824

November In Puerto Rico, the United States reacts to an incident by dispatching Commodore Porter's fleet to Fajardo. Porter goes ashore with a contingent of Marines to retaliate for an insult to the American flag.

November 14 In Puerto Rico, two U.S. naval vessels, the *Beagle* and *Grampus*, enter the harbor at Fajardo Bay to demand an apology from the Spanish for an insult to an American naval officer and the American flag a few weeks before. Captain David Porter notes two Spanish cannons directed at his ships and promptly dispatches Marines to knock out the guns. The assault team scales the 80 foot cliff without opposition and destroys the firing mechanisms of the guns. The 14 man squad moves rapidly to join the main force of approximately 200 Marines and sailors who landed near a main road and begin to approach the town of Fajardo under a white flag. The Spanish defenders offer the Americans an apology and shortly thereafter, the Americans depart.

Captain Porter is suspended from duty for a period of six months after a hearing on the 12 July 1825. The court-martial board which suspends Porter simultaneously commends him for his competence against the pirates operating in the West Indies. Captain Porter, rejecting the outcome of the court-martial board, feeling it too harsh a punishment, decides to resign from the Navy. Porter subsequently becomes the commander of all Mexican naval forces and serves in that capacity until 1829, when he returns to the U.S. to become the consul general to the Barbary Coast countries.

1825

January 20 The U.S. has maintained a naval presence in the Mediterranean since the Barbary Wars when the American Navy established itself as a power to be reckoned with.

The armadas are necessary to insure freedom of the seas for merchant vessels. The squadron has been bolstered because of a conflict between the British and Algerians during 1824 and because of piracy in the area near the Grecian Archipelago. The Americans are simultaneously working out a treaty with Turkey during this time.

February 12 Creek Indian Chief William McIntosh signs the Treaty of Indian Springs in Georgia. This treaty cedes all Creek Territory in Georgia to the United States. Chief McIntosh is killed by the other Creeks, who think he has betrayed them.

March 4 John Quincy Adams is inaugurated as sixth president of the United States.

1826

January 24 Creek Indians sign a new treaty with the United States, allowing them to keep more land than stated in the Treaty of Indian Springs.

July 4 Two former presidents of the United States die on this day, the 50th anniversary of the Declaration of Independence, which had been signed in 1776 initiating the American Revolution. They are John Adams (age 91) and Thomas Jefferson (age 83).

1827

November 15 The Creek Indians cede the balance of their Western Georgia lands to the United States.

1829

March 4 General Andrew Jackson, the hero of the Battle of New Orleans of 1815, is inaugurated as seventh president of the United States.

March 23 President Andrew Jackson issues an ultimatum to the Creek Indians; either conform to the laws of Alabama or move across the Mississippi River.

May 19 A treaty of peace is agreed upon between the U.S. and Brazil. The treaty emphasizes commerce, friendship and navigation rights.

July 29 The Indian tribes Chippewa, Ottawa and Potawatomi cede lands to the United States.

1830

May 7   A treaty is signed between the U.S. and Turkey which gives the U.S. free access to navigation in the Black Sea.

June 30   Chief Black Hawk agrees to relocate his Fox and Sauk tribes west of the Mississippi River.

September 15   The Treaty of Dancing Rabbit Creek forces the Choctaw Indians to cede almost 8 million acres east of the Mississippi River to the United States.

1831

January   The *Friendship*, an American merchant vessel, enters the harbor at Quallah Battoo, Sumatra, to receive a cargo of pepper. As the crew waits, a band of Malay pirates storm the vessel and massacre many of the crew and seize the vessel. President Andrew Jackson will subsequently dispatch the USS *Potomac* to retaliate.

July 4   James Monroe, the fifth president of the United States, dies.

1832

January 1   The USS *Lexington*, having been dispatched previously to the vicinity of the Falkland Islands off the coast of Argentina, South America, sends a contingent of Marines and sailors ashore to insure the protection of Americans on the islands.

February 5–6   The USS *Potomac* sails into Sumatra to avenge the murders of American seamen; two American Navy men were killed, 11 wounded. The natives suffer 150 killed. The USS *Potomac*, which earlier received orders to set sail for China, actually departed New York several months before, heading for the Indian Ocean to avenge the atrocities against the merchant vessel *Friendship*, captured by Malay pirates the previous year.

Within five miles of Quallah Battoo the *Potomac* anchors leisurely, posing as a lucrative Danish East Indian vessel, but during the early morning hours of February 6, the Americans display their true intent. Landing boats are dropped into the sea and 280 Marines and sailors zip silently toward the four enemy forts protecting the village. The defenders are greeted by the first rays of sunshine coupled with four separate assault teams. The fighting is vicious as the Americans push forward. In short order, the strongholds fall. The Marines, outnumbered at Tuko de Lima, crash through the walls knocking out the cannons and forcing the enemy to scatter.

The last remaining obstacle, Fort Duramund, is assaulted by sailors and Marines who charge through the smoke-filled village, seizing the fort in a flash. The Malays who fled to the jungle watch as their forts and village burn in retaliation for the assault against the vessel *Friendship*. The victorious Americans are back on board the *Potomac* by 10 A.M. They take time to solemnly bury one seaman and two Marines who fell during the battle. Before departing the following morning, the *Potomac*, with the Stars and Stripes in full view, moves close to the shores of Quallah Battoo and commences firing its deadly long range 32-pounders, leaving the Malays with a final reminder of the visit.

March 24   The Creek Indians cede all their lands east of the Mississippi River to the United States.

April 6 BLACK HAWK WAR   Chief Black Hawk, in a futile attempt to regain the lands of his tribe, begins raids into the Wisconsin Territory. The conflict lasts until August 2.

May 9   A group of Seminole chiefs cede their lands in Florida to the United States and relocate west of the Mississippi River.

July 10   In Washington, D.C., Congress authorizes the building of Naval Hospitals in Brooklyn, New York and Pensacola, Florida.

August 2 BLACK HAWK WAR   The Illinois militia and Regulars commanded by Colonel Henry Atkinson defeat the Indians under Chief Black Hawk, ending the Black Hawk War. General Scott, U.S. Army, arrives on August 7 with reinforcements.

September 21   Chief Black Hawk, who manages to escape from the Illinois Militia, surrenders on August 27, 1832. His tribes, the Fox and Sauk, sign another treaty agreeing to remain west of the Mississippi.

December 18   A treaty regarding commerce and navigation is reached between the United States and Russia.

1833

March 4   Andrew Jackson is inaugurated to his second term as president.

October 31   *In naval activity,* U.S. ships are still in the vicinity of the Falkland Islands and Argentina, South America. A contingent of Marines and sailors are debarked at Buenos Aires, Argentina, to insure the well-being of American citizens in the area during a period of unrest.

1834

July 3   In Massachusetts, a figurehead of President Jackson is placed on the USS *Constitution* at the Charlestown Navy Yard; however, during the night, someone secretly boards *Old Ironsides* and beheads "Old Hickory." Anti-Democrats simultaneously complain and demand a different figurehead for the vessel.

July 7   Joseph Dana Webster (later a Union general) joins the army at the rank of 2nd lieutenant. He becomes a topographical engineer and serves for the duration of the Mexican war. In July 1849 he is promoted to first lieutenant.

1835

January 30   In Washington, D.C., President Jackson survives an assassination attempt. Richard Lawrence fires two pistols at the president; both misfire. Lawrence is subsequently admitted to an insane asylum.

May   In Washington, D.C., due to a directive by President Andrew Jackson during his second term, the army and Marines are instructed to begin changing their uniforms back to the styles worn during the Revolutionary War. This change was based on tradition and Jackson's strong belief in a positive image of the military. The Marines are finally in receipt of their new uniforms and are "Changing Back to the Green" while stationed aboard the USS *Brandywine* off the coast of Valparaiso, Chile. The sloops *Fairfield* and *Vincennes* and two additional schooners have been on patrol in the Pacific for almost a year when they meet the supply ship transporting their new attire

June 30   In Texas, tensions continue to mount between the Texans and Santa Anna. Santa Anna intends to rule over the Mexicans and Texans while the Texans are readying their independence. Fort Anahuac, garrisoned by Mexican troops, is overpowered by Texans, led by Colonel William B. Travis. During the fall, an outbreak of violence develops between the Texans and Mexican cavalry in the vicinity of Gonzales. By the early part of 1836 Santa Anna mobilizes an enormous army to stamp out the insurrection and marches on the Alamo.

October 2   In Texas, the Texans have been ordered previously by the Mexican government to abandon their cannon, used primarily against hostile Indian attacks. The Texans, quite reluctant to abide by this ultimatum, find themselves staring down a Mexican force of dragoons, intent on forcibly seizing the cannon at Gonzalez. Out of the fog, the Mexicans receive a pugnacious response which startles the dragoons. One volley of the coveted cannons and the dragoons turn about and retreat. This becomes the first step in the movement for independence from Mexico.

December 5–9   In Texas, Texans marching into the Mexican stronghold of San Antonio assault the enemy fortifications and for three days, a vicious close combat battle ensues. Finally, on the night of December 8, the Texans drive the Mexicans under General Cos to surrender and agree to terms. The

Mexicans depart on the 25th, Christmas Day, withdrawing across the Rio Grande, leaving all the supplies and artillery to the Texans. It is not over for Texas, rather just beginning, as Santa Anna is about to send a massive army to destroy the Alamo.

December 15   In Texas, American Texans profess their intent to secede from Mexico.

December 28   In Florida, the Seminoles under Osceola slay approximately 110 American soldiers marching from Fort Brooke to Fort King. Only two men under Major Francis Dade survive the massacre. In other activity, hostile Indians attack a contingent of American troops at Withlacoochee. Approximately 40 Indians are slain.

December 29   A treaty is signed by the Cherokee Indian tribe to cede all their lands east of the Mississippi to the United States.

1836

January 3   In Texas, a resolution from American settlers in Texas is dispatched to Mexico City via Stephen Austin. The purpose of the resolution is to request annexation to the United States. The request is turned down and the courier detained in prison.

January 20   A peace treaty is signed between the U.S. and Venezuela.

January 21   In Washington, D.C., President Jackson's order sends General Scott to assume command of all forces in the area near Texas. Scott finally arrives at his headquarters at St. Augustine, Florida, on February 22, 1847, after stops in South Carolina and Georgia.

January 22   In Florida, U.S. naval vessels, including the *Constellation*, arrive at Fort Brooke (Tampa Bay) to bolster the defenses and prepare against additional Indian attacks such as the massacre of December 1835. The Marines subsequently depart with the soldiers to track and kill as many Indians as they can locate. The campaign force returns during early April after a few skirmishes with the Indians. The swamplands of Florida make it difficult to deal with the Indians.

February 23 to March 6   In Texas, Mexican President Santa Anna, with an army of over 3,000 men, leads an attack on the Alamo. The gallant defenders — including Davy Crockett, Jim Bowie and William Travis, outnumbered by more than 20 to 1— refuse to capitulate to the hordes of Mexican troops that have the mission surrounded. The defenders hold out spectacularly, neutralizing the superior numbered enemy with accurate marksmanship and stamina. The savage attacks are repulsed continually as the walls of the mission are pummeled with artillery. The defenders, waiting reinforcement, see their ammunition depleting at an alarming rate. Finally the bastion is overwhelmed on March 6 in a brutal attack by Santa Anna's army. These valiant men refuse to strike the colors. They give their lives in extraordinary fashion with the fire of liberty flashing from their rifles. As the last shots are fired, the Alamo falls on March 6, but the memory of these men lives on. From this battle came the slogan "Remember the Alamo," the famous Texas battle cry.

After the fall of the outpost, Santa Anna stacks the bodies of the defenders, soaks them with oil, and sets them afire. The Texans subsequently raise enough men to fight Santa Anna. The Texans win a major victory at San Jacinto on April 21.

March 1   In Texas, during the early morning darkness, a valiant contingent of 32 volunteers creep through Mexican lines and reach the Alamo. No other men arrive to aid the struggle against Santa Anna's siege.

March 2   Texas adopts a declaration of independence from Mexico.

March 4   The Texans, having declared independence, appoint Sam Houston as commander of the army.

March 5   In Texas, Colonel Travis informs the defenders of the Alamo the cause is lost and suggests choices: "Surrender, attempt to escape, stay and fight." One man chooses to escape and does so. The rest accept their destiny and prepare for the worst. The following day, in a futile one-sided battle, the Alamo falls after an hour and a half of furious combat to Santa Anna, who is unmerciful. One of the survivors, Susana Dickenson, recounted her husband's plea: "Great God, Sue! The Mexicans are inside our walls! … If they spare you, save my child."

March 17   Texas adopts a constitution.

March 27   Texans, under the command of Captain James Fannin, defending Goliad are devastated by Mexican troops under Santa Anna. (The Americans had surrendered as prisoners of war to Mexican General Urrea. Santa Anna countermands General Urrea's order, and directs more than 300 men be shot.)

April 20   In Washington, D.C., the Wisconsin Territory is established by Congress. It is acquired from the western part of the Michigan Territory.

April 21 THE BATTLE OF SAN JACINTO Texans rally behind General Sam Houston, beating the Mexicans decisively at San Jacinto and capturing Santa Anna during the battle. The Texans got their revenge as Mexicans are saying "Me no Alamo," "Me no Goliad."

May 19   Approximately 100 Comanches raid the Texas settlement of Parker's Fort in Limestone County, Texas. John Parker is savagely mutilated (his genitals ripped out) and scalped. Granny Parker is tied to the ground, lanced and raped. Five people are killed and five women and children are kidnapped. The two women captives, Elizabeth Kellogg and Rachel Plummer, are the first known white women taken captive by Comanches. Both were raped that night in full view of the three children.

May 24   In Washington, D.C., Colonel Archibald Henderson, commandant of the Marine Corps, reports to the War Department in compliance with an agreement reached between himself and President Andrew Jackson to lend the assistance of the available Marines to fight the Indians in the southeastern states. Colonel Henderson posts a sign on his office in Washington and departs on 10 May with the 1st Battalion of Marines. Henderson arrives in Columbus, Georgia, on 23 June, where his Marines begin supporting the army fighting the Creeks in the area.

June 15   Arkansas is admitted to the Union as the 25th state.

September   Texans vote affirmatively on annexation by the United States.

October 22   Sam Houston is inaugurated as the first president of the Republic of Texas. He won the election in a landslide victory over Stephen F. Austin on September 5. Although Texas is a republic, there is strong sentiment among the Texans to become a state.

1837

January 26   Michigan is admitted to the Union as the 26th state.

January 27   In Florida, a contingent of U.S. soldiers and Marines led by Colonel A. Henderson clash with the Indians in the vicinity of Hatchee-Lustee. The confrontation culminates with one of the few victories against these elusive Indians who thrive in the swamps. An agreement is signed during March concluding a settlement of sorts with the Seminoles. A bona fide treaty has never been signed with the Seminoles ending the war, but this agreement authorized by General Jesup, commanding general of the Army of the South, supposedly ended the hostilities.

March 4   In Washington, D.C., Martin Van Buren is inaugurated as the eighth president of the United States.

March 6   The Seminoles agree to move from their tribal lands in Florida to locations west of the Mississippi. Osceola, their chief, convinces them

to resist, prompting U.S. troops under General Jesup to seize Osceola and confine him in prison at Fort Moultrie, where he will remain until his death.

April 16   In naval activity, the USS *Natchez* intercepts a Mexican war ship off the coast of Brazos de Santiago and seizes the vessel in retaliation for the Mexican seizure of two merchantmen.

July 20   Mexico, since its independence from Spain, had to find ways of increasing its treasury. American citizens who used Mexican ports were imprisoned and their boats seized. A special messenger is dispatched to Mexico requesting redress for Americans who have been affected by the government of Mexico. The Mexican government responds on the 29th: "Anxious wish not to delay the moment of that final and equitable adjustment which is to terminate the existing difficulties between the two governments" that "nothing should be left undone which may contribute to the most speedy and equitable determination of the subjects which have so seriously engaged the attention of the American government; that the Mexican government would adopt, as the only guides for its conduct, the plainest principles of public right, the sacred obligations imposed by international law and the religious faith of treaties;" and that "whatever justice and reason may dictate respecting each case will be done."

December 5   In Washington, D.C., President Martin Van Buren, in response to the Mexicans ignoring the U.S. attempts for redress, issues the following:

> Although the large number [of our demands for redress,] and many of them aggravated cases of personal wrongs, have been now for years before the Mexican government, and some of the causes of national complaint, and those of the most offensive character, admitted of immediate, simple, and satisfactory replies, it is only within a few days past that any specific communication in answer to your last demand, made five months ago, has been received from the Mexican minister. For not one of our public complaints has satisfaction been given or offered; that but one of the cases of personal wrong has been favorably considered, and that but four cases of both descriptions, out of all those formally presented and earnestly pressed have as yet been decided upon by the Mexican government. On a careful and deliberate examination of the contents [of the correspondence with the Mexican government] and considering the spirit manifested by the Mexican government, it has become my painful

duty to return the subject as it now stands, to Congress, to whom it belongs, to decide upon the time, the mode, and the measure of redress.

December 25 Battle of Lake Okeechobee (Battle of Grassy Lake) Colonel Zachary Taylor departs from Fort Basinger with about 800 troops in search of Seminoles and Miccosukee Indians. Taylor has been informed that his troops are in a section of Florida that is Indian-controlled and they are waiting on the Americans to ambush them. Captured Indians have also told them that the Seminoles intend to fight to the death. The Missouri regiment was to start the engagement, supported by the 6th Regiment and a small detachment of Delaware Indians. The signal is given and the Americans attack, but they are stuck by devastating fire by Indians holding concealed positions. The fire causes them to panic and withdraw right through the formation of the 6th Regiment.

The officers of the 6th Regiment immediately charge the Seminoles as best they can, cutting through the mud and saw grass. But the charge, heroic as it is, takes the lives of Lt. Colonel Alexander R. Thompson and Captain Joseph Van Swearingen. Lieutenant Walker is hit five times but survives.

Taylor's 1st Regiment comes up and, supported by the 4th, they push the Seminoles from their concealed positions and into the swamp, where they disappear. The Americans take high casualties, including Colonel Richard Gentry, commander of the Missouri Regiment.

1838

January In Washington, D.C., President Van Buren instructs American citizens not to violate American neutrality laws and particularly emphasizes that they are forbidden from assisting Canadians in a state of rebellion against the British government. The insurrection of the Canadian rebels is short-lived and ends by mid-October.

May 15 Colonel Taylor, recently promoted to brigadier general, succeeds General Jesup as commander of the army in Florida.

June 12 The Territory of Iowa is formed from portions of Wisconsin Territory. In other activity, Andrew Jackson Smith (later Union general) graduates from West Point at about this time. He is appointed as lieutenant of the 1st Dragoons and for the next 23 years he serves in the West. At the outbreak of the Civil War, he was commissioned colonel of the 2nd Cal-

ifornia cavalry, but declined the appointment. He afterward becomes chief of cavalry under General Henry Halleck.

July 23 All shore Marines have departed Florida and have been dispersed or returned to Washington. A substantial number of Marines remain on board ships in Florida waters as part of the Florida Squadron, the "Mosquito Fleet."

August 19 In naval activity, in an unusual voyage, three American vessels depart Hampton Roads, Virginia, embarking on a venture known as the Wilkes Expedition. The vessels *Peacock*, *Porpoise* and *Vincennes*, sail into the South Pacific to the Fiji Islands and the Gilberts, not returning home until July 1842.

October 12 Texas withdraws its request for annexation to the United States.

1839

January 2 The USS *John Adams* sends a landing party of Marines and sailors ashore to protect Americans on the island of Muckie, Sumatra. Another contingent of Marines and sailors attached to the USS *Columbia* debark later in the day to bolster forces already there.

April 11 In Washington, D.C., in the capital, a convention of delegates is selected for the purpose of "the ad-

justment of claims of citizens of the United States of America upon the government of the Mexican republic." In conjunction, the convention does not get organized until August 1840.

May General Macomb holds a council with the Indians. He is of the opinion that a peace had been concluded; however, on 23 July they attack Colonel Harney's command of 28 men at Charlotte's Harbor. Colonel Harney loses more than one-half of his command.

September 25   France signs a peace treaty with the Republic of Texas.

November 11   Virginia initiates the Virginia Military Institute, the first state-supported military college. In 1851, Thomas Jonathan (later Stonewall) Jackson becomes a teacher of natural philosophy at the institute, located in Lexington, Virginia. He remains there until 1861, when he takes up arms for the Confederacy.

1840

March 9   Mook-War-Ruh and twelve other Comanche war chiefs arrive in San Antonio with their families for a peace parley. They return two captives, including one brutalized woman, Matilda Lockhart. Her nose had been burnt to the bone, both nostrils wide open and denuded of flesh. She had also been sexually abused. The Texans demand release of all other captives and hold the chiefs. A fight starts as the Indians attempt to escape. This encounter is known as the Council House Fight. Sixty-five Indians are killed during the confrontation.

March 26   A woman held captive by the Comanches, Mrs. Webster, steals a Comanche horse and escapes with one of her children from the Comanche camp, arriving at San Antonio. Booker Webster, her son, and one five-year-old child, survive. All other white captives were "skinned, sliced and horribly mutilated, finally being burned to death." (This disaster was described by Booker Webster.)

April 16   The USS *Otsego*, patrolling off the east coast of Florida, waits offshore as a detachment of Marines and sailors engages a band of Indians for several hours.

May 1   General Taylor, who requested to be transferred earlier in the year, on this day is relieved of duty in Florida. He is later transferred to Louisiana and from there he is dispatched to the Rio Grande.

July 12   The U.S. Navy, performing its operation in concert with the Wilkes Expedition, experiences difficulties with a detachment that has gone ashore at Sualib Bay, Fiji Islands. Marines and sailors are dispatched expeditiously from the USS *Peacock* and *Vincennes* to take retaliatory measures against the natives who attack the expedition. Another retaliatory raid occurs on 26 July.

August   In Washington, D.C., the convention of delegates established in April 1839 finally gets organized. By the terms of the convention, their duties are to end within eighteen months. Nevertheless, it takes four months to cover the preliminaries. During December 1840, the main subject was taken up. The claims were at that time found to be so numerous that it would be impossible to take then all up before the convention is scheduled to dissolve (February 1842).

August 4   Comanches under Buffalo Hump bypass San Antonio with a war party of over 1,000 braves. The Texas Rangers, led by Ben McCulloch, follow their trail, sending riders in all directions to raise a militia force, which pursues them for their actions.

August 6   The Comanches encircle the town of Victoria, Texas, and massacre several people on the outskirts; however, the town is able to blockade the streets, preventing total disaster. The Indians fear house-to-house fighting and retreat, taking with them 2,000 horses and mules.

August 7   Buffalo Hump's warriors move swiftly, leaving death and destruction as they raid along Peach Creek toward the gulf.

August 8   Comanches are off to raid Linville, Texas (near San Antonio). The savages take captive Daniel Boone's granddaughter, Mrs. Crosby, kill her baby and throw her over a horse for their later pleasure. Most of the other settlers in Linville escape to safety to wait in boats. The Indians loot and burn the town.

The Texas Rangers arrive as Linville is being burned. McCulloch, having picked up additional men, now leads a force of over 100. He pushes on toward the coast, pursuing Buffalo Hump.

August 10–12   Texans from all over are converging on Plum Creek, knowing Buffalo Hump and his braves must cross at that point. Tonkawa Chief Placido and 14 warriors join the Texans as scouts. The Texans devastate the Comanches, pursuing them for 15

miles toward Austin, Texas. The Indians tie their captives to trees as they flee, filling the Texans with arrows.

October 1840   Vengeful Texans under Colonel John M. Moore, on the trail of the Comanches since the Battle of Plum Creek, finally discover a Comanche camp near the Red Fork of the Colorado. In revenge for the Linville massacre they attack, killing Indians at will. The Indians lose approximately 130, including women and children. The Texans suffer one fatality.

November 13   Great Britain signs a treaty with the Republic of Texas. The treaty is commercial in nature, but recognizes Texas as a nation.

December   In Washington, D.C., the convention established during April 1839 to get satisfaction for American citizens from the Mexican government finally brings the main subject into discussion. The number of accredited claims as noted by the convention amounted to more than $2 million. In the meantime, the claims ran up to more than $9 million and there were more $3 million was given to the convention before it dissolved (February 1842).

December 31   Marines and sailors attached to the Florida Squadron are assigned to the army to assist in an operation which is to venture into the Florida Everglades to attack Indian villages. The expedition will return to their base in November 1841 without ever seeing any Indians.

1841

February 25 The United States Exploring Expedition in the South Pacific has encountered additional problems with the natives on the islands. A contingent of approximately 70 men, including Marines and sailors, are debarked at Upolu, Samoa, where they land and torch three villages in retaliation for the natives having murdered an American sailor. On April 6 American Marines and sailors land at Drummond's Island (Gilberts), known as Tabiteuea to the natives, and attempt to rescue a missing sailor. The Americans, upon receiving opposition and no attempt by the natives to release the sailor, burn two villages. The Americans return to the ships without the sailor.

March 4 William Henry Harrison is inaugurated as ninth president of the United States. He dies of pneumonia on April 4. Vice President John Tyler is sworn in on 6 April as the tenth president.

1842

February In the capital, the convention that was selected to get claims against the Mexican government settled is dissolved. The convention anticipated that it would receive more than $2 million. However, the American claims that were not considered amounted to more than $3 million. The sum was acknowledged by the Mexican government; however, it also requested a postponement, to which the convention agreed.

June 20 The U.S. Navy disbands the Florida Squadron, which has been on duty during and after the Indian difficulties, which occurred at Fort Brooke, Florida, in 1835. Navy personnel, including Marines, are reassigned to Norfolk, Virginia. The Florida Indian campaign will be officially terminated on 14 August 1842 without benefit of a peace treaty.

June 25 General Alexander Macomb, commander-in-chief of the Army, dies.

August The Senate ratifies the recently negotiated treaty between the U.S. and Great Britain concerning boundary disputes over each ones North American possessions. The treaty was negotiated by Daniel Webster and Lord Ashburton.

August 9 The United States and Great Britain agree to share the responsibility of policing the coast of Africa with their navies to eliminate the slave trade by intercepting the vessels running slaves.

August 14 This day marks the end of the second war against the Seminoles in Florida.

September 11 San Antonio, Texas, is attacked by the Mexican Army, and the city is captured.

October 2   The sloop USS *Concord* is destroyed when it crashes into the rocks while passing through the Mozambique Channel.

October 20   Commodore T. Catesby Jones, U.S. Navy, under the impression that war had broken out between the United States and Mexico, decides to speed from their location in Peru toward California with his East Pacific Squadron. The USS *United States* and the USS *Cyane* rush into the port of Monterey and quickly demobilize the Mexican garrison. Commodore Jones raises Old Glory and is prepared to claim Monterey for the United States when he is informed no war has been declared. After making several apologies, Jones lowers the Stars and Stripes and departs the harbor.

1843–1844   The *St. Mary's* (second) is built at the Washington Navy Yard. It is commissioned in the fall of 1844, with Commander John L. Saunders in command. Later the warship is at Philadelphia awaiting orders to sail with Commodore Robert Stockton. However, tensions began to rise between Mexico and the United States during the winter of 1845.

1843

January 30   In Washington, D.C., in response to the Mexican government, a new convention is appointed. By the terms of this convention "all the interests due on the awards which had been made in favor of the claimants, under the convention of the 11th of April, 1839 were to be paid to them on the 30th of April, 1843, and the principal of the said awards, and the interest accruing thereon, were stipulated to be paid in five years, in equal installments every three months." The Mexican government could not hold up to its part of the convention. The impasse began to bring about proposals for yet another convention. However, Texas becoming a state and the coming war between U.S. and Mexico caused the convention to be postponed.

June   The Mexicans and Texans who have been skirmishing since the Alamo incident arrive at an agreement and declare a truce. It does not improve the situation. Mexico is concerned about the possibility of Texas becoming a state and the United States is bickering about whether to accept the Republic of Texas as a state. This ultimately leads to war with Mexico during 1846.

November 29 to December 16   The U.S. dispatches a naval squadron, commanded by Commodore Matthew Perry, to forestall difficulties with various chiefs of the African nations. Perry's attempts to negotiate solutions which will eliminate the slave trade and piracy bring himself and detachments of servicemen ashore several times in areas that are today in the region known as Liberia. On one such occasion, the natives under King Ben Crack-O, at the village of Little Bereby, Nigeria, betray the trust of the two parties. The Americans respond to the treachery of the 15th with a severe response, first, King Crack-O is shot by a Marine and then the town is burned to the ground. Within two days, Perry's men debark again and burn seven additional villages in retaliation for the betrayal.

December 14   Marines and sailors retaliate against Africans on the Ivory Coast for attacks against the merchant ships *Mary Carver* and *Edward Barley*. The expedition is led by Matthew C. Perry. King Crack-O is slain and Little Bereby is burned.

1844

February 28   The USS *Princeton*, one of the first U.S. steam warships, is making a trial run down the Potomac. On board are several dignitaries, including President John Tyler and his cabinet. During the test voyage, an accidental explosion, involving a new type of gun, causes tragedy. The president escapes death but the malfunction of the gun kills Secretary of State Abel P. Upshur, the secretary of the navy and several congressmen.

April 12   A treaty of annexation signed by the joint commissioners is rejected by the United States Senate.

April 22   In Washington, D.C., President Tyler submits a treaty to the Senate for ratification accepting the annexation of Texas. The treaty was signed by representatives of the United States and Texas a few days earlier. The United States Senate rejects the Texas annexation treaty on 8 June 1844.

June   The USS *St. Louis*, commanded by Captain Tilton, while stationed near Canton, China, debarks a detachment of Marines which is to go ashore to protect the lives of Americans during a period of turmoil.

July 3   A trade agreement is reached between the United States and China.

December 7   Jose Joaquin Herrera is elected interim president of Mexico.

1845

March 3   Florida is admitted to the Union as the 27th state.

March 6   In Washington, D.C., the Mexican minister, subsequent to the passing of the joint resolution by Congress, protests against the annexation of Texas. He finishes his speech and afterward demands his passports that he could return to Mexico.

March 3   Florida is admitted to the Union as the 27th state.

March 4   James K. Polk is inaugurated as eleventh president of the United States.

March 28   Mexico breaks diplomatic relations with the United States. Tensions are rising over the situation in Mexico, especially since President Polk has expressed strong intent on the annexation of the Republic of Texas to the United States.

May 28 General Zachary Taylor leads an American force from Louisiana into Corpus Christi, Texas, to protect the southwestern border against an anticipated attack from Mexico. (Texas has not yet become a state, but President Polk treats it as one anyway.)

April 5 The president of Mexico, Jose Joaquin Herrera, exiles Santa Anna. He is sent to the island of Cuba.

Spring Brevet Captain John C. Frémont, later Union general (Corps of the U.S. Topographical Engineers) begins his third tour across the continent. He is charged with discovering a route from the Rocky Mountains to the mouth of the Columbia River.

June 15 In Washington, D.C., the president orders General Zachary Taylor to head for either the mouth of the Sabine or the Gulf of Mexico, whichever he judges the proper place to defend the western frontier of Texas. General Taylor is to disembark at a place in or near Rio Grande del Norte. The orders also make it clear that unless war erupts between the U.S. and Mexico, Taylor is to only defend Texas.

June 26 Lieutenant George Thomas (later Union general) departs from Fort Moultrie, South Carolina, with his company. He is under orders to report to General Taylor. Company E arrives in New Orleans on 19 July. On the 24th, it sails for Texas.

July 4 Texas holds a state convention in San Felipe de Austin and ac-

cepts the dictated terms of American statehood.

July 30 General Zachary Taylor receives new orders from the president. They instruct him to continue to avoid contact with Mexican forces, but he is also instructed to take up positions along the Rio Grande and west of the Nueces River. General Taylor, in Texas, is informed that the USS *Lexington* is to sail from New York with reinforcements. The vessel is to head for Corpus Christi. In the same letter, Taylor is ordered to communicate with the vessels *Dolphin, Harney* and the *On-ka-hy-e*, once they are put into active service.

August 6 Reinforcements, the 7th Infantry and three companies of dragoons are dispatched to Texas to reinforce General Taylor. The letter being carried by the troops asks Taylor "what auxiliary troops, in case of an emergency, he could rely upon from Texas." The letter informs Taylor that 1,000 rifles and 10,000 muskets had been issued for Texas. It also authorizes the general to accept volunteers from Alabama, Louisiana, Kentucky, Mississippi and Tennessee.

September In Washington, D.C., President Polk directs the secretary of state to inquire of the Mexican government through the U.S. Consul in Mexico "if it would be willing to receive an American envoy, entrusted with ample powers to terminate all difficulties." The Mexican government, on 15 October, through its foreign minister, responded to the U.S. inquiry. The Mexican government said that they were acceptable; however, they also suggested that the U.S. fleet at Vera Cruz should be withdrawn during negotiations. The U.S. Agrees with the Mexicans and withdraws its fleet. The U.S. envoy arrives at Vera Cruz on 30 November 1845.

October 10   The United States Naval Academy at Fort Severn, Annapolis, Maryland, is formally opened. The institution is headed by Franklin Buchanan. The institution begins with five instructors and three midshipmen.

October 11   The U.S. 5th Infantry (5 companies) arrives at Corpus Christi, Texas. The regiment is commanded by Lieutenant Colonel McIntosh. It reports to General Zachary Taylor.

Captain John Frémont.

November 30   In Mexico, the American envoy arrives at Vera Cruz. He discovers that the country has changed and that it is unfavorable to the United States. President Herrera, never inclined to peace, is opposed by General Paredes, who has built his rebellion on the assertion that Herrera had consented to the annexation of Texas to a hostile country, the U.S. Nevertheless, the American consul was not received by the government of Mexico.

December   In Washington, D.C., U.S. Senator Cass offers a resolution and delivers a tough speech concerning the boundary dispute with Great Britain over the Oregon and British Northwest possessions. This action initiates the Democratic phrase "54° 40 or fight." In other activity, the great potato famine in Ireland forces

many Irish people to begin to settle in America. This will bring over a million and a half people from the Emerald Isle to the U.S. over the next four years.

December 2   In Washington, D.C., President Polk addresses Congress, stating that the U.S. holds claim to all of Oregon and re-emphasizes a determination to prevent any other nation from colonizing the U.S., known as the "Polk Doctrine."

December 10   In California, John Frémont reaches Sutter's Fort with his command. Before Frémont had reached the Sierra Nevada Mountains, he had split his force. He sent one part under T. Talbot farther south to search for a pass. Meanwhile, Frémont, guided by Kit Carson, crosses the mountains south of Lake Tahoe and enters California, passing through El Dorado County.

December 29   Texas is admitted to the Union as the 28th state.

December 30   Jose Joaquin de Herrera resigns as president of Mexico. General Paredes assumes the post without any opposition.

1846

January   The Army begins construction of Fort Jefferson in the Tortugas Islands in the Florida keys. Construction continues for over 30 years but is never totally completed. The fort is used as a Union prison during the Civil War. It was from this fort that the USS *Maine* sailed to Cuba in 1898 on that fateful voyage which would bring war between the United States and Spain, and in which Samuel Mudd, the accused accomplice of John Booth, the assassin of Lincoln, is incarcerated.

January 7   **In California,** Captain John Frémont departs from Sutter's Fort. He proceeds up the San Joaquin valley to meet Talbot at a rendezvous point to which both agreed. Nevertheless, after failing to hook up with Talbot, he returned to Sutter's Fort. Frémont, however, sent Kit Carson to locate Talbot. In the meantime, Frémont heads for Monterey where the American consul, Thomas A. Larkin, introduced him to the Mexican commander, General Castro. In turn, Castro gave his permission for Frémont to remain in the San Joaquin valley until he could "recover sufficiently" before continuing his trek to Oregon. Castro, however, also told Frémont that he would have to take his word because a Mexican officer's word "was as good as a written statement." Afterward,

Frémont returned to Fisher's farm where his command had paused. While there, a Mexican Californian noticed some animals who were thought to be Mexican. The man was hurried away, but he headed for San Jose to find the alcade Don Dolores Pacheco. Frémont was sent a summons to appear to answer charges. Frémont did not appear; however, he did send a letter on 21 February:

> You will readily understand that my duties will not permit me to appear before the magistrates in your towns on the complaint of every straggling vagabond who may chance to visit my camp. You inform me that unless satisfaction be immediately made by the delivery of the animals in question, the complaint will be forwarded to the governor. I will beg you at the same time to enclose to his excellency a copy of this note. I am, very respectfully your obedient servant. John S. Fremont, U.S. Army.

January 12   **In California,** Captain Archibald Gillespie and his Marines construct a primitive fort at what is now downtown Los Angeles on Fort Hill. It is named the Post at Los Angeles and it is a 400 foot long breastwork. The fort's plan was initiated by 1st Lieutenant William H. H. Emory (Corps of Topographical Engineers).

General Kearny had ordered the fort to be built; however, on the 23rd of April, the plans are modified and a larger fort is constructed. This is supervised by 2nd Lieutenant John W. Davidson of the 1st Dragoons. The post, designated Fort Moore on 4 July 1847, is never completed. It is named in honor of Captain Benjamin Moore of the 1st Dragoons, who was killed at the Battle of San Pasqual in San Diego County on 6 December 1846. The garrison was withdrawn in 1848 by the order of Captain William Tecumseh Sherman and the post was abandoned during 1849. A large mural now stands at the intersection of Hill Street close to Sunset Boulevard marking the location of the fort.

January 13   In Texas, President James Polk orders General Zachary Taylor to move from Corpus Christi to the Rio Grande River. General Taylor moves his troops (almost 4,000 men) after negotiations with Mexico break off. His instructions from the president are to "take the defensive position, don't treat Mexicans as an enemy but take the necessary precautions in the event hostilities might occur." Lieutenant John Bankhead Magruder (later Confederate general) is based at Corpus Christi; however, later he participates at the Battle of Palo Alto and Battle of Resaca-de-la-Palma.

March 1   In Mexico, the American consul at Vera Cruz sends a note to the foreign minister of Mexico requesting that he be able to present his credentials to the new government. Mexico responds on 12 March. The American consul's request is rejected. He demands that his passport be returned.

Afterward, he returns to the United States.

March 5–7   In California, General Castro sends Frémont a letter dated 5 March expressing his displeasure that the Americans have not left California. On the following day, John Frémont, having failed to depart from California, instead reaches a fortified camp on the top of Hawk's Peak. On the 7th, General Castro, with his army of 200 to 300 Californians, marches out from his camp to intimidate Frémont. Nevertheless, Castro manages to keep the distance between him and Frémont's force to ensure that none of Frémont's sharpshooters could fire at his force. In the meantime, the American consul, Thomas O. Larkin, at Monterey becomes concerned that Castro could endanger Frémont's force. He sends a letter to the American consul at Mazatlan asking if there are any U.S. warships at that point. Upon receipt of the letter, Commodore Sloat dispatches Captain Montgomery of the USS *Portsmouth* to depart for Monterey.

March 6   In California, John Frémont is informed that General Castro had abandoned his fortifications at Santa Clara and is headed for Los Angeles. Frémont decides to continue his pursuit of the Mexican general.

March 8   In Texas, General Taylor departs Corpus Christi for the Rio Grande. They depart with four separate detachments; first, Colonel Twiggs, followed by three brigades, Captain James Duncan on the 9th, Lieutenant James S. McIntosh on the 10th, and Colonel Whistler's Brigade on the 11th, leaving Corpus Christi virtually deserted. This march includes about 2,300 men, the 3rd, 4th, 5th, 7th and 8th Regiments, the 2nd Dragoons, three light batteries and one battalion of foot artillery. Lieutenant Robert Selden Garnett (later Confederate general) becomes an advisor to General Taylor. Later he participates at the Battles of Monterey and Buena Vista.

March 11   In California, Captain John Frémont, having abandoned the fortified camp (Hawk's Peak), joined with Talbot's detachment in the San Joaquin Valley and moved to Peter Lassem's trading post near the northern line of California while en route to Oregon. The force remained there until 14 April. While at the trading post, Frémont was informed that a number of Indians had expressed hostilities against the small amount of white settlers. A few volunteers from Reading's trading post joined with Frémont's men, and they moved against the Indians. Only a few of the Indians escaped by swimming across the river.

March 11–24   In Texas, General Taylor, upon orders, breaks camp at Corpus Christi and proceeds toward the Rio Grande, where he establishes Fort Texas (later Fort Brown) opposite Matamoros. On the 20th, Taylor's force, which is composed of about 2300 troops (3rd, 4th, 5th 7th and 8th Regiments of Infantry; 2nd Dragoons, three light batteries and one battalion of foot artillery) arrives at the Arroyo Colorado, about thirty miles east of the Rio Grande. The Mexicans under General Mejia are there to meet him.

General Edmund Pendleton Gaines (Frost, *The History of Mexico and Its Wars*).

The Americans are informed that if he crosses the stream it will be considered an act of war. Nevertheless, the army under Taylor sends word to Meija that if the Mexicans block passage, the American guns will be used against them. Artillery is placed to cover the crossing and the army begins to cross. Surprisingly, the Mexicans do not try to block passage. The army proceeds to Matamoros, but it pauses on the 24th.

March 21   In Washington, D.C., General Gaines, the superior officer of the section, is passed over. General Scott (later Union general) is known

Troops landing at Point Isabel (Frost, *The History of Mexico and Its Wars*).

to have suggested General Taylor for the position. On this day, orders are sent to General Taylor at Fort Jesup in Louisiana to prepare to move his force into Texas.

March 24   **In Texas,** General Taylor has received information that the Mexicans took possession of Point Isabel on the Brazos Santiago. General Taylor had planned to make camp at Point Isabel from where he could be easily maintain his base of supplies from land or sea. Taylor leaves his main body along the Matamoros Road, about half of his army, while he moves the remainder of his force to Point Isabel. As Taylor's force approaches Point Isabel, he and his dragoons meet a delegation of citizens protesting why a foreign army is moving into a country claimed by Mexico. As the general is responding, some troops rush up to inform him that the station is on fire. General Taylor postpones his response. Colonel David Twiggs and a detachment of dragoons speeds to Matamoros to save a few of the public buildings. However, the citizens and the Mexicans abscond.

General Taylor arrives shortly afterward and directs Colonel Twiggs to fortify the place. General Taylor places Major Monroe in command. Monroe has two companies of artillery with six brass 6-pounders, two long 18-pounders along with two ships' guns. His command is composed of 450 troops. After Taylor finishes with the work of command of the fort, he heads back to his main body under General William Jenkins Worth, which is encamped near the intersection of the Matamoros and Point Isabel Roads. Afterward, Taylor brings the main body to the Rio Grande. They arrive on the 28th.

March 28   In Washington, D.C., President Polk issues orders through the secretary of state, Mr. Marcy, which directs General Taylor to "be put in a position where they may most promptly and efficiently act in the defense of Texas, in the event it should become necessary or proper to employ them for that purpose."

In Texas, General Zachary Taylor arrives at the Rio Grande, where the U.S. flag is placed on the river embankment opposite Matamoros. Richard Taylor (later Confederate general), the son of Zachary Taylor, acts as his secretary during the war.

American soldiers fortify the left bank of the Rio Grande, while Mexicans are preparing for battle on the opposing bank. These fortifications become Fort Texas. In conspicuous view of Matamoros, the "Stars and Stripes" is raised along the banks of the Rio Grande, while "The Star Spangled Banner" and "Yankee Doodle" are being played.

In naval activity, the USS *Dolphin,* under Captain Pope, and the USS *Marion,* Captain Simonds, attached to the African squadron, are operating in the water off Moravia. On this day, the *Marion's* boat capsizes while crossing the bar of the Messurado River. Midshipman Joseph T. Bartlett of Maine and a seaman, John Johnson, both drown.

April   In Texas, Mexican governor Jose Castro declares that the purchase or acquisition of land by foreigners who had not been naturalized as Mex-

ican citizens will be considered as "null and void, and they will be subject to be expelled whenever the country might find it convenient." The American settlers in California take offense at the governor's actions. They decide to take things into their own hands. This is known as the Bear Flag Rebellion.

Early April   In Texas at General Zachary Taylor's camp, a mysterious letter appears from the commander-in-chief of the Mexican army, Pedro de Ampudia. It focuses on the English and Irish soldiers along with the French, German and Poles, and it attempts to convince them to switch sides in the war. De Ampudia then says: "Now, then come with all your confidence to the Mexican ranks; and I guarantee to you, upon my honour, good treatment, and that all your expenses shall be delayed until your arrival in the beautiful capital of Mexico." Prior to receiving this message, some U.S. troops had deserted. Several had made it to Matamoros. In order to halt this practice, orders were issued to "shoot every one who should leave his lines, and several were thus put to death."

April 1   *In naval activity,* the frigate USS *Potomac,* which had embarked at Norfolk, arrives at Vera Cruz, Mexico. The American squadron by the 5th will include the USS *Cumberland* and *Potomac,* both frigates, and the sloops of war *Falmouth, St. Mary's* and *John Adams.* Later, the USS *Brandywine,* a frigate in ordinary at the Gosport navy yard, is to be fitted out and sent to join the others at Vera Cruz.

In other activity, Lieut. G. S. Blake

takes command of the USS *Perry*, a brigantine at Norfolk. He is to ship out to the Pacific. Also, the USS *Constitution* (Old Ironsides) is operating in the Pacific. One of the officers aboard writes in a letter:

> The Constitution was out about ten days from Macao, on her way to Manilla, and found herself near a fleet of six British vessels, becalmed. A few light cats-paws fanned us along until we were within two miles of them, and then the wind left us. We were all thus becalmed in sight of each other. We made them out to be a large line of battleship, two frigates, one brig and two steamers; their nation as yet unknown, as there was no wind to throw out their ensigns. Presently one of the steamers began firing up, and shortly afterwards bore down for us. We were just exercising our crew at general quarters, (always keeping up our discipline, you perceive), when she came within hail. From her we learnt that the vessels composed the East India squadron of H.B.M. under command of rear admiral sir Thomas Cochrane, K.C.B., that they had been seven months down among the islands, and the whole squadron were short of bread, "grog," water, and other necessaries, and they desired to know if we could furnish them with the stores required, to last them one week. No sooner asked than done. No sailor ever stops to count the biscuit in his locker when he sees a hungry customer. Then a lively scene occurred, gratifying, I assure you, to both sides. Our guns had to be secured, and, indeed, we must have presented rather a hostile appearance to Mr. Bull; in fact, one of the officers good humoredly observed, he "thought we were going to blow him out of water." We turned to with light hearts, and broke out the provisions and sent them on board, while we entertained the officers in very gallant style, in fact doing the clean and genteel thing by them. I don't recollect ever spending a more pleasing time that I did the two short hours they were with us; and when they left, it was like parting with friends of long standing.

On the following day, the mountains of Luzon were spotted.

April 3 *In naval activity,* the Texas ship *Invincible*, carrying eight guns and commanded by Jeremiah Brown, encounters the Mexican brigantine *Montezuma* in the port of Matamoros at the mouth of the Rio Grande. At about 10 A.M., Captain Brown orders his crew to raise the Texas flag and open fire on the *Montezuma*, which carries ten guns. The *Montezuma* and the *Invincible* exchange blows, but the *Invincible* is able to outsail the *Montezuma*. On the *Invincible*'s second pass, the *Montezuma* bursts into flames and runs aground on a sandbar. Its crewmen escape into the water while the *Invincible* maintains a blistering bombardment that destroys the ship.

In related activity, the *Invincible* engages and seizes the American merchant ship *Pocket*. Afterward, Captain Brown discovers the cargo contains weapons and supplies headed to the Mexican army. Furthermore, Mexican naval officers are captured and are carrying documents written in Span-

Colonel Truman Cross (Frost, *The History of Mexico and Its Wars*).

ish. The Americans take the *Pocket* to Galveston where the supplies are given to General Sam Houston.

April 4 In Texas, four heavy guns arrive to reinforce Taylor's fortification. Taylor has them promptly positioned on the town of Matamoros.

April 9 In Texas, U.S. General William Jenkins Worth resigns from the army. He later rescinds the resignation and re-joins General Taylor after hostilities break out.

April 10 In Texas, American Colonel Truman Cross (quartermaster) rides out of General Taylor's camp on his customary ride, but he never returns. A search party led by Lt. Porter is ambushed by bandits, mortally wounding Lt. Porter. About one week later, a Mexican comes into camp and informs the Americans that he is aware of an American officer. American troops finally find Colonel Cross' remains about a week later. They discover that he was dragged from the road to the thicket subsequent to the murder. His corpse was stripped of its clothing and in turn vultures had torn the flesh from the body. His corpse was identified by his teeth. Cross' remains are taken to Fort Texas, where he is buried at the base of the flagstaff.

April 11 In Texas, Mexicans issue an ultimatum to General Zachary Taylor, insisting American troops withdraw or face an armed conflict. General Taylor rejects the ultimatum, declaring his intent to remain. In related activity, General Pedro de Ampudia arrives in Matamoros. He also had with him a large army.

April 12 In Mexico, General Pedro de Ampudia sends a letter to Zachary Taylor demanding that he "by explicit and definite orders of my government, which neither can, will, nor should receive new outrages, I require you in all form, and at the latest in the peremptory term of twenty-four hours to break up your camp and retire to the other bank of the river, while our governments are regulating the pending question in relation to Texas." General Taylor responds to the letter on the same day, essentially rejecting de Ampudia's request. Nevertheless, at the appointed time, the Mexicans fail to take any offensive action against Taylor's force.

April 17   In California, Lieutenant Archibald Gillespie arrives at Monterey where he joins Commodore Sloat, giving him secret orders from Washington to take appropriate action if hostilities start between Mexico and the United States.

April 17–20   In Texas, Lt. Porter (4th Infantry) and Lt. Dobbins (3rd Infantry) both depart from General Taylor's camp in the morning of the 17th. On the second day out, Lt. Porter encounters a group of Mexicans. A Mexican "snapped his piece at him." Porter responds by emptying both barrels of his gun. The Mexican then disappears into the woods. Meanwhile, the Americans seize the Mexicans' camp, along with ten horses and saddles. Porter, the same day, encounters another Mexican party at about 4 P.M. in the midst of a heavy rain. The Mexicans open fire, killing one private. The Americans' wet ammunition prevents them from returning fire. The sergeant along with four privates returned to camp on the following day.

On the 20th, thirty dragoons depart Taylor's camp in search of the remainder of the detachment, but return because the horses cannot ma-neuver through the thicket. During the search, the detachment encounters Lt. Dobbins' party. He tells the dragoons that his party will continue to search for Porter for another day or so. In the meantime, Porter's party had all returned to camp. The following letter (in part), dated the 24th, adds the following particulars: "The whole of Lieutenant Porter's party have been returned to camp, except himself and the soldier who was killed by the first fire of the Mexicans in the encounter of the 19th. Private Arns, who came in last of the company, states that he was within five or six feet of Lieutenant Porter when he fell. He received a ball which penetrated his thigh, and no doubt parted the artery. He immediately laid down, and expired very soon afterwards. The private previously killed lay within five yards of him." It was noted also that the first attack by the Mexicans numbered about 150 men and that the second numbered even more. It was later determined that American casualties would have been much higher, except for the attacks being made in the dark.

April 19   In naval activity, General Taylor issues orders to the brigantine *Lawrence* along with the cutter *Santa Anna* to chase and intercept two ships en route to Matamoros. Both vessels are taken to Brazos Santiago.

April 20   In Mexico, General Arista, the commander-in-chief of the Mexican army, pens a letter dated 20 April to the troops of Zachary Taylor: "Besides, the most of you are Europeans, and we are the declared friends of a majority of the nations of Europe. The

north Americans are ambitious, over-
bearing, and insolent as a nation, and
they will only make use of you as vile
tools to carry out their abominable
plans of pillage and rapine. I warn you
in the name of justice, honour, and
your own interests and self-respect, to
abandon their desperate and unholy
cause, and become peaceful Mexican
citizens. I guarantee you, in such case,
a half-section of land, or three hundred and twenty acres, to settle upon,
gratis. Be wise, then, and just and
honorable, and take no part in mur-
dering us who have no unkind feelings
for you. Lands shall be given to officers, sergeants, and corporals, according
to rank, privates receiving three hundred and twenty acres, as stated."

April 22   In Mexico, General Pedro
de Ampudia, in a letter to General
Taylor, complains that the U.S. has
prevented two vessels from arriving at
Matamoros. The letter also protests
that two Mexicans whose boat strayed
into the Americans' camp were being
held as prisoners. De Ampudia insists
that neither man is part of the Mexican army and urges the Americans to
release them. On the same day, General Taylor tells de Ampudia that the
Americans had captured two men who
were detained at Brazos Santiago, but
that they were to be released. He also
tells de Ampudia that the boat that
had carried the two men down the
river had arrived empty. The Mexicans
later attempted to retrieve the boat.
The guard at the place fired upon the
Mexicans, but there is no trace of
them on the following morning. Taylor tells de Ampudia the boat would
be returned to him.

April 23   In Mexico, President Mariano Paredes issues a proclamation. He
tells the Mexican people that the U.S.
has invaded their territory and that
American naval squadrons have blocked
their ports. At Laredo, Texas, some
Mexican troops were disarmed.

Hostilities, then, have been commenced by the United States of
North America, beginning new con-
quests upon the frontier territories
of the Department of Tamaulipas
and New Leon, and progressing at
such a rate, that troops of the same
United States threaten Monterey, in
upper California. No one can doubt
which of the two republics is responsible for this war; a war which
any sense of equity and justice,
and respect for the rights and laws
of civilized nations, might have
avoided. I have commanded the
general in chief of our forces on the
northern frontier to repel all hostilities offered to us, and calling upon
the God of battles, he will preserve
the valour of our troops, the un-
questionable right to our territory,
and the honour of those arms which
are used only in defense of justice.
Our general will govern himself by
the established usages of civilized
warfare. I solemnly announce that
I do not declare war against the
United States of America, because
it pertains to the august Congress of
that nation, and not to the execu-
tive, to settle definitely the reparation which so many aggressions
demand. But the defence of the
Mexican territory, which the United
States troops invade, is an urgent
necessity, and my responsibility
would be immense before the nation
if I did not give commands to repel

Thornton's Skirmish (Frost, *The History of Mexico and Its Wars*).

those forces who act like enemies, and I have so commanded. From this day commences a defensive war, and those points of our territory which are invaded or attacked will be energetically defended.

In other activity, General Taylor is informed by his spies that about 2,500 Mexicans had crossed from Mexico onto the Texas side of the Rio Grande above the American fort, while another 1,500 had crossed to the American side of the Rio Grande below the fort. General Taylor dispatches two detachments, one above the fort (Captain Thornton) and the other (Captain Croghan Ker) below it.

Captain Thornton rides to a point within three miles of the Mexican camp. His guide refuses to go farther, stating that the land is infested with Mexicans. Nevertheless, Thornton continues to move with his command. Thornton comes upon a house (Carricitos Ranch), which he approaches by using a pair of bars to enter through a chaparral fence. The Mexicans, who are hiding, wait until the entire command enters the compound, then they open fire. Thornton attempts to swing his command around and get out of the way. Meanwhile, Captain Hardee (later Confederate general) suggests to Thornton how to get out of the trap, while the Mexicans continue to fire. Thornton races toward the fence and jumps it, but his horse, which is shot, falls into a precipice and lands on top of Thornton. Thornton remained insensible for about six hours.

Captain Hardee assumes command. He attempts to escape by making it to the river and swimming it; however, the ground is too boggy. He is unable to make it to the river. Afterward, a Mexican officer rides up to Hardee and asks him to surrender. Hardee agrees to surrender if the Mexicans treat him and his men as prisoners of war. The officer returns to his commanding general, General Anastasio Torrejón, who agrees. Hardee surrenders. Captain Hardee, Captain Thornton and Lieutenant Kane along with the other soldiers are captured. The Mexicans celebrated

Captain Benjamin McCulloch (Frost, *The History of Mexico and Its Wars*).

the victory with great enthusiasm but treat the Americans kindly.

In related activity, Captain Herr had ridden to the point where the Mexicans were supposed to have crossed, but the information given to Taylor had been false. Subsequent to the capture of Thornton's command, the Mexicans began to ford the river where they spread out between General Taylor and Point Isabel.

April 25   In Mexico, American cavalry troops under Captain Thornton suffer casualties when attacked by a Mexican cavalry unit. General Zachary Taylor informs Washington and American President Polk uses this as a reason for war.

April 26   In Texas, General Taylor writes to the governor of Louisiana, Isaac Johnson. He requests four regiments of volunteers from Louisiana and asks that General Persifor Smith is selected to lead the regiments. Leroy Augustus Stafford (later Confederate general) joins with the Rapides Volunteers, Company E, 3rd Louisiana Infantry. Subsequent to it mustering out of service, he comes under the command of Ben McCulloch and his Texas rangers.

April 27   In Texas, General Taylor issues an order that details the funeral services for Colonel Cross, to be held on the following day. The funeral escort will be "a squadron of dragoons and eight companies of infantry, to be organized and commanded by Colonel David Emanuel Twiggs."

In naval activity, the USS *Monmouth,* a steamer, sails for Port Lavacca and Galveston, where it is to present a requisition from General Taylor for the governor of Texas, James Pinckney Henderson. Taylor is seeking four regiments, two of cavalry and two infantry.

In other activity, Major L. J. Beall writes to his brother about the death of his son-in-law,

> He was sent out on this duty somedays, when he met with a Mexican sentinel who snapped his piece at him and retreated to the woods, being perused by the men, they came on a camp, where they found nine horses belonging to the Mexicans, which they mounted. On their way back to Gen Taylor's camp they were surrounded by forty Mexicans, and fired upon. Pat Flood was killed, Porter wounded, but not before he had discharged both barrels of his guns with effect. This occurred during the heavy rain, and the men with Porter were unable to discharge their guns, and retreated to the chaparral, only one man remaining near enough to see what took place afterwards. Flood was surrounded immediately and stabbed with knives, and … they served Porter in the same manner after he had fallen from his horse.

April 28   On April 28 Captain Catlett writes from onboard the steamer *Monmouth* off St. Joseph's to the people of Galveston:

> Gentlemen: I am the bearer of a communication from Gen. Taylor to Gov. Henderson, requesting to be immediately reinforced by twenty companies of foot Riflemen. My destination is Victoria, and thence to Austin. I was instructed by the General to send an express from the former place by land to your city with communications to Lieut. Kingsbury, and at the same time to spread the information through the country. But it having been left discretionary with me, and the Monmouth being available, I have determined to send the communications by her, and also to write to you, in order to facilitate as much as possible the sending on of troops. Gen. Taylor is in a very precarious situation at his camp near Matamoros, and an attack is feared on the post at Point Isabel. I believe a reinforcement of two hundred men would save that place. This is vastly important, as a larger amount of commissariat and ordnance stores are deposited there, and if that place should fall, General Taylor will be left without resources of any kind. I was instructed by Gen. Taylor to send out from Victoria expresses in such directions as I might deem most advisable, so as to have all the men possible on their march to his relief without awaiting orders of the Governor. You will have it in your power to send to the Lower Brazos, Houston and Montgomery sooner than an express can go from Victoria. I therefore leave that to you, knowing that it will be promptly - attended to. I shall send to Matagorda, Texana, Richmond and San Felipe. If you have an opportunity, please send to Washington. I shall send there from La Grange.
>
> The place of rendezvous for the foot companies is suggested by the General at Galveston; that of the mounted men at Corpus Christi; at which place there will be provisions and forage. No party less than 400 should think of going through on

the direct road to Matamoros, as there is a large force of Mexicans on the Aroyo Colorado, for the purpose of cutting off reinforcements in that direction. Small parties can cross from Corpus Christi on to Padre's Island. Arrangements are made for crossing from the lower point of the Island to Point Isabel. If two hundred men could be raised even temporarily at Galveston, I am decidedly of the opinion it would be better to send them forthwith by the Monmouth — the security of Point Isabel is of the last importance.

From the best information we could obtain, the force of the Mexicans is set down at seven thousand certain and reports go as high as twelve thousand. All communication is now cut off between the camp and Point Isabel, except by running the gauntlet. I came out in the night of the 26th with a guide, and was prowling all night through chaparral, swamps and lakes. Capt. Baker will be able to give all the particulars of what has happened, the situation of Point Isabel, &c. &c.

In haste, your obedient servant.
W.G. CATLETT.

Late April Commodore Robert Stockton sails for Galveston, Texas.

May In Texas, American Captain William Henry, just finishing two battles himself, remarks after seeing the victorious defenders of Fort Texas: "I would have rather fought 20 battles, than have passed through the bombardment of Fort Brown" (Fort Texas re-named).

May 1 In Texas, General Taylor marches 26 miles to the seacoast for the purpose of overseeing construction

of Fort Polk. Taylor leaves 500 men behind as a garrison, commanded by Major Jacob Brown at Fort Texas, later re-named Fort Brown.

In related activity, Mexican General Mariano Arista begins to position his artillery soon after Taylor departs from the area.

In naval activity, the steamship *Galveston* arrives in New Orleans, Louisiana, with news of General Taylor's conflict on the Rio Grande and his request for four Louisiana regiments.

May 2 In Louisiana, The Louisiana newspaper *Picayune* runs a headline emphasizing the need for men to meet the Mexican threat:

WAR!!
TO ARMS! TO ARMS!!
THE WAR HAS BEGUN IN EARNEST!
THE ENEMY IS UPON OUR SOIL!!
LOUISIANA VOLUNTEERS
THE HOUR HAS ARRIVED.

May 3 In Texas, American Captain William Walker, a commander of the Texas Rangers who joins Taylor's army, departs to check on the status of Fort Texas, returning on the 5th of May, with news that the fort has repulsed the attackers with only minor damage.

May 3–9 DEFENSE OF FORT TEXAS Fort Texas defends against a relentless Mexican artillery assault. Second Lieutenant Thomas "Stonewall" Jackson (later Confederate general) is tasked with getting the fort's artillery in place. There is no attack immediately. The Mexicans open with their seven cannon early on the 3rd and it is matched by American guns. The exchange lasts for about fifteen minutes. Nevertheless, one of the Mexican guns is silenced after it is shot from its carriage and another gun is also disabled. Afterward, the Mexicans begin to fire shot and shells from the lower fort along with a mortar battery that is nearby. The shelling continues until 7:30 P.M. The Americans cease fire because they are costing themselves ammunition while only damaging the buildings in Matamoros.

Captain Walker had arrived between 3:00 A.M. and 4:00 A.M. He was hailed by the sentinel and responded that they were "friends from Frantone." Following a short delay, he and the six rangers who accompanied him were permitted to enter the fort. Once inside, Walker delivers messages from General Taylor to the commander, Major Brown. In the meantime, Captain Walker and his rangers depart from Point Isabel in the early afternoon. Walker rides to a point where Captain May, with about 100 troops, had been waiting. Initially, it was believed that Walker had been captured, but when he was spotted riding toward the troops under Captain May, it became apparent that he was not. Walker informs Captain May that Captain Seth Brown was able to hold the fort at Point Isabel. The Mexicans did not commence fire on the 4th, which allowed the garrison to complete the defenses of the fort.

On the 5th, fire was reopened by cannon reported to be in the field on the east side of the Rio Grande. A response was made by the 6-pounder cannon in the howitzer batteries late in the afternoon. Shortly afterward, the Mexican cannon ceased fire. Meanwhile, other cannon in Matamoros opened up and the fort was hit from all sides, but they too were silenced.

The Americans had cancelled the Mexican guns, but they were now bracing for an attack. Lieutenant Hanson, after spotting some Mexican

Major Brown is killed (Frost, *The History of Mexico and Its Wars*).

troops, requests permission to move out of the fort to reconnoiter. Permission is granted. After he leaves the fort, Hanson encounters one Mexican party, but it flees rather than engage. The other Mexican troops then attempt to surround him, but Hanson is able to outmaneuver them and return to the fort. By that time, the Mexicans had begun to surround the post. Nevertheless Taylor had earlier directed Brown to fire his two 18-pounders at intervals as a signal.

On the 6th, the Mexicans resume their fire. At about 10:00 A.M. the fire mortally wounds Captain Jacob Brown, the American commander. Captain Brown's right leg is shattered. He is immediately tended to and his leg amputated, but he survives only three more days. The Mexicans continue their bombardment of the fort until about noon and then cease until about 2 P.M. In the meantime, a band of Mexicans who had moved to the rear of the fort the night before approach the post, but Lieutenant Lowd's battery commences fire and repulses them. At about 5 P.M. on the 6th, the Mexicans call for a parley. Two officers under a white flag approach the post. Commander Hawkins sends Major Sewell and Lieutenant Britton out to meet with them. The Mexicans give the Americans a message from General Mariano Arista: "The principle, which Mexicans observe above all other nations, obliges me to summon you, as all your efforts will be useless, to surrender, in order to avoid, by a capitulation, the entire destruction of all the soldiers under your command. Haw-

kins, the American commander is given one hour to reply." Hawkins calls for the officers and holds a council. The unanimous response is "to defend the fort until death." Captain Hawkins informs General Arista of his response: "Sir, Your humane communication has just been received, and, after the consideration due to its importance, I must respectfully decline to surrender my forces to you. The exact purport of your despatch I cannot feel confident that I understand, as my interpreter is not skilled in your language; but if I have understood you correctly, you have my reply above."

After receiving the reply, the Mexicans again commence fire with their cannon. The Americans are not able to respond due to the shortages of ammunition. The Mexicans, if they

General Mariano Arista (Jenkins, *History of the War Between the United States and Mexico*).

attacked, would also not be able to respond. On the night of the 6th, the Americans brace for an attack which does not come. On the 7th, both sides are more active. The Mexican cannon hits the post from nearly every direction, while the Mexican cavalry is forming in the field to display an intent to attack. Orders are issued throughout the fort not to fire upon the Mexicans unless they come to a point within 80 yards of the post. The Mexicans, however, do not approach within the 80 yard marker.

In the evening, a small contingent under Captain Joseph King Fenno Mansfield moves out of the post to cut down the chaparral. The Mexicans had been using the heavy shrub as cover. At about midnight, the garrison is awakened by the sounds of muskets and the blaring of bugles. The garrison prepares for an attack, however, everything goes quiet after a short time. At daybreak on the 8th, the musket firing resumes and continues until the afternoon. The fort sustains no damage.

On the 9th, the Mexican batteries resume their firing upon the fort and it continues until the afternoon. The Mexican batteries all become silent, while inside the post, the troops start to become jubilant. In the afternoon, the heavy guns of General Taylor are heard by the garrison, which then knows that Taylor's force is engaging the Mexicans. Later that night, a Mexican comes into the post and gives an account of the Battle of Palo Alto.

Theophilus Hunter Holmes (later Confederate general) participates at the defense of Fort Texas. Later, he participates at the Battle of Monterrey and Vera Cruz. Also, 2nd Lieutenant Earl Van Dorn participates at this siege. Still later he sees action at Cerro Gordo, Contreras, and at Mexico City. Van Dorn is brevetted first lieutenant on 3 March 1847, and on 20 August 1847, he is brevetted major for his actions at Contreras and Churubusco. Joseph King Fenno Mansfield (later Union general) participates at this battle; he serves as chief engineer of General Taylor. Later, he participates at Monterrey and at Buena Vista, where he is awarded the brevet of major, lieutenant colonel and colonel in the regulars. Lieutenant George Henry Thomas (later Union general), an artillery officer, participates at the defense of Fort Texas. Afterward, he participates at the Battle of Resaca de la Palma, Monterrey and Buna Vista; he is brevetted three times for his gallantry.

May 4 *In naval activity,* the USS *Mississippi,* a frigate commanded by Captain Fitzhugh, is ordered to leave Pensacola for Vera Cruz at 4 P.M. Also, on or about this day, the USS *St. Mary's,* a sloop commanded by Commander Saunders, is ordered to sail from Pensacola to reinforce Americans at Point Isabel. In other activity, William Wallace Burns (West Point 1847) is assigned recruiting duty.

May 7 BATTLE OF PALO ALTO   General Zachary Taylor's Army of Occupation Order of Battle: 3rd, 4th, 5th and 8th U.S. Infantry Regiments; the 2nd U.S. Artillery Battalion (serving as U.S. Infantry); 2nd U.S. Dragoons (200 troops); Duncan's Battery (four

Battle of Palo Alto (*A Sketch of the Life and Character of Gen. Taylor*).

6-pounders, 50 men); Ringgold's Battery (four 6-pounders, 50 men); Heavy Battery (two 18-pounders, 30 men). The Mexican Order of Battle: General Mariano Arista, Lancer Brigade (General Torrejon, 700 men); 7th Line Cavalry, 8th Line Cavalry, Light Cavalry, Presidial Irregular Company, Ranchero Irregular Company; 2nd Light Infantry (500 men), 1st Line Infantry (500 men); 6th Line Infantry (500 men); 10th Line Infantry (500 men); and Tampico Coastal Guard Battalion (500 men). The Mexican force also includes 14 small cannon (4-, 6-, and 8-pounders, 200 men).

In other activity, following a hazardous journey that carried him through Indian country, Captain Gillespie is able to contact Captain Frémont at Klaymath Lake, Oregon. He delivers a secret message from President Polk.

May 7–8 BATTLE OF PALO ALTO   In Texas, General Taylor, unaware of Mexican General Arista's planned ambush at Palo Alto, departs from Point Isabel on May 7 at about 7 P.M. General Taylor issues the order for the main body to march on Matamoros. After marching about seven miles, they make camp. The number of guards is increased. On May 8, they resume the march until about noon, when they discover the Mexican army at Palo Alto. It is formed in an unbroken line over a mile long. Taylor pauses to get water for his horses and troops, then he forms for battle. On his far right are the 5th Infantry (Lt. Colonel McIntosh) artillery under Major Samuel Ringgold, 3rd Infantry (Captain L. M. Morris), two 18-pounders (Lt. Churchill), and 4th Infantry (Major G. W. Allen). The 3rd and 4th Regiments composed the

Battle of Palo Alto (Tomes, *Battles of America by Sea and Land*).

Third Brigade, which is commanded by Lt. Colonel Garland. The right wing is also bolstered by two squadrons of dragoons (Captain Croghan Ker and Captain Charles May). The left wing is composed of a battalion of artillery (Lt. Colonel Thomas Childs), the light artillery under Captain James Duncan and the 8th Infantry (Captain William Montgomery). The units of the left wing form the First Brigade, commanded by Lt. Colonel Belknap.

At about 2 P.M., the Americans initiate their march toward the enemy. Their artillery is trailing. During the advance, Lieutenant Blake, topographical engineer, volunteers to reconnoiter the enemy's lines. He moves out in front and discovers that the Mexican artillery is deployed in the intervals between their infantry and cavalry. Suddenly, the Mexican artil-

lery commences fire. Taylor halts his advance and orders his artillery to respond. The 8th Infantry had pulled back to prevent the left flank from being overrun. In the meantime, Ringgold's artillery responds to the Mexican fire, while the battery under Captain Duncan is brought up in advance of the line, while Captain May's squadron detaches to protect that battery as well as the left flank.

Mexican cavalry with two pieces of artillery are moving to outflank the right flank. The 5th Infantry is dispatched to hold the line. With the support of Lieutenant Randolph Ridgely and part of Ringgold's battery along with Captain Walker's volunteers, the enemy is repulsed. In the meantime, the 5th Infantry was able to repulse a charge by Mexican cavalry. The 3rd Infantry was detached and sped to the right flank to further bolster it.

The heavy firing from the American artillery set the prairie on fire, which nearly conceals the two opposing armies. Taylor directs his troops on the right to advance because the Mexican left had been driven back and the road is open. The Mexicans also cease their artillery fire. Taylor directs his 18-pounders to advance to new positions where the Mexican cavalry had been stationed. The First Brigade is directed to take new positions to the left of the 18-pounders. The 5th Infantry advances to its new positions on the far right of the new lines. In the meantime, the Mexicans take advantage of the lack of fire to adjust their lines. After a cessation of about one hour, the two sides resume the fight.

The 4th infantry is directed to support the 18-pounder battery, which it does despite taking enormous fire from the Mexican artillery. A few men, including Major Ringgold, are seriously wounded. Ringgold is struck by a 6-pound shot while mounted. The shot enters his right thigh, passing through the holsters and upper part of the shoulders of his horse, and then striking his left thigh in the same line. His wound is mortal. Major Ringgold spends the night with Doctor Byrne of the U.S. Army and lives for sixty hours. Captain Page sustains a serious wound but survives. Page, unable to speak, is shot in the lower jaw "with part of his tongue and palate ... shot away." The Mexicans in the meantime put together a charge that advanced toward the 18-pounders. Once the

Mexican cavalry approaches the range of the 18-pounders, a vicious bombardment hit them, causing the Mexicans to disperse.

Near darkness a volley is sent into the square. Lt. Roland Luther is hit by a shot and slightly wounded. However, discharges originating in the square quickly silence the small arms fire. Afterward the Mexicans are driven back and foiled at every turn.

In the meantime, the Mexicans push against the American left, but Captain Duncan is able to sense the danger. His artillery is repositioned and the attempt is repeatedly repelled, saving the left flank. Duncan's battery is supported by the 8th Infantry and Captain Croghan Ker's squadron. The Mexicans are again driven back. Nevertheless, they continue their futile attack until dark. At that time, the Mexicans retired into the chaparral, bringing an end to the slaughter.

During the fighting, John Bankhead Magruder's company loses two men. The Mexican cannon fire remains heavy for about five hours and in one instance, two men had their bayonets shot off their muskets as the cannon balls pass "just over their shoulders and between their heads." The cannon balls "fell in the centres of the square and ricocheted out again without touching anyone." On the following morning the Mexicans retreat. The Mexicans leave their wounded and dead on the field. Their losses amount to more than 500.

After the battle, General Taylor visits with each of the wounded to make sure they receive the care they deserve. Afterward, Taylor calls for a council and gathers all of his officers. They number 13 and all but four are in favor of the army advancing the next day. Of the other four, some want to entrench where they stand to wait for reinforcements, while others want to retire to Point Isabel. General Taylor inserts: "I will be at Fort Brown before night, if I live."

Taylor estimates American casualties as nine killed, 44 wounded and two missing. Major Ringgold, who was killed, was interred initially at Fort Polk and later at Greenmount Cemetery at Baltimore, Maryland. Captain Page and Lieutenant Luther, both of whom sustained wounds, survived. U.S. Captain Edmund Kirby Smith, ecstatic over Taylor's victory, remarks: "It is a glorious fact for the army that there were no volunteers with us." American Captain Henry remarks after Taylor's victory: "We only asked for an opportunity, few as we were, to prove to our country, she had a safe anchor in our small but gallant force."

Taylor's force is victorious and Mexican General Mariano Arista retreats to a better defensive position at Resaca de la Palma. Captain Duncan, when asked by General Taylor for his opinion of fighting, responds, "We whipped 'em today and we can whip 'em tomorrow!" Mexicans had 320 killed and 380 wounded.

Major Brown, badly wounded, issued this order: "Men go to your duties, stand by your post. I am but one among you." He is among those killed. Major Jacob Brown's body is later exhumed and moved to the National Cemetery at Pineville, Louisiana.

Bushrod Rust Johnson (later Confederate general) participates at this battle. First Lieutenant Thomas Jordan (later Confederate general), 3rd Infantry, also takes part. Later he participates at Resaca de la Palma, and at Vera Cruz he is quartermaster. Lieutenant Lafayette McLaws participates at this battle. Subsequently, McLaws takes part at Vera Cruz and Monterey. Afterward, his health fails and he is sent back to the United Sates on recruiting duty. Afterward, McLaws is engaged in convoying trains to Mexico City. Lieutenant John Clifford Pemberton (later Confederate general) participates at this battle. Later, on 4 August, Pemberton becomes an aide-de-camp to Brigadier General William J. Worth. He keeps the position until 1 May 1849. Pemberton also participates in the Battle of Resaca, Battle of Monterrey, Vera Cruz, Cerro Gordo, San Antonio, Churubusco, Molino del Rey, Chapultepec and Mexico City. Pemberton is brevetted to captain on 21–23 September 1846 and to major on 8 September 1847.

Captain Daniel Ruggles (later Confederate general), 5th Infantry, participates at this battle. Later, he takes part in the Battle of Resaca de la Palma before being attached to recruiting duty which lasts into the following year. In 1847, Ruggles participates at the Siege of Vera Cruz, the capture of San Antonio and the Battles of Churubusco and Molino del Rey. Ruggles is brevetted as major on 20 August 1847 for his gallantry at Contreras and Churubusco, then on 13 September 1847, he is brevetted as lieutenant colonel for his actions at Chapultepec and the capture of Mexico City. Lieutenant Carter Littlepage Stevenson (later Confederate general), 5th U.S. Infantry participates at this battle and later at the Battle of Resaca de la Palma. During 1847–1848 he is engaged in recruiting service at Detroit, Michigan.

Lieutenant Benjamin Alvord (later Union general), 4th Infantry, participates at this battle. Later he participates at the Battle of Resaca and is brevetted captain for his gallantry at both battles. Afterward, he is assigned recruiting duty (1846–1847), followed by his participation at the Battle of Vera Cruz. Afterward, he is engaged at the defense of a convoy at Paso de Ovejas, Cerro Gordo, Las Animas and the affair at Huamantla. George Meade (later Union general) participates at this battle, the Battle of Resaca de la Palma and Monterrey. William Reading Montgomery (later Union general) also takes part. Later, he participates at Resaca de la Palma and Molino del Rey.

Christopher Columbus Augur (later Union general) participates at this battle and at Resaca de la Palma. Lieutenant William Thomas Harbaugh Brooks (later Union general) is also involved in this battle. Captain Robert Christie Buchanan (later Union general) participates as well. Subsequently, he participates at Resaca de la Palma and Molino Del Rey. Buchanan won the brevets of major and lieutenant colonel during his time in service. Patrick Edward Connor (later Union general) takes part in this battle. Second Lieutenant Lawrence Pike Graham, General George Meade's brother-in-law, participates at this battle and at Resaca de la Palma. He is brevetted for gallantry at both battles. Captain George Archibald McCall (later Union general) takes part in this battle and at Resaca Del Palma; he is brevetted major and lieutenant colonel for his gallantry. Randolph Barnes Marcy (later Union general) participates. Later, he is involved in the Battle of Resaca de la Palma; he is afterward assigned to recruiting. Thomas Hewson Neill (later Union general) of the 5th Infantry does not participate in the war; he is employed along the frontier. Lieutenant Thomas Gamble Pitcher (later Union general), who had served in Texas prior to the war with Mexico, is a participant; he is a member of the 5th Infantry. Second Lieutenant John Cleveland Robinson (later Union general), quartermaster, 5th Infantry, participates. He serves for the duration and participates at Resaca de la Palma, Monterrey and the capture of Mexico City. John Henry Hobart Ward (later Union general), 7th Infantry, takes part. He serves as a private, corporal, sergeant and sergeant major during the conflict and is wounded at Monterrey, Mexico. Lt. Colonel Alpheus Starkey Williams (later Union general) serves as first lieutenant of the 1st Michigan Infantry during the latter part of the war.

In other activity, the United States Navy has secured Point Isabel for the purpose of establishing a supply base for the Army troops. This naval detachment is under the command of Commodore David Conner. The Mexicans offer only token resistance to U.S. naval forces during the entire confrontation. Mexico acquired two ironclads, the *Guadalupe* and the *Montezuma*, but neither see battle during the conflict. The much superior American Navy certainly lends great assistance to the American Army, by strangling the Mexican supply line with a blockade along the Gulf Coast, preventing supplies from entering Mexico by sea.

May 8   In Florida, the USS *Mississippi*, a steamer, arrives at Pensacola from Vera Cruz. Doctor Wood, U.S. Navy, who is carrying dispatches from the squadron to the government, is a passenger.

In other activity, Marines and seamen attached to the Home Squadron occupy Port Isabel, Texas. They are to defend the fort if attacked by the Mexicans.

May 9 THE BATTLE OF RESACA DE LA PALMA   General Zachary Taylor advances toward Fort Brown. His advance proceeds to a point about four miles from the post when his force once again encounters the Mexican army standing on ground the Mexicans thought impregnable. Their artillery is placed where it could inundate the entire road on which Taylor's army would pass. The Americans determine the dangers involved with trying to pass through the dry bed or gorge which gave it the name Resaca de la Palma. General Taylor, once seeing the positioning of the Mexican artillery, orders his supply train to halt. Four pieces of artillery are left there to defend the wagons.

In the meantime, Taylor continues to advance. Captain George A. McCall is sent on a mission to determine exactly where the Mexican artillery is placed. His infantry is shortly thereafter engaged in a bloody contest. McCall's troops are able to best the Mexicans in a vicious engagement. However, Taylor is pressed to send up Captain Charles A. May to guarantee it. Taylor insists that May has to "take that battery with his squadron of dragoons, if he lost every man." May accepts the challenge.

Captain May sets out to determine if the Mexicans have artillery, but they are not fired upon. He arrives back at American lines without discovering the artillery. Lieutenant Jacob E. Blake offers to go out alone to check on the Mexican guns. He and another officer move up to a point about eighty yards from the Mexicans lines. After peering through eyeglasses, the two men are able to spot the artillery. Shortly thereafter, two Mexican officers ride out toward them. Blake, after being informed of the two riders, tells the other officer to draw his weapon and train it on the two Mexicans. Blake and the other officer then gallop along the Mexican lines where they again search for artillery, then they return. As soon as Blake and the other officer returned to their lines to report what they had found, the Mexican artillery commenced firing.

Captain May arrives at a point where he is halted by Lieutenant Randolph Ridgely, who explains that the Mexicans had just reloaded their weapons and that if he charged, the Mexican artillery would decimate his command. Ridgely then says, "Stop, til I draw their fire." The fire is commenced by each of Ridgely's guns and

Captain May's second charge (Frost, *The History of Mexico and Its Wars*).

they take a toll on the Mexicans. The Mexicans return horrendous fire. The initial shot from the Mexican battery knocks over one man and three horses at the first place. The enemy fires too high, as on the day before. The 5th and 6th Infantry move up and deploy along the line about twenty paces from the Mexicans.

At that instant, May initiates his charge. The first and second platoons are nearly decimated, but the near impenetrable fire does not harm him. May is galloping through the grape and bullets as if he were invulnerable. May's horses pass through the battery so quickly that May is compelled to make another run through the battery.

May charges the battery and drives away the cannoneers. He seizes the guns and causes the Mexican veterans to take flight. During the assault, the Mexicans sustain high losses. On his second charge, May comes upon Mexican General Romulo de la Vega, who remains at his guns and is dodging the strokes of one of his men. When May appears, la Vega hands him his sword.

The Mexicans flee in all directions, pursued by Captain Ker's dragoons and Duncan's artillery. The Americans seize many Mexicans and capture eight pieces of artillery as well as much baggage and public property. Captain May transfers the general to an officer, then races to General Taylor to tell him that his men had seized the battery as ordered, as well as General de la Vega. Captain May gives De la Vega's sword to Taylor. Later that night when Lieutenant Magruder introduces General de la Vega to

General Taylor, the general conveys "his deep regret that such a misfortune should have happened to an officer whose character he so highly esteemed." Taylor then returns his sword. Other notables who participated in the battle include Lew Wallace, later a general in the Civil War.

Colonel Belknap leads his brigade into the midst of the battle, where he seizes a Mexican standard. He waves it back and forth until his horse trips over the dead bodies which are lying everywhere. When the horse trips, Belknap is thrown. A soldier trying to help him get back on his horse is shot in the lung, while at about the same time, a bullet shoots the Mexican flag away. Suddenly the colonel is holding only the pole. In the meantime, American cavalry attack General Arista's right wing and Taylor's infantry assault just afterwards, causing great confusion among the Mexicans, who retreat in disarray. The retreating Mexicans must pass American artillery, which creates more problems for them. The Americans, although greatly outnumbered, win an overwhelming victory. The victory elevates General Taylor to a prominent position as national hero. Mexicans total 547 killed or wounded. Americans have 33 dead and 89 wounded.

The wounded and killed American officers include Lieutenant Inge (2d Dragoons), Lieutenant Cochran (4th Infantry) and Lieutenant Chadbourne (8th Infantry). Officers wounded include Lieutenant Colonels McIntosh, Lieutenant Colonel Payne, Captain Montgomery, Captain Hooe, Lieutenant Gates, Lieutenant Maclay, Lieutenant Selden, Lieutenant Burbank, Lieutenant Jordon, and Lieutenant Fowler.

Following the victory, General Zachary Taylor dispatched Captain Carr (dragoons) with a guard to inform the fort at Point Isabel with the news. The detachments were carrying so many Mexican flags that the garrison assumed that the detachment was Mexican and about to attack the fort. The garrison fired upon the detachment, but no one was injured.

After the battle at La Palma, the Americans capture Mexican General Arista's personal papers. Included in the papers is a government directive instructing General Arista to bring General Taylor to Mexico City immediately following his capture.

Participants in this battle include Bushrod Rust Johnson (later Confederate general) and Lieutenant William Thomas Harbaugh Brooks (later Union general). Brooks is promoted to first lieutenant of the 3rd Infantry on 21 September 1846.

In California, John Frémont is informed that an American officer, Lieutenant Gillespie of the U.S. Marine Corps, is following the command. Later that day, Lieutenant Gillespie delivers secret orders to Frémont. And Frémont is also informed that hostile Indians are waiting for him. Gillespie had destroyed the dispatches, but not before memorizing them. Frémont is ordered to return to California. Frémont's return to California prevents Sir George Seymour from claiming California for the British when he sailed into Monterrey.

In other activity, Captain Jacob Brown, the commander of Fort Texas, dies at 2 P.M. General Taylor says in his official dispatch regarding the death of Brown: "The field work opposite Matamoros has sustained itself handsomely during a cannonade and bombardment of one hundred and sixty hours. But the pleasure is alloyed with profound regret, at the loss of its heroic and indomitable commander, Major Brown, who died to-day from the effect of a shell. His loss would be a severe one to the service at any time, but to the army under my orders it is indeed irreparable." Captain Edgar S. Hawkins is named commander after the death of Brown.

In activity elsewhere, the New Orleans *Bulletin* publishes that about thirty troops had deserted from General Taylor's force and that "ten or twelve of them were shot in endeavoring to make their escape."

In yet other activity, Simon Bolivar Buckner (later Confederate general) is promoted to 2nd Lieutenant, 6th Infantry. During the Mexican War, he participates at the siege of Vera Cruz, Battle of Cerro Gordo, and the Battle of Churubusco, where he was wounded. He also participated at the battles of Contreras and Molino del Rey. At the latter, he was brevetted a captain for his gallantry. He also participated in the seizure of Mexico City. Buckner is designated as quartermaster general of the 6th Infantry on August 9, 1847.

May 10   In Texas, Captain Edgar S. Hawkins, who succeeded Captain Brown at Fort Texas, states in a memorandum to W.W.S. Bliss, assistant adjutant-general, Army of Occupation, Texas:

Sir:— I have the honor to report that on the morning of the 6th instant, during the third day of the bombardment of this fort, its gallant commander, Major Brown, received a severe wound, which caused his death at 2 o'clock on the 9th instant. I immediately assumed command, and have the honor to report the result of the bombardment since 7 o'clock, P.M., on the fourth, at which time Captain Walker left with a report of the result up to that time. At 9 o'clock, P.M., on the fourth, firing of musketry was heard in our rear, about three or four hundred yards distance, and apparently extending a mile up the river, the firing very irregular; this continued until half-past 11 o'clock, P.M. The garrison was under arms, batteries and defences all manned and continued so during the night. On the fifth instant, at 5 o'clock, A.M., the fire was recommenced from the enemy's batteries, which was immediately returned from the 18-pounder battery, and 6-pounder howitzer placed in embrasure on the southeast bastion; the firing was kept up one hour, receiving during that time about fifty round shot and shells from the enemy. The batteries on both sides ceased firing at the same time; our expenditure of ammunition was thirty rounds of both caliber. At 8 o'clock, A.M., Valdez, a Mexican, came in and reported that a party of dragoons had been driven back from the prairie to the point, and also a party to the fort; that he had seen thirty deserters from Arista's army, who stated that the Mexicans were without subsistence stores; that they were tired and left for their homes; that it was stated in the Mexican camp that General Mariano Arista had received an express from Mexico, informing him that another revolution had broken out in Mexico, and that he could receive no support from the government. At 9 o'clock, A.M., it was reported that a reconnaissance of officers, escorted by mounted men of the enemy, was going on in rear within eight hundred yards of the fort, and that other parties, mounted and infantry, were at the same distance, extending from the bend of the lagoon to the river. Lieutenant Hanson, 7th infantry, asked permission to take the dragoons and go and look at them; this was granted, and in an hour he returned, reporting that the enemy was establishing a battery at the cross roads; his appearance among them created great alarm, and they were soon concentrated at a distance under cover of their work. Every man at work today strengthening their defences. Several parties of cavalry and infantry seen to-day occupying our old encampment. At 11 o'clock, P.M., musketry was heard in our rear from bend of lagoon to the river. The troops all at their places in the bastions during the night.

May 11   In Texas, General Taylor departs from Fort Brown en route to Point Isabel to confer with Commodore David Conner, commander of the American Gulf Squadron. While there, he sends a letter to Washington. Taylor informs his superiors that the Mexican Army is nearly totally disorganized, he is preparing to invest Matamoros, and he is about to open the navigation of the river. Taylor also mentions that Lieutenant Blake of the Topographical Engineers, "after rendering distinguished service in my staff, during the affair of the 8th instant, accidentally shot himself with a pistol the following day, and expired before night." Taylor also mentioned that he had exchanged prisoners with the Mexicans to recover the command of Captain Thornton. Taylor stated that the wounded prisoners were sent to Matamoros and the wounded officers were placed on parole. Taylor closed his letter by saying that General de la Vegas, having turned down a parole, and a few other officers were sent to New Orleans to report to General Edmund Pendleton Gaines. General Taylor remained at Point Isabel until the 13th.

May 12   In Louisiana, General Edmund Pendleton Gaines authorizes Colonel William B. Lewis to raise a regiment or a battalion of mounted gunmen. The regiment is afterward to rendezvous at Opelousas. The regiment is to be raised for service of the United States for a period of six months for duty along the Rio Grande.

May 13   In Washington, D.C., Congress approves a Declaration of War with Mexico. "By the act of the republic of Mexico, a state of war exists between that government and the United States." The war further divides the North (anti) and the South (pro), pulling the United States closer to civil war. The president's declaration announcing war with Mexico was copied nearly word for word from

James Madison's proclamation of June 19, 1812, which declared war with Great Britain.

In other activity, General Zachary Taylor departs from Point Isabel and returns to Fort Brown. After advancing only a short distance, Taylor was informed that the Mexicans were forming at Barita, located below Matamoros. Taylor returns to Point Isabel to formulate his plan.

May 14   In Texas, General Taylor departs from Point Isabel en route to Fort Brown. He is thankful when he sees the faces of the reinforcements who had just arrived from New Orleans. The troops had earlier been requested by Taylor and came from Louisiana and Alabama. Taylor's entourage includes 600 troops, an artillery train and about three hundred wagons. He arrives at his destination on the night of the 15th. Zachariah Cantey Deas (later Confederate general) serves with the Alabama forces.

May 15   *In naval activity,* the USS *Augusta*, a schooner, sails from Point Isabel to New Orleans. It is transporting dispatches. At 6 A.M. the *Augusta* crosses the bar at Brazos Santiago.

In other activity, Albert Gallatin Blanchard (later Confederate general) is appointed captain of Louisiana Volunteers. He participates in the Battle of Monterrey and the siege of Vera Cruz. On 9 April, he is reinstated in the U.S. Army as a captain, but he declines. Nevertheless, he is re-appointed in the United States Army with the rank of major, 12th Infantry, on 27 May 1847. Also, Milledge Luke Bonham (later Confederate general and governor of South Carolina) takes part in the war. He serves as lieutenant colonel and colonel of the 12th U.S. Infantry. In December 1861, he is appointed major general and commander of Army of South Carolina, then later, on 19 April 1861, he is named brigadier general in the Confederate Army. In December 1862 he is elected governor of South Carolina. During February 1865, he is appointed brigadier general of cavalry in the Confederate Army. Also, Harry Thompson Hays (later Confederate general) serves with the 5th Louisiana Regiment.

May 16   *In naval activity,* the *Augusta*, a steam schooner that left Point Isabel on 15 May, is hailed by the steamer *Galveston*, which transfers Colonel C. Doane with dispatches from General Taylor. Elsewhere, the USS *Princeton*, a steamer commanded by F. Engle, having been repaired at the Charlestown Navy Yard, is ordered on or about this day to proceed to Pensacola. Captain French Forrest, aboard as a passenger, is to succeed Captain Dulaney, commander of the USS *Cumberland*, which is in the Gulf of Mexico.

In Alabama, the "relief volunteers" of Montgomery, commanded by Captain Elmore, had arrived at Mobile to discover that the Louisiana numbers had been filled. On the 16th, after the regiment dispatched an agent to New Orleans to gain acceptance from General Edmund P. Gaines, the regiment went over to New Orleans as part of the Louisiana volunteers. In addition, another company from Alabama went with them to claim the same privilege of being received without pay. The other company, with men were from Mobile and Tuscaloosa, was commanded by Col. W. H. Platt.

In Missouri, the St. Louis Volunteers, about 600 strong, march to the Jefferson Barracks from where they will depart for Texas.

May 17 **In Mexico,** Lieutenant Colonel Wilson, 1st Infantry, leads the two companies of volunteers from Louisiana under Captain F. Stockton and Captain G. H. Tobin and the one from Alabama. He is en route from Barita to Matamoros. Meanwhile, General Taylor insists on an interview with Mexican General Pedro de Ampudia. The general, however, sends General Thomas Reguena. He arrives at Taylor's camp and speaks of an armistice, but Taylor demands unconditional surrender of the town. Reguena agrees to return an answer by 3:00 P.M. that day, but he never returns. All the while, Taylor is aware that the city has been loaded with war supplies and de Ampudia is wasting time to get the supplies removed. Taylor, however, is prepared to cross the river. He dispatches troops to secure boats that could be used for the crossing. Later that night, his army moves within three miles of Matamoros to camp. The army begins to cross at dawn.

May 18 **In Mexico,** the American consul in Vera Cruz is ordered by the Mexican government to leave within eight days.

In naval activity, Marines and seamen attached to the USS *Cumberland* and the USS *Potomac* are landed on the south side of the Rio Grande.

They become the first U.S. forces to land in Mexico.

May 18–23 **In Mexico,** American soldiers cross the Rio Grande unopposed and occupy Matamoros on the 18th, raising "Old Glory." Mexican General Arista had evacuated the city at about dusk on the previous night. The east bank of the river is defended by two 18-pounders and three batteries of artillery. To alleviate the boredom of the advance, Colonel Twiggs directs the bands to play "Yankee Doodle." Captain Walker of the Texas Rangers and Lieutenant Hays (4th Infantry) along with ten volunteers are first to cross. They are to report on the positions and the number of the enemy near the river if possible.

Shortly after Lieutenant Hays crosses, the flank companies of the 3d, 4th, and 5th Infantry follow. After these commands cross, Captain Smith of the artillery battalion crosses with two companies. Captain Ker's squadron of dragoons then crosses. Next, Ridgely's artillery is dismounted and taken over in sections. Meanwhile, the infantry crosses and advances, then occupies a hedge fence to cover the crossing.

About two hours later, a group of civilians come out of Matamoros to request a meeting with General Taylor. They are sent over the river with an officer because General Taylor had not yet crossed. The group is anxious to inform Taylor that General Arista and his Mexican troops had fled from Matamoros; however, they are also interested in finding out what Taylor has in store for the city. Taylor informs the group that the civil and religious rights of the people would be respected. Once General Taylor is informed of the Mexican army's flight, he directs the forces that have not yet crossed the river to return to Fort Brown and cross there.

In the meantime, while the group is speaking with General Taylor, Captain Ker's dragoons move to Fort Paredes, where they raise the American flag to signal the occupation of Matamoros. Also, the separate regiments that had crossed the river advance to their encampments. During the evening a small guard is established in Matamoros.

Lieutenant George Stephens, while crossing the river at the head of his command, 2nd Dragoons, is pushed from his horse by the current. Attempts to save him fail. His body is recovered two days later. Once the Americans had crossed, Major Ed Bliss approaches the fort in front of the town and demands its surrender. The alcalde inquires about the public buildings and is told that all private property would be protected and that all religious and civil rights were to be protected; however, the alcalde is then told that all public buildings were to be given up. The alcalde tells General Taylor that he could take possession and that he would meet no resistance. The place is taken and Taylor's army encamps outside the town.

General Taylor sends Captain Walker on a mission to observe the Mexican Army's retreat. A skirmish develops between the Americans and the vanguard. The Americans kill a few and take 25 prisoners. Taylor's camp is about one mile from the city of Matamoros, and his troops are not permitted to enter. The American capture about 300 Mexicans that are convalescing in the hospital.

Also, due to the large number of printers who have joined the service, it is not long before Matamoros gets its own printing press into action. The *Flag* becomes a prominent newspaper.

Lieutenant Alfred Pleasonton (later Union general) participates at this battle as a member of the 2nd Dragoons. He also participates at Resaca de la Palma and is later promoted to first lieutenant. Lieutenant Benjamin Stone Roberts (later Union general) also takes part.

In naval activity, the frigate USS *Raritan* arrives at Vera Cruz where it joins the squadron. Commodore David Conner transfers his flag to the USS *Raritan*. On the 23rd, Conner departs Vera Cruz. Conner's USS *Raritan* is accompanied by the USS *Cumberland*, USS *Potomac* and the USS *Falmouth*. The USS *John Adams*, a sloop of war, is the only vessel that remains in port at Sacrificios.

May 19   In Texas, Governor James Pinckney Henderson and some of his staff depart from Austin for the Rio Grande. One company of volunteers from Montgomery, commanded by Captain (later colonel) Jo. Bennet, departs from Galveston for the Rio Grande on the 29th and later, a company composed of about 60 mounted riflemen commanded by Captain Early leaves from Washington County. In the absence of Henderson, Albert Clinton Horton becomes acting governor. Henderson returns to his duties as governor on 13 December 1846.

May 19–22   In Texas, Lt. Col. Garland, commanding cavalry of about 250 dragoons and regulars, sets out from Matamoros in an attempt to catch the Mexican army under de Ampudia. The cavalry is ordered to capture baggage and take prisoners. However, on the 22nd, Garland returns to Matamoros due to the condition of his horses and the condition of the land, particularly the absence of water. Before returning, his force captures twenty-two troops. The Americans sustain two wounded. One ammunition wagon and clothing for an artillery company is also seized.

May 20   In Mexico, the United States begins the naval blockade of Vera Cruz. In other activity, at Guadalajara in the province of Jalisco, a revolution erupts. The battalion of Lagos, other bodies of the military, along with the people attack the palace of the governor. The assault happens so quickly there is hardly time for the artillery to fire. One man is killed and another wounded. The governor is compelled to surrender and is permitted to leave for Mexico City. The people of Jalisco begin to proclaim General Don Antonio Lopez de Santa Anna "as the chief of the grand enterprise for which this plan is entered into."

May 21   In Kentucky, the Louisville *Journal* publishes that some manufacturing establishments were forced to close due to a shortage of workers because of men joining the army.

May 23   Two companies of U.S. artillery from Pensacola, one company from Fort Wood and another from near New Orleans are directed by General Edmund P. Gaines to head for the Rio del Norte. They will leave New Orleans on the 5th. In other activity, a chief of the Creek Indians, while in Washington, offers, according to the *Pennsylvanian*, the service of two thousand Creek warriors in the war with Mexico.

May 24   In Kentucky, Governor Owsley is pleased by the Louisville Legion, eight companies, who depart for New Orleans on or about this day. The Kentucky regiments (two infantry and one cavalry called for) had been raised in about four days and only 13 days after the declaration of war with Mexico. Robert Hall Chilton (later Confederate general) serves as captain of the 1st Kentucky Rifles. John Stuart Williams (later Confederate general) serves initially as a captain with the 6th U.S. Infantry and later as colonel of the 4th Kentucky Regiment. Also, Edward Henry Hobson (later Union general) serves as a member of the 2nd Kentucky Infantry Regiment.

In naval activity, the USS *St. Mary's* bombards Tampico, Florida. The Marines aboard the vessel participate in the bombardment. In other activity, the Mexican schooner *Juanita* is seized by the USS *Flirt,* a schooner. It is taken to Brazos as a prize. In other activity, the *Montezuma* and the *Guadalupe,* both steamers, have escaped from Vera Cruz and arrived at Havana, Cuba, under British colors on this day. Roger Weightman Hanson (later Confederate general) signs up as a first lieutenant. He serves for the duration in John Williams' company. John Stuart Williams (later Confederate general) serves initially as a captain with the 6th U.S. Infantry and later as colonel of the 4th Kentucky Regiment. Also, Cassius Marcellus Clay (later Union general) serves with the 1st Kentucky Cavalry. James Streshly Jackson (later Union general) serves in the 1st Kentucky Cavalry Regiment as a private; he had helped to form the regiment and later he is made third lieutenant (9 July 1846). Later he resigns from the service on 10 October, 1846. Lieutenant Walter Chiles Whitaker (later Union general) enters the service with the 1st or 3rd Kentucky Regiment.

May 27   In California, John Frémont arrives at Marysville Buttes, where he remains for about one week. While there, Frémont succeeds in

Captain Samuel Walker (Frost, *The History of Mexico and Its Wars*).

gaining volunteers for his force. In other activity, about 260 volunteers commanded by Captain Stewart, Piper and Steiner break up their camp at Baltimore's Howard's Park. The march through Baltimore and report to the commandant of district volunteers, whom they expect to speed up their arrival at the frontier.

In other activity, Washington Lafayette Elliott (later Union general) is commissioned into the regular army as second lieutenant of mounted rifles. Later, he participates at the Battle of Vera Cruz. Afterward he is struck by illness; when he recuperates he is assigned recruiting duty. In other activity, Andrew Porter is appointed first lieutenant of mounted rifles. He serves in the Mexican war and is promoted to captain on 15 May. He participates at Contreras and at Churubusco, where he receives the brevet of major. Afterward, he participates at Chapultepec, where he is brevetted lieutenant colonel.

May 28   In Texas, Captain Samuel Walker, having only recently arrived at Point Isabel, is directed by Major Munroe to open communication with General Taylor. On this day, Walker, with his command of about 75 Texas Rangers, sets out to hook up with General Taylor. After moving about 12 miles, his command is struck by a Mexican force. His troops, many of whom are fresh, retreat. The engagement lasts about fifteen minutes. The rangers are able to make it to Point Isabel. The rangers claim that about thirty of the attackers were killed.

In other activity, 2nd Lieutenant Hamilton Prioleau Bee (later Confederate General and brother of Barnard Bee) serves as a member of the Benjamin McCulloch's 1st Regiment of Texas Volunteers, then he is transferred to Mirabeau B. Lamar's Texas cavalry, where he is a first lieutenant. Also, Captain Thomas Green (later Confederate general) arrives in Texas at about this time as part of Zachary Taylor's command. However, as the clerk of the Supreme Court of Texas, he is unable to remain with the army for the duration. He serves in a regiment commanded by Colonel Jack Hays. Walter Paye Lane (later Confederate general) serves under Colonel Hays as a first lieutenant in the 1st Texas Regiment Texas Mounted Riflemen in June of this year. He participates in the Battle of Monterrey. Lane is later promoted to major and receives command of a battalion. William Miller (later Confederate general) of Louisiana serves in the army of Zachary Taylor.

In naval activity, the USS *Aurora,* a schooner, sails from Point Isabel en route to General Taylor's camp with dispatches for the general.

May 29   In Maryland, three companies of volunteers, eager to serve in the war, decide to take cars into the capital to report to the secretary of war; however, the city is not prepared for the influx. The president asks Governor Thomas G. Pratt of Maryland to make the companies part of the District of Columbia Battalion, which Pratt accommodates. Governor

Pratt then commissions William H. Watson lieutenant colonel of the battalion. Another company, from Baltimore, joins the battalion within a few days. They sail for the Rio Grande River on 11 June aboard the USS *Massachusetts.* James Jay Archer (later Confederate general) accepts a captain's commission for service with a Maryland regiment.

In other activity, the Galveston *News* reports that 15 Americans, including two women and a child, were murdered by a band of Mexicans. The party left Corpus Christi on the 2nd or 3rd of May and arrived at Little Colorado just before the Battle of Palo Alto. The Mexicans, after confronting the party and disarming it, stripped them and robbed them. The Mexicans also raped the women before cutting their throats. One in the party, Rogers, who saw both his father and brother savagely murdered, feigned death. His throat injury was not fatal. He had the presence of mind to let the Mexicans, believing him to be dead, throw him into the Colorado River. Once in the river, he swam to the opposite bank and escaped. Afterward, he made it to the Rio Grande River, where he was taken prisoner and sent to a hospital in Matamoros. Subsequent to the seizure of Matamoros, Rogers was exchanged.

May 29–30   In Texas, Captain Samuel Walker, far from being discouraged by the debacle, offers to carry messages from Major Monroe to General Taylor, provided that four men accompany him. Six rangers immediately volunteer. Major Monroe agrees and on the following day, Walker again sets out to find Taylor. Walker does reach Taylor's camp outside of Matamoros and informs him of the conditions at Point Isabel.

May 28   In Rhode Island, Captain Swartwout, 2nd Artillery Regiment, at Fort Adams receives orders to move with his regiment to New York from where they will depart for the Rio Grande. William Farquar Barry (later Union general) moves with the 2nd Artillery Regiment; however, he becomes very sick. When he recuperates he is assigned staff duty. Also, Joseph Farmer Knipe (later Union general) serves as a sergeant with the 2nd Artillery.

May 30   Two volunteer companies have been organized in Indiana at New Albany, and at Evansville two corps have been raised. In Illinois, at Quincy, three volunteer companies are raised. In Tennessee, the Nashville *Whig* published on the 19 May that "volunteers from every part of Tennessee are daily tendering their services to Governor Brown…. Tennessee will be ready to furnish more than her quota of any number that may be needed." Another Tennessee newspaper, the Nashville *Banner*, states: "Five thousand Tennesseans will be ready for whenever their services are required." John Wilkins Whitfield (later Confederate general) serves as captain of the 1st Tennessee and later as lieutenant colonel of the 2nd Tennessee. William Bowen Campbell (later Union general) is colonel of the regiment. Also, Isham Nicholas Haynie (later Union general) serves with the 6th Illinois Regiment.

In other activity, the Cincinnati papers publish that 1,000 men from that city are waiting for orders. Elsewhere, George Pickett (later Confederate general) on or about this day is promoted to second lieutenant, 2nd Infantry. Afterward, he is transferred to the 7th Infantry and finally to the 8th Infantry. He participates in all of the principal battles of General Winfield Scott. Pickett is brevetted first lieutenant for bravery at Contreras and Churubusco, and at Chapultepec he is brevetted captain. He later participates in the capture of Mexico City.

In naval activity, a letter from an officer in the U.S. Navy, dated at Pensacola, states: "We shall probably sail, as soon as we are provisioned, for Vera Cruz, but I doubt if any attack will be made on the castle, as they have prepared it so well for defense; and if their practice should be equal to the fire on Gen. Taylor's camp they would sink the whole of our navy. When the French attacked the castle, there were only twenty-five guns of small caliber at the point of attack; they have now over two hundred pieces, thirteen mortars, and Paixhan guns in quantities, on new batteries, at the same point, and one of our engineer officers says that if they were served well no fleet could ever make any impression."

June   In California, Commodore Sloat, commanding the USS *Savannah*, sets sail for Monterey, California. Following the orders of Commodore Sloat, Commander John B. Montgomery dispatches a landing party to raise "Old Glory" over San Francisco on 8 June, followed by the seizure of Monterey on 7 July.

Early June   In California, Mexican General Mariano Vallejo, commandant of the northern frontier at Sonoma, offers 170 horses to Castro, who is then organized at Santa Clara. Once the settlers hear the horses are to be used to uproot their claims, they began to mobilize an armed force to stop the transfer. This force is commanded by Ezekiel Merritt.

June 2   In New Orleans, the *Picayune* publishes the following: "The enormous forced loans which the government had imposed upon the clergy, the latter had declared itself totally unable to meet. The Metropolitan church was ordered to furnish a subsidy of $98,000 per month; the Mechoacan $35,000; of Puebla $40,000; of Guadalajara $2,000; of Durango $15,000, and of Oajaca $8,000. These great sums per month show that the president is determined to prosecute the war with energy. He will never be able to collect such loans."

In other activity, the New Orleans *Commercial Times* announces: "By the arrival of steamer *Mary Kingsland* from Brazos, which place she left on the 27th ult., eight hours after Galveston, we are put in possession of the following items of intelligence: "On the 26th, a reinforcement of 600 Texans arrived at Point Isabel; 400 mounted rangers and 200 infantry, from Padre Island. Amongst the latter is a German company, 80 strong, from Point Lavaca. It is confidently stated that Arista is concentrating his forces at Reinosa. The troops that went by the *Mary Kingsland*, were to march on the 28th for Matamoros, by way of Bocca Chica and Barita."

The U.S. brigantine *Lawrence* is the only vessel of war left at the mouth of the Rio Grande.

June 3   In California, American Colonel Stephen Kearny receives orders to capture Santa Fe and then proceed with his men to California.

June 5   In Mexico at Matamoros, a contingent of four companies of the 1st Infantry along with some volunteers, commanded by Lt. Colonel Wilson, departs from Barita en route to Reinoso, about 60 miles above the Rio Grande River. After reaching it, the column proceeds to Camargo, about thirty miles farther. Both towns surrender without any resistance. Lieutenant Robert Seaman Granger (later Union general), 1st U.S. Infantry, participates at this battle; on 8 September 1847 he is promoted to captain.

June 6   *In naval activity,* the British steamer HMS *Terrible*, according to an article in Wilmer and Smith's *Times*, is dispatched to Oregon.

In other activity, General John Ellis Wool, having been authorized by the president, is heading to the northwestern states to muster the quota of troops. In addition, Wool is to get the troops to the Rio Grande.

June 8–12   In California, Captain John Frémont is informed by William Knight of Knights Landing that Lt. Francis de Arce had passed over the Sacramento River with about eighty horses. On the morning of the 9th, eleven men commanded by Captain Ezekiel Merritt depart from Frémont's camp. They succeed in surprising the Mexicans on the morning of the 10th before daybreak and they capture all of Castro's men. The Mexicans are permitted to continue their journey to San Jose, minus the horses, which are driven into Frémont's camp on the 12th.

In naval activity, the USS *Truxton* is re-commissioned on this day at Norfolk, Virginia. On 15 June it anchors in Havana harbor. It remains there until 2 August, when it departs from Cuba and joins with the American blockading fleet at Sacrificios Island.

June 9   In California, Ezekiel Merritt, known as Stuttering Zeke, leads a small party of about ten men who intend to capture horses that are meant for Castro at Santa Clara. The Americans seize the horses. Afterward they take them to Captain Frémont's camp. The party, which now stands at about twenty men, then departs to attack Sonoma.

Elsewhere, Darius Nash Couch (later Union general) graduates West Point at about this time. He is promoted to brevet second lieutenant, 4th Artillery. Afterward he serves in the Mexican War and participates in the Battle of Buena Vista.

June 10   In Texas, Governor Henderson, leading about 1,000 troops, arrives at the Rio Grande. The Texans are accompanied by seventeen warriors of the Tonkaway tribe. At Matamoros, the Mexicans become alarmed. They believe that General Taylor is going to let the Indians swarm upon the town.

June 11   In California, a group of Americans heads for Sonoma. They arrive on 14 June and take control of the town without meeting any opposition. The Americans take prisoners,

including General Mariano Vallejo. Most are taken to Sutter's Fort, but about 25 are left at Sonoma.

June 13   In Mexico, in a letter dated this day the minister of the treasury urges the necessity of the money that Mexico has assessed from the clergy. He claims it is "the duty of the clergy to submit to the hardship forced upon all by the national calamities." He tells the archbishop that "the government has appropriated all revenues which were mortgaged, suspending, without exception, all payments to its creditors; that it withheld a fourth part of the salaries of all its employees; that all classes were called upon to make sacrifices, and the clergy must not be exempt." He then calls for a loan of $2,400,000, payable in twelve monthly installments. The archbishop replies on the 15th that he would call for an ecclesiastic convention on this day to "to meet that morning, before whom the matter would be laid; and that he would co-operate to the extent of his powers." It is determined that the churches cannot meet the contribution.

In other activity, the Arkansas volunteers are mustered into U.S. service. Five days later, the regiment, composed of 800 men commanded by Archibald Yell, march off to San Antonio, Texas, to join with General Taylor.

June 14   In California, Americans who had settled in California defiantly declare independence from Mexico, stating they are the "Republic of California." This is also known as the Bear Flag Republic because of the flag used as their colors. At dawn, about twenty Americans arrive at the home

of General Mariano Vallejo in Sonoma. They knock loudly on the
door, demanding that the general surrender. He answers the door after getting dressed, then invites three of the
men in for breakfast. Two hundred
and fifty muskets along with nine
brass cannon are surrendered. Vallejo
is afterward sent to Sutter's Fort, but
he returns after the U.S. takes control
of California. Vallejo subsequently
serves as a delegate to the California
Constitutional Convention and later
as a state senator.

Colonel John Frémont, who moved
into Mexican Territory through the
Sierra Madre Mountains into California, arrives during the hostilities
in the latter part of June. He assumes
command of the American settlers in
early July. After the capture of Sonoma, Captain Merritt resigns. John
Grigsby is elected captain, but Sonoma is placed under the command
of Captain William B. Ide. Captain
Ide sends a two-man detachment to
the Fitch ranch in search of powder.

June 17   In Mexico, Colonel Wilson, with a 300-man contingent of
regulars and about 350 volunteers,
takes Barita without encountering resistance. The Americans' taking of
Barita on the southern side of the Rio
Grande River is the first seizure of a
post in Mexico.

June 18   In Mexico, a contingent of
about 200 seamen and Marines, commanded by Captain Aulick and attached to the USS *Cumberland* and
the USS *Potomac*, enter the Del Norte
where they are to cooperate with an
army detachment under Lt. Colonel
Wilson in setting up a post at Barita.

In other activity, Lieutenant John
Bankhead Magruder (later Confederate general) is promoted to captain,
1st Artillery. He is placed on recruiting duty (1846–1847), but afterward,
Magruder returns to Mexico and participates in the siege of Vera Cruz and
the Battle of Cerro Gordo, the latter
in which he is brevetted major on 18
April 1847. He also participates at the
skirmishes at La Hoya and Ocalaca,
the Battle of Contreras, Molino del
Rey and Chapultepec, where he is
again brevetted as lieutenant colonel
for his gallantry. Magruder also participates in the capture of Mexico
City. Also, Lieutenant John Milton
Brannan participates with the 1st
Artillery at this battle. Later, he participates at Contreras and at Churubusco, where he is brevetted as
captain for his gallantry.

June 19 General Zachary Taylor
crosses the Rio Grande and enters
Mexico.

June 20   In California, Sergeant
Gibson and a four-man detachment
search for a missing detachment and
for another two-man detachment that
went in search of the first detachment.
Gibson was able to collect powder, but
he failed to learn of the fate of his
comrades. While moving back to
Sonoma, his detachment is attacked at
Santa Rosa by four men. Two of the
bandits are seized and returned to
Sonoma. From the prisoners back at
Sonoma, Captain Ide is able to learn
the fate of his men. The first two had
been murdered, but the second two
were being held as prisoners. Murdered men Cowie and Fowler were
tied to trees by 13 Californians and

were the object of thrown knives. When the Californians got tired of tossing knives, they threw stones and other projectiles. Both men were discovered still tied to the trees. They were buried in Santa Rosa. One of the prisoners was Bernardino Garcia (later known as Three Fingered Jack), the bandit who was killed by Harry Love's rangers on 27 July 1853.

June 21   In Ohio, General John Ellis Wool, while at Camp Washington, reviews the troops. On the following day, the men are inspected and mustered into U.S. Service by Captain Shriver. Afterward, they are to head south to the Rio Grande.

June 22   In Texas, The USS *Alabama*, a steamer, arrives at Galveston. The *Alabama* drops off supplies for a military depot recently established at Robinson's ferry along the Trinity River. The vessel departs Galveston the next day and sets a course for Brazos Santiago.

June 23   Mexican General Castro sets out from Santa Clara en route to Sonoma in California.

June 25   In California, the force of General Castro enters Sonoma at about 2:00 A.M. In the meantime, Lt. Ford with about 23 men departs from Padilla's ranch, which he had just seized. Ford leaves an eight-man detachment to guard the horses (about eighty captured). The small detachment, while approaching a house, is attacked by a large Mexican force. Ford orders his command to form in platoons and his riflemen are able to hold off the attack. The Mexicans depart from the field and afterward, Ford

rescues two men left in the house. Eleven Mexicans are left lying on the field.

June 26, 1846   In Washington, D.C., the president is authorized to appoint two major generals and eight brigadier generals. They include William O. Butler (Kentucky) and General Robert Patterson (Philadelphia), major generals.

June 27–29   In Alabama, John R. Coffee, a private in the Jackson County Company, is elected colonel. The 1st Alabama Regiment leaves for Point Isabel from Mobile on the 29th. William Henry Forney (later Confederate general) serves as a lieutenant in the 1st Alabama Regiment and participates in the Battle of Vera Cruz.

June 27–30   In Kansas around the 27th, Colonel Stephen Kearny, with 1,500 to 1,800 frontiersmen, leaves Fort Leavenworth to assault Santa Fe, New Mexico, as they travel to California to fight the Mexicans. Kearny's force is handicapped by mules. Many of his troops are forced to ride them.
    Captain Waldo and Captain Reed depart from the post on the 22nd. Lieutenant Colonel Ruff departs this day with the companies of Captain Walton, Parsons, Captain Moss, and Captain Johnson. On the 29th, Colonel A. W. Doniphan and Major Gilpin depart with the companies under Captain Hudson, Captain Rogers, and Captain Harrison. In addition, the companies of Captain Agney and Captain Murphy also depart on the 29th. Captains Richard Weightman's and A. W. Fischer's companies of flying artillery leave on the 30th. Lieutenant John Wynn Davidson (later

Union general) participates in this expedition.

In other activity, General Taylor at Matamoros is awaiting transports so he can advance to join with the corps. Most of Taylor's regulars are on the river's right. However, Captain Desha's regiment, the Washington Regiment and Jackson Regiment of Louisiana are on the river's left. The Alabama companies, St. Louis and Louisville Legions are at Brazos Island. Col. Dankin's, Peyton's, Davis', and Featherston's regiments of Louisiana volunteers are at Brazos.

Elsewhere, a company of mounted men commanded by Captain L. Balloo leaves Brazoria, Texas, for the Rio Grande on or about this day. Also, William Hemsley Emory (later Union general) serves with General Kearny during the war; he is brevetted twice for his gallantry.

June 28 In California, John Frémont's command captures three men, each a Californian. The three had been acting as spies for General Castro. All of them are summarily shot in retaliation for the executions of the two soldiers captured earlier at Santa Rosa.

June 30 The Kentucky 2nd Regiment departs from Louisville in two transports and goes to New Orleans. The Kentucky cavalry regiment, commanded by Colonel Humphrey Marshall (later Confederate general), is scheduled to depart for Memphis on 2 July by ship if available, or by an overland route to Memphis and from there through Arkansas.

In naval activity, the USS *Neva,* after arriving at Matamoros, is ordered to St. Joseph's to get overhauled. The 7th Infantry, which is ordered to Reynosa, instead is disembarked at Matamoros. The distance to Reynosa by water stands at about 180 miles and by land about 80 miles.

In other activity, the U.S. Marine Corps stands at 1,167 men, 41 officers and 1,126 enlisted men. Also, Lieutenant Abner Monroe Perrin (later Confederate general) of South Carolina takes part in the war. He serves as a lieutenant in the infantry. Elsewhere, Colonel Stephen Kearny is promoted to brigadier general.

Late June In California, Captain John Frémont launches an attack against San Solito (present-day Sausalito), which contains the Castile de San Joaquin. Frémont orders the seven cannon at the castle to be spiked. In addition, Frémont dispatches a small detachment to patrol the narrows of San Francisco Bay to prevent Mexican forces from passing.

July The treaty between the U.S. and Great Britain regarding boundary lines between Oregon and the British Northwest possessions is ratified in London.

July 1–4 In California, John Frémont, Lieutenant Gillespie and twenty men cross the bay and capture the presidio. After spiking the guns there, the troops get supplies from an American bark, *Moscow.* The Americans are also able to collect a large store of ammunition left there under guard by the USS *Portsmouth.* They leave for Sonoma on the 2nd, arriving there on the 4th.

July 2 In a letter dated this day at Pittsburgh, Captain John Saunders informs General Taylor that he has purchased five light draught steamers for service on the Rio Grande. The vessels are the *Corvette, Colonel Cross, Major Brown* and the *Rough and Ready.* Saunders had been authorized by Taylor to purchase the boats.

July 3   The USS *Forward,* USS *Woodbury* and the USS *Van Buren,* escorting a large fleet of merchant ships, arrive at the bar of Brazos. In other activity, Captain Samuel Walker, a Texas Ranger, is named captain of the U.S. mounted riflemen, but he declines the appointment.

July 3–4   *In naval activity,* the USS *St. Mary's,* recently detached from Commodore Robert Stockton's squadron, is ordered to proceed from Galveston, Texas, to join Commodore David Conner's squadron. The next day it heads to New Orleans to escort transports that are carrying troops under General Zachary Taylor.

In other activity, Lieutenant Thomas Leonidas Crittenden (later Union general) serves as an aide to General Taylor and later as colonel of the 3rd Kentucky Infantry Regiment.

July 4   **In Mexico,** Lieutenant Braxton Bragg of the artillery, while at Matamoros, raises a toast to the heroine of Fort Brown: "During the whole of the bombardment the wife of one of the soldiers of the 8th Cavalry, Sarah Borginis, whose husband was ordered with the army to Point Isabel, remained in the fort, and though the shot and shells were constantly flying on every side, she disdained to seek shelter in the bomb-proofs, but labored the whole time cooking and taking care of the soldiers, without the least regard to her own safety. Her bravery was the admiration of all who were in the fort." Borginis was issued a musket and she never missed a target. General Taylor brevetted her a colonel, making Borginis the first female colonel of the U.S. Army. After the war, she moved to El Paso, where she opened a hotel. She later moved to Arizona, opened a saloon in Yuma and ran it until her death in 1866. She was interred with full military honors at Fort Yuma.

In other activity, at dawn at Fort Brown and the other encampments, the celebration of the country's independence is breaking out. The 18-pounders, which have been quiet since the 8th of June, blast the sounds of the guns. They receive a response from Paredes, and Bragg's, Duncan's and Ridgely's guns also join in the celebration. The Stars and Stripes is flying over the headquarters of General Taylor and "Hail Columbia" is heard and interrupted by the cheers of thousands of troops.

Braxton Bragg (later Confederate general), 3rd Artillery, is brevetted three times during the war. Edward Dickinson Baker (later Union general) is appointed as colonel of the 4th Illinois Regiment. Baker later participates at the siege of Vera Cruz and afterward, he commands a brigade at Cerro Gordo. James Winning McMillan also serves as a member of the 4th Illinois as a sergeant, and later, he serves as a private in a Louisiana battalion. Richard James Oglesby (later Union general) serves as 1st Lieutenant, Company C, 4th Illinois Regiment.

In other activity, a company of volunteers raised by James Craig (later Union general) is mustered into federal service at Fort Leavenworth, Kansas, and it is known as Company C, Powell's battalion, Missouri Mounted Volunteers. Too late to join Colonel Doniphan's march to New Mexico, the company is ordered to Fort Kearny on the Missouri River at Nebraska City. The company is assigned to protect the wagon trains that move west on the Overland Trail. Leonard Fulton Ross (later Union general) serves as lieutenant in the 4th Illinois Regiment.

July 5   In California, American Colonel John C. Frémont assumes command of the Americans in their struggle against the Mexicans. This day in Sonoma, Frémont reviews his battalion, which has grown to about 250 men.

In Texas, a company commanded by Captain Arnold arrives at Galveston on the *Samuel M. Williams*, a steamer. They receive their arms. Another company from Jaspar and Jefferson counties arrives from Sabine by water on the 6th. They are commanded by Captain James Cheshire. The company is received and departs for Point Isabel on the *Vesta*, a schooner.

In Mexico, Lieutenant Colonel Wilson, 1st Regiment U.S. Cavalry, Captain Price's Texas Rangers and Captain Thomas' artillery initiate their advance to Reynosa, along the Rio Grande, between 60 and 70 miles above Matamoros. The alcalde along with citizens of that place visited with General Taylor several days before and informed him that the townspeople welcomed the Americans. They also made it clear they would be happy to have the Americans protect them. En route back to their homes the townspeople were intercepted by General Antonio Canales, a partisan. He robbed them and murdered the alcalde.

Colonel Wilson arrived at the town after advancing four and one-half days. Once there, he sent

Colonel Baker.

Colonel Edward Baker (Frost, *The History of Mexico and Its Wars***).**

word to General Taylor that no opposition had been encountered during the advance. Colonel Wilson had been directed by Taylor to fortify the town; however, after checking it out, he determined that the plaza was surrounded by "heavy buildings." Wilson occupied the town and afterward with only some trouble, he placed it into a state of defense. Later, the inhabitants arrived back in town and went to their homes with a sense of relief that the Americans would protect them. Shortly after Reynosa is occupied, steamers head up the Rio Grande bringing supplies and provisions.

June 5–6   In Alabama, the Mobile *Register* reports that three companies of the Georgia regiment, commanded by Major Williams, arrived. The units consist of the Georgia Light Infantry (Captain A. Nelson), Texas Rangers (Captain Nelson), and the Sumter Volunteers (Captain J.A.S. Turner). On the 6th, the USS *Amaranth*, USS *Lowndes* and USS *Eurea* arrive. They are transporting the remainder of the regiment. The Macon Guards (Captain Holmes), Columbus Guards (Captain Davis), Richmond Blues (Captain Dill), the Jasper Greens (Captain McNair), Crawford Guards (Captain Jones), Fannin Avengers (Captain Sargent) and the Canton Volunteers (Captain Grambling) are commanded by Colonel Jackson.

In other activity, James Holt Clanton (later Confederate general) serves with the Alabama forces as a private in Captain Rush Elmore's company of Colonel Bailie Peyton's regiment. He serves for six months; then he reenlists in the Palmetto Regiment of South Carolina. Clanton arrives in Mexico City soon after it is occupied by the Americans. Also, John Donovant (later Confederate general) serves as a sergeant in the Palmetto Regiment. Arthur Middleton Manigault (later Confederate general) also serves in the Palmetto regiment as a lieutenant. He participates with General Scott on his advance to Mexico City.

July 6   In California, John Frémont departs from Sonoma with about 180 troops en route to attack General Castro's camp at Santa Clara. On the 10th, Captain Jack Scott, who had galloped from Sonoma, carries the news that on the 7th, Commodore Sloat had captured Monterey and that on the 8th, Captain Montgomery had seized Yerba Buena. A 21-gun salute carried out by a brass cannon is fired while the Bear Flag comes down and the Stars and Stripes is hoisted.

In other activity, Captain Montgomery dispatches a launch under the command of Lieutenant N. B. Harrison to inform Commodore John D. Sloat of the ongoing war in northern California (Bear Flag War). Sloat does not react; rather, he orders the men to remain in the launch and wait to take dispatches back to Captain Montgomery. The dispatches direct Montgomery not to offer assistance to the Americans engaged in the insurrection. In the meantime, other officers, including R. M. Price, the purser on the *Cyane*, persuade Sloat of the magnitude of what is occurring in northern California. The orders for Captain Montgomery are changed.

Capture of Monterey, California (Frost, *The History of Mexico and Its Wars*).

In naval activity, the HMS *Clyde,* a steamer, departs from Vera Cruz and sails to Cuba. At the same time, the frigates USS *Cumberland, Raritan* and the *Potomac,* the corvette *John Adams,* the brigantine *Somers* and the steamers USS *Princeton* and USS *Mississippi* are at Vera Cruz.

July 7   In California, American Commodore Sloat, aboard the *Savannah* and with five smaller vessels, arrives in Monterey and claims California for the United States. He orders a force of 250 Marines and sailors to go ashore at 10 A.M. to raise "Old Glory"

above the Customs House. Commodore Robert Stockton replaces Commodore Sloat and continues directing the Navy's role during the conflict in California. R. M. Price reads a proclamation in English and Spanish proclaiming California as part of the United States, ending the Bear Flag War.

Henry Hayes Lockwood (later Union general) serves on the USS *United States* and participates in the capture of Monterey. Edward Otho Cresap Ord (later Union general) and his West Point classmate Lieutenant Henry W. Halleck (later Union general) along with Lieutenant William Tecumseh Sherman (later Union general) are sent to Monterey during 1847. Halleck is credited with maintaining law and order in Monterey during the latter part of the war.

July 8 In California, Doctor Robert Semple — trained as dentist, lawyer, M.D., and river boat pilot and the founder of Benicia — is ordered to seize the old fort at San Joachim, which is near the mission of San Francisco. He does seize it and returns to Sacramento with a prisoner, Captain R. T. Ridley. Afterward, he moves to Sutter's Fort, where his prisoner is delivered.

July 9–11 The HMS *Rose*, a British sloop of war, arrives at Brazos Santiago. The USS *Tampico* and the USS *Flirt*, a schooner, also arrive.

Commodore Robert Stockton (*A Sketch of the Life of Com. Robert F. Stockton*).

July 9–29 *In naval activity,* on the 9th, sailors and Marines debark and seize the town of Yerba Buena (present day San Francisco) without incident. On the same day, Marines and seamen aboard the USS *Portsmouth* occupy the town of Sonoma, California. Navy Lieutenant Joseph Warren Revere, a grandson of Paul Revere, hoists Old Glory above the town. Revere (later Union general) after the war lives in California and enters the Mexican army, where he is involved in organizing their artillery units. This action is followed by crewmen of the USS *Cyane* landing and capturing San Diego, California.

July 10 In Ohio, Colonel George Morgan's regiment of volunteers departs Cincinnati. They are aboard two steamboats headed for New Orleans. By this time, all of the Ohio volunteers are en route to the Rio Grande. In other activity, the 3rd Regiment of Ohio volunteers arrives at New Orleans.

July 11 In Washington, D.C., President Polk, with the advice and consent of the Senate, appoints the following general officers: Robert Patterson (Pennsylvania) and William O. Butler (Kentucky) as major generals; Thomas L. Hamer (Ohio), Joseph Lane (Indiana), James Shields (Illinois), Thomas Marshall (Kentucky), Gideon J. Pillow (of Tennessee, later Confederate general), and John A. Quitman (Mississippi) as brigadier generals; Captain George A. McCall, (4th Infantry) assistant adjutant general, with the brevet rank of major; Brevet Captain William W.S. Bliss, assistant adjutant general, to be assistant adjutant general with the brevet rank of major; First Lieutenant Randolph Ridgely (3rd artillery) to be assistant adjutant general, with the brevet rank of captain; First Lieutenant George Lincoln, of the 8th Infantry, to be assistant adjutant general with the brevet rank of captain; and First Lieutenant Oscar F. Winship (2nd dragoons), to be assistant adjutant general, with the brevet rank of Captain. Winship had been selected in place of W.W.S. Bliss, who was promoted. Also, Charles Ruff (mounted riflemen, 3rd Dragoons) of Missouri is promoted to captain. Bela M. Hughes declines to accept.

General George McCall (Frost, *The History of Mexico and Its Wars*).

Colonel George Morgan (Wilcox, *History of the Mexican War*).

In naval activity, on or about this day, the USS *Pennsylvania* (120 guns) and the USS *North Carolina* (74 guns), at Norfolk and the USS *Ohio* receive orders to prepare for active service. Elsewhere, the *Preble,* a sloop of war, is awaiting a crew. It is to sail to the Gulf of Mexico. Also, the Texas sloop of war *Austin* is towed from Galveston on 24 May. It is bound for Pensacola to get repairs. Once ready for service, it will become the USS *Austin,* commanded by George N. Hollins. The *Whiteville,* a steamboat, is acquired by Captain Sanders and expected to act as a transport along the Rio Grande. It departs from Cincinnati on 30 May en route to New Orleans.

In yet other activity, the Mexican government had contracted for three vessels, which are being built in New York at the Brooklyn navy yard. However, the U.S. government has taken over the ships. The three schooners are the *Reefer* (Lieutenant Commander J.S. Sterrett); the *Petrel* (Lieutenant Commander T.D. Shaw) and the *Bonita* (Lieutenant Commander T.G. Benhain). The three vessels are fitting out for service in the Gulf of Mexico.

July 13–15   In Canada, the HMS *Athol,* a troop ship, arrives at Halifax with a contingent for the rifle brigade. In other activity, the *Arabian,* another troop ship, arrives on the 15th from Cork, Ireland. The *Arabian* is transporting contingents for the 33rd, 77th and the Newfoundland Veterans.

July 14 U.S. Forces occupy Camargo, in Tamaulipas, Mexico.

July 14–18   In Mexico, Captain Duncan is ordered to proceed to Cerralvo. His reconnaissance mission takes him to the town of Punta Aguada at the halfway point between Mier and Cerralvo. Captain Duncan, having been informed that Canales often used this town as a meeting place, has his force surround the town, then move against the center. Music is coming from within the town. Duncan, with a detachment of rangers, enters the party and orders all in attendance to stand. After it is determined that there are no prisoners to be taken, Duncan orders the music to resume. Duncan returns to Mier on the 18th. He reports that his expedition is a success.

July 15   In California, Commodore Robert F. Stockton arrives and reports to Commodore Sloat. Stockton requests that he receive command of the land forces and Sloat agrees. In other activity, Maxcy Gregg (later Confederate general) serves as major in the 12th U.S. Infantry; however, he does not see any action.

July 16   In Iowa, a Mormon battalion is raised at Council Bluffs. Four companies (more than 400 men) are completed and a fifth company is partially raised. Jefferson Hunt is selected as captain of Company A. Jesse D. Hunter is named captain of Company B. James Brown is captain of Company C. The captain for Company D is Nelson Higgins and Company E's captain is Daniel C. Davis. The first order issued: "In virtue of authority given me by the Col. commanding the army of the west, I hereby assume the command of the Mormon Battalion, raised at this place for the service of the United States. Therefore, companies now organized will be held in readiness to march at the shortest notice, and as soon as the fifth company be filled all will be ready for movement. J. ALLEN, LT. COL. U.S. A., COMMANDING."

Also, George Stoneman (later Union general) is appointed quartermaster for the Mormon battalion.

July 17   In California, John Frémont's force arrives at the San Juan Mission, about thirty miles from Monterey. Purser Fauntleroy arrives with a company of mounted Marines. Fauntleroy is also carrying orders from Commodore Sloat. In accordance with the orders, Frémont, along with Gillespie, arrives at Monterey on the following day to report to Sloat. Commodore Sloat, while interviewing Frémont, expresses anger with Frémont when the latter is asked about his reasons for aiding the rebels. Frémont responds that he acted on his own authority. Sloat then informs Frémont that he might as well "continue to prosecute the war on his own responsibility." Sloat tells Frémont that will turn over the "control of affairs to his junior officer (R. F. Stockton) and return to Washington."

In other activity, according to the Detroit *Advertiser*, "An order was received yesterday by Col. Riley, from the war department, to move the 2d regiment of infantry, stationed on the frontier, at once to Point Isabel, Texas. The company at this post and one at Fort Gratiot will march forthwith. Orders have been dispatched to the companies to Lake Superior to

follow Company C, Captain Byrne, stationed at Mackinac, [to] remain at that post. The other companies are at Buffalo, Fort Niagara, and Sackets Harbor."

Elsewhere, General Zachary Taylor issues a proclamation:

After many years of patient endurance, the United States are at length constrained to acknowledge that a war now exists between our government and the government of Mexico. For many years our citizens have been subjected to repeated insults and injuries, our vessels and cargoes have been seized and confiscated, our merchants have been plundered, maimed, imprisoned, without cause and without reparation. At length your government acknowledged the justice of our claims, and agreed by treaty to make satisfaction, by payment of several millions of dollars; but this treaty has been violated by your rulers, and the stipulated payments have been withheld. Our late effort to terminate all difficulties by peaceful negotiation has been rejected by the Dictator Paredes, and our Minister of Peace, whom your rulers had agreed to receive, has been refused a hearing. He has been treated with indignity and insult, and Paredes has announced that war exists between us. This war, thus first proclaimed by him, has been acknowledged as an existing fact by our president and Congress, with perfect unanimity, and will be prosecuted with vigor and energy, against your army and rulers; but those of the Mexican people who remain neutral will not be molested.

Your government is in the hands

of tyrants and usurpers. They have abolished your state governments, they have overthrown your federal constitution, they have deprived you of the right of suffrage, destroyed the liberty of the press, despoiled you of arms and reduced you to a state of absolute dependence upon the power of a military dictator. Your army and rulers extort from the people by grievous taxation, by forced loans and military seizures, the very money which sustains the usurpers in power. Being disarmed, you were left defenceless, an easy prey to the savage Comanches, who not only destroy your lives and property, but drive into a captivity more horrible than death itself your wives and children. It is your military rulers who have reduced you to this deplorable condition. It is these tyrants, and their corrupt and cruel satellites, gorged with the people's treasure, by whom you are thus impressed and impoverished; some of whom have boldly advocated a monarchical government, and would place a European prince upon the throne of Mexico. We come to obtain indemnity for the past, and security for the future; we come to overthrow the tyrants who have destroyed your liberties;- but we come to make no war upon the people of Mexico, nor upon any form of free government they may choose to select for themselves. It is our wish to see you liberated from despots, to drive back the savage Comanches, to prevent the renewal of their assaults, and to compel them to restore to you from captivity your lost wives and children. Your religion, your altars and churches, the property of your churches and citizens, the em-

blems of your faith and its ministers, shall be protected, and remain inviolate. Hundreds of our army, and hundreds of thousands of our people, are members of the Catholic Church. In every state, and in nearly every city and village of our Union, Catholic churches exist, and the priests perform their holy functions in peace and security, under the sacred guarantee of our Constitution. We come among the people of Mexico as friends and republican brethren, and all who receive us as such shall be protected, whilst all who are seduced into the army of your dictator, shall be treated as enemies. We shall want from you nothing but food for our army, and for this you shall always be paid in cash the full value. It is the settled policy of your tyrants to deceive you in regard to the policy and character of our government and people. These tyrants fear the example of our free institutions, and constantly endeavor to misrepresent our purposes, and inspire you with hatred for your republican brethren of the American Union. Give us but the opportunity to undeceive you, and you will soon learn that all the representations of Paredes were false, and were only made to induce you to consent to the establishment of a despotic government. In your struggle for liberty with the Spanish monarchy, thousands of our countrymen risked their lives and shed their blood in your defence. Our own commodore, the gallant Porter, maintained in triumph your flag upon the ocean, and our government was the first to acknowledge your independence. With pride and pleasure we enrolled your name on the list of independent republics, and sincerely desired that you might in peace and prosperity enjoy all the blessings of a free government. Success on the part of your tyrants against the army of the Union is impossible, but if they could succeed it would only be to enable them to fill your towns with their soldiers, eating out your substance, and harassing you with still more grievous taxation. Already, they have abolished the liberty of the press, as the first step toward that monarchy, which it is their real purpose to proclaim and establish.

Mexicans we must treat as enemies and overthrow the tyrants, who, whilst they have wronged and insulted us, have deprived you of your liberty, but the Mexican people who remain neutral during the contest shall be protected against their military despots.

BY THE REPUBLICAN ARMY OF THE UNION. Z. TAYLOR, MAJOR GEN.

July 18 In Virginia, at Fort Monroe, General Edmund Pendleton Gaines is compelled to undergo an inquiry, ordered by President Polk. Officers ordered to undertake the hearing are Brevet Brigadier General H. Brady, Brevet Brigadier General G.M. Brooke and Colonel J. Crane. Brevet Captain J.F. Lee, recorder, is also ordered to Fort Monroe. The inquiry is to determine the conduct of Major General Gaines in calling upon governors of states for volunteers, in organizing and mustering certain volunteers, and in giving orders to officers since 1 May 1846 for "subsistence, stores, &c., and for payment to certain individuals or bodies of men, &c."

In Mexico, volunteers arrive at Brazos Santiago from Tennessee. Other volunteers who had arrived earlier from New Orleans have moved to Barita. However, two regiments remain at Brazos Santiago awaiting transportation. The volunteers from Texas are close to Point Isabel and are being organized by their governor. Elsewhere, the regular army at Camargo, composed of seven infantry regiments and two batteries of artillery, commanded by General William J. Worth, forms for a grand review. This is the first time the U.S. military has been displayed under the flag since the last war. General Taylor, General John A. Quitman and General Gideon Johnson Pillow also attended the review.

In other activity, the Arkansas regiment (Yell's Mounted Devils) with Colonel Archibald Yell advances through Shreveport and from there across Texas to San Antonio.

July 20 In Virginia, at Fortress Monroe, General Edmund Pendleton Gaines, acting as his own defense attorney, succeeds in gaining an acquittal at his court-martial. Earlier, Gaines had dispatched troops into Texas when he was informed that General Taylor was at Fort Brown. Washington had initially charged that Gaines had "exceeded his authority."

In naval activity, the USS *Columbus*, ship of the line, and the USS *Vincennes*, a sloop, enters Yedo Bay, Japan, with diplomats who will open negotiations on a treaty.

Elsewhere, Lieutenant Abner Doubleday (later Union general), who served in the 3rd Artillery, transfers to the 1st U.S. Artillery Regiment during this year. Afterward, he joins with General Zachary Taylor in Texas. Ebenezer Dumont (later Union general) serves with the 4th Indiana volunteers as captain and lieutenant colonel. Thomas John Lucas (later Union general) serves during the war as a 2nd lieutenant in the 4th Indiana volunteers.

July 21   In Washington, D.C., a board of naval officers convenes to determine the best mode of seizing the Mexican fortress of San Juan de Ulua by a naval attack. Attending are Commodores Charles Stewart, Jacob Jones, Charles Morris, L. Warrington, John Downes, Jesse Wilkinson, Thos. Ap. C. Jones, William B. Shubrick, Charles W. Morgan, Lawrence Kearney, F. A. Parker, Daniel Turner, M. C. Perry, Joseph Smith, Captain G. W. Storor, Isaac McKeever, Charles S. McCauley, S. H. Stringham, Isaac Mayo and Samuel L. Breese. Member E.A.F. Lavallette was not in attendance; he was en route from Memphis.

July 23   In California, Commodore John Drake Sloat sails for Washington. He leaves Commodore Robert Field Stockton in command of the forces on the sea (sailors and Marines) as well as the army. Also, Stockton dispatches the USS *Cyane*, commanded by Commodore Samuel Francis Dupont, to take Frémont and his force to San Diego.

July 25   *In naval activity,* the USS *Potomac* is caught by a series of high winds five or six miles from the pass of St. Louis. The steamer is lost, but the cargo is only damaged. The schooner USS *Lavina* is also wrecked, but the USS *Flirt* saves its crew.

July 28–August 2   In Mexico, President Mariano Paredes turns his government over to the vice president and goes into hiding. On August 6 the vice president resigns. The Federalists restore the constitution on the 22nd. Afterward, Valentin Gomez Farias, deposed as vice president by the Centralists in 1834, assumes temporary control of the Mexican government.

July 29   Marines and seamen aboard the USS *Cyane* occupy San Diego, California.

July 31   Captain John R. Vinton, leading one company of the 3rd Artillery, advances into the town of Mier. They stack arms in the plaza while the inhabitants look on as spectators.

August   In Texas, General Kearny, anticipating a Mexican attack in the vicinity of Apache Pass, moves with caution; however, the Mexicans are evacuated. A single Mexican peasant on a mule laughingly tells Kearny: "Armijo and his troops have gone to hell and the canyon is all clear."

In other activity, four companies of Missouri Volunteers are received this month. They muster out during August of the following year. Thomas Turpin Crittenden (later Union general) participates with this regiment.

August 1   The Mormon battalion arrives at Fort Leavenworth, Kansas. Lt. Colonel James Allen becomes sick with fever. Captain Jefferson Hunt is given temporary command of the battalion. Colonel Allen died on August 23 at the fort.

Colonel Alexander M. Mitchell (Frost, *The History of Mexico and Its Wars*).

Commodore Robert Stockton sails toward San Pedro, the port of Los Angeles, California. He pauses at Santa Barbara where he takes possession of the presidio there without any resistance.

August 5   General Zachary Taylor and his staff depart from Matamoros, Mexico, for Camargo aboard the USS *Whiteside*. The vessel is also carrying some regulars and a contingent of Texas infantry.

August 6   Marines and seamen aboard the USS *Congress*, a frigate, land and occupy San Pedro, California.

August 6–7   **In Mexico,** General Taylor crosses the San Juan River at Camargo on the 6th. On the 7th, he places General Robert Patterson in command at Camargo, then he de-

parts for Cerralvo. Lieutenant Seth Williams (later Union general) serves for the duration of the war as aide-de-camp to General Patterson. The 1st Mississippi Rifles, commanded by Colonel Jefferson Davis, the 1st Tennessee, commanded by Colonel Campbell, the 1st Ohio, commanded by Colonel Alexander M. Mitchell, and the Baltimore Battalion, commanded by Lieutenant Colonel W. H. Watson, are greatly reduced in numbers due to sickness and injuries. General Taylor has decided to take only those who can handle the march. He discharges those who are sick or discontented.

In other activity, William Barksdale (later Confederate general) is with the 2nd Mississippi Regiment as an enlisted man and later as an officer. He is the quartermaster. Charles Clark is an officer with the 2nd Mississippi Regiment. Upon the resignation of Reuben Davis, Clark is elected as its colonel. Thomas Hindman (later Confederate general) also serves with the 2nd Mississippi Regiment. Captain Douglas Hancock Cooper (later Confederate general) serves with the 1st Mississippi Rifles. Also, Thomas Harrison (later Confederate general) joins with the 1st Mississippi Rifles. Carnot Posey (later Confederate general) also serves with the 1st Mississippi Rifles. Ferdinand Van Derveer (later Union general) joins the 1st Ohio as an enlisted man (first sergeant) and later he is promoted to first lieutenant and then captain. He participates in the capture of Monterey, California.

Colonel Jefferson Davis (Frost, *The History of Mexico and Its Wars*).

August 7 Commodore Robert Stockton sends a force of approximately 350 men to assault the Camp of the Messa, Gust (outside of Los Angeles), which is defended by 500 Mexicans. The Mexicans retreat without a fight. In other activity, the squadron of Commodore Conner sails to Alvarada, Mexico. Marines aboard the vessel are to participate in the expedition; however, due to the arrival of inclement weather, the squadron departs on the following day.

August 8 BATTLE OF CANONCITO **In New Mexico,** Manuel Armijo, the governor of Santa Fe, is trying to avoid battle with the Americans; however, he is prodded to mount a defense at a narrow pass, Apache Pass, about 10 miles from Santa Fe. On 14 August, Armijo decides not to fight. The New Mexican army retreats to Santa Fe. Armijo leaves for Chihuahua. There is no fighting at Canoncito.

August 9–10 In California, Santa Barbara and San Pedro fall to the Americans when contingents of the USS *Congress* debark and capture the two towns. The Marines who accompany Commodore Stockton are drilled in infantry tactics, particularly cavalry attacks. While in Los Angeles, the Mexicans come into Stockton's camp under a flag of truce, but the real reason is probably to get a number of American troops. Nevertheless, the Marines under Stockton march over the hill in such a way that their numbers appear to be multiplied by about ten. General Castro requests an armistice, but Stockton through the envoys emphatically say no. In the meantime, General Castro, once informed of Stockton's decision, abandons his camp and moves to Sonora.

In naval activity, the USS *Cyane* encounters a Mexican vessel, the brigantine *Juanita,* at San Diego and captures it on the 9th. The next day it seizes the Mexican vessel *Prima Vera,* another brigantine.

August 11 Commodore Robert Stockton departs from San Pedro and moves into Los Angeles. Stockton's force takes the city without firing a shot.

August 13 Marines and seamen march into Los Angeles against no opposition. Commodore Robert Stockton sends the following message to the secretary of the Navy in Washington, D.C.: "The flag of the United States is flying from every commanding position in the territory of California."

August 14–22 *In naval activity,* the USS *Truxton* is en route to aid the USS *John Adams* off Tampico, Mexico. It gets caught in a nasty storm about 100 miles from its destination. The *Truxton* moves toward land, but it gets too close to the Tuxpan Reef and runs aground. Mexicans attempt to get the crew to surrender but the offer is rejected. The next morning, the *Truxton* dispatches a cutter to Anton Lizardo to get help, but none arrives. On the 16th, a sail is spotted and a cutter is sent to investigate. It turns out to be a Mexican ship, which is captured by the cutter. It sails its prize toward the

Truxton, but the reef interferes. In the meantime, Lieutenant Carpender dispatches the cutter to Anton Lizardo with a message that he will surrender. The prize drops the Mexican crew off at Tuxpan before heading to Anton Lizardo.

En route the prize spots another ship on the 18th that ignites a prolonged sea chase, but late on the night of the 18th, the ship is captured. Afterward, both ships sail for an American anchorage and despite getting separated during the night, both reach their destination. The first arrives on the 22nd and the second on the 23rd. In the meantime, the USS *St. Mary's,* which had picked up the cutter (with the message requesting help) from the *Truxton* enters the harbor at Anton Lizardo. In addition, Commodore David Conner orders the USS *Falmouth* and the USS *Princeton* to the reef which had caught the *Truxton.* On the 20th, the *Princeton* arrives at the site of the grounded brigantine. It sends a boat ashore under a flag of truce and discovers that Lieutenant Carpender and his crew had surrendered several days before. The crew, except for two lieutenants and nineteen men, are captured.

August 15 General Kearny captures Las Vegas, New Mexico. The annexation of New Mexico by the United States is announced by General Kearny. Alexander Brydie Dyer (later Union general) accompanies General Kearny on this expedition. Lieutenant John Dunlap Stevenson (later Union general) also participates.

August 16 General Kearny captures San Miguel, New Mexico. In other activity, General Santa Anna returns to Mexico following his exile in Cuba.

August 18   In New Mexico, Americans enter and occupy Santa Fe with no opposition, raising "Old Glory." As the Stars and Stripes are being raised, nearby cannons give a resounding salute. This flag-raising ceremony culminates a 1,000 mile march from Fort Leavenworth, Kansas, which gives the Americans control of a strategic city with no casualties, nor the firing of a single shot. On the same day, Commodore Robert Stockton declares the annexation of California by the United States. Kearny sets up a civilian government for New Mexico before leaving for California in four weeks.

**August 19   The first U.S. troops depart from Camargo en route to Monterrey, Mexico.

**September 2   Marines aboard the USS *Cyane*, a sloop, participate in the capture of the Mexican sloop *Solita* while operating off San Blas.

**September 3   Marines aboard the USS *Cyane* participate in the capture of the Mexican brigantine *Susanna* off San Blas.

**September 7   Marines participate in the capture of the Mexican brigantine *Malek Adhel* by the USS *Warren*, a sloop, while operating off Mazatlan, Mexico.

September 9   In Mexico, General Taylor enters the village of Cerralvo. His train — 1st and 2nd Divisions, commanded by Generals David Twiggs and William Worth — winds over the hills for miles. He has brought light artillery but his heavy artillery was left behind at the Rio Grande. In other activity, a Mexican rider appears at Cerralvo. He is carrying dispatches, sent by General de Ampudia, for the people of Mexico.

**September 14   Marines aboard the USS *Cyane* participate in the capture of nine Mexican vessels off the coast of La Paz, California.

**September 16   The 1st Division arrives in the vicinity of Merine, Mexico, where it makes camp to await the remainder of the army.

September 17   In Mexico, the Spanish consul at Monterrey has a letter delivered to General Taylor. He inquires whether the property of locals is to be respected. Taylor responds that he would be "responsible for nothing, if the town was taken by assault."

September 18   In Mexico, on the morning of the 18th, the 1st Division, followed shortly thereafter by the remaining divisions, commanded by General William Jenkins Worth and the Texans under General Henderson, advance. By about noon, the divisions pass through the village of Aqua Frio and from there they pass through San Francisco. At San Francisco General Taylor is informed that General Pedro de Ampudia is prepared to defend Monterrey until the death. In the meantime, the advance arrives at St. Domingo. After passing through, Monterrey comes into sight.

Also, a great alarm is spreading through the Mexican mule drivers because of a report that General Canales is to the rear of the American columns. The horsemen that started

General William O. Butler (Frost, *The History of Mexico and Its Wars*).

General Pedro Ampudia (Frost, *The History of Mexico and Its Wars*).

the rumor were General Henderson's brigade (George T. Wood's and John Coffee "Jack" Hay's regiments) of mounted Texans.

September 19   In Mexico, General Taylor advances to a point north of the city with his army, which encamps just outside of Monterrey in a section known as Walnut Springs. Monterrey is naturally protected to the south by the Rio Santa Catarina River and the Sierra Madre Mountains. A solitary road that runs south along the river to Saltillo serves as the primary source for re-supplying the army and as the primary road for retreat. General Pedro de Ampudia is defending the city with a large amount of fortifications, including the Citadel north of the city. To the northeast, an earthwork known as La Teneria stands. The eastern approach to Monterrey is guarded by Fort Diablo. The western approach is defended by Fort Libertad, which is at the top of Independence Hill. Fort Soldado stands atop Federation Hill on the opposite side of the river and slightly south; it protects the rod to Saltillo.

General Taylor's reconnaissance of the area by Joseph

K.F. Mansfield reveals that General de Ampudia is unable to provide support and that his reserves will have great difficulty in filling the gaps that separate them. Taylor, after being briefed on the situation, discerns that the Mexican strong points can be isolated and seized. He plans to execute a double envelopment of Monterrey. Although the situation calls for a siege, Taylor had left his heavy artillery at the Rio Grande. He re-organizes his army into four divisions under General William Jenkins Worth: Brigadier General David Twiggs, Major General William Butler, and Major General J. Pinckney Henderson. General Taylor sets up headquarters in the Wood of San Domingo, just outside of his objective, Monterrey, Mexico. Earlier, while General Taylor was overseeing the movement of his troops, one of the batteries at Monterrey, fires three shots, one of which passes just over the head of General Taylor before it plows deeply into the ground. American reconnaissance informs General Taylor of the Mexican defenses at Monterrey, which will make a successful attack extremely difficult. The city has become a tremendous fortress defended by over 7,000 Mexican troops.

In other activity, the government decides that it has to get a payroll shipment to Monterrey. General Patterson orders 250 troops to act as escort. The detachment is the Jasper Greens from Colonel Jackson's regiment, commanded by Captain Chase. The regimental quartermaster at Camargo writes: "They [the Georgians] were fine looking men and I heard it said the choice companies of the regiment including the celebrated Jasper Greens were composed almost entirely of Irishmen, of which a Georgian reminded in my presence 'Give the Jasper Greens some whiskey and they will charge into Hell.'"

In other activity, Captain Allison Nelson (later Confederate general) of Georgia forms the Kennesaw Rifles of Georgia. Lieutenant Roswell Sabine Ripley (later Confederate general) participates at this battle. Later he takes part at the Battle of Vera Cruz and Cerro Gordo. On 3 March 1847, he is promoted to first lieutenant, 2nd Artillery. Later, he participates at the battles of Contreras, Molino del Rey, and Chapultepec and the capture of Mexico City. Ripley is brevetted as major on 13 September 1847. He is appointed as aide-de-camp to Major General Gideon Johnson Pillow on 6 August 1847. Lieutenant Ulysses S. Grant (later Union general), 4th Infantry, participates at this battle. Afterward Grant's regiment is transferred to General Scott's command. Later he participates at Molino del Rey, Chapultepec and the capture of Mexico City. Also, Conrad Feger Jackson (later Union general) at about this time is appointed as a lieutenant in the revenue service. He is later sent to deliver a message to General Scott. Joseph Haydn Potter (later Union general) takes part at this battle. Afterward, Potter is assigned to recruiting.

September 20–22   In Mexico, as part of his master plan to seize Monterrey, Taylor dispatches General William Jenkins Worth's 2nd Division

and the Texas division
(about 2,700 troops) to
make a wide sweep
against the western and
southern defenses of
Monterrey at 1400. Gen-
eral Worth is to sever the
Saltillo Road and enter
the city from the west.
The sweep is to permit
General Worth to avoid
General Pedro de Ampu-
dia's lines, which other-
wise could reinforce the
defenders on the west.

At 0600 on the 21st,
Worth's column comes
under attack at a point
slightly west of Inde-
pendence Hill. More
than 200 Mexican lanc-
ers form a line and open
their charge. It is met by
Texans who dismount
their horses and seek
positions behind a fence. The Mexicans are unable to penetrate the Texas
defense. Before the Mexicans can
form for yet another assault, Colonel
Duncan pushes his 8-pounders past
the American defenders. Once they
are at the front, the fire pours into the
Mexican line with devastating effect.
After losing about thirty troops, the
Mexicans withdraw.

Once the Mexicans retire and the
American fire subsides, General Worth
resumes his advance. However, Mexican artillery posted on Federation
Hill (Federacion Hill) begins to pound
the Americans. The spectacular bombardment inflicts only slight casualties. Nevertheless, General Worth decides his 2nd Division will have to

Americans' charge at Monterrey, Mexico (*A Sketch
of the Life and Character of Gen. Taylor*).

eliminate the enemy on the hills before he can finish his sweep.

A strong storming party — composed of about 300 Texas Rangers
under Captain Charles F. Smith, bolstered by General Persifor Smith's
2nd Brigade along with the 5th and
7th Infantry Regiments — is designated as the attack force. At 12:30
P.M., the assault force crosses the
Santa Ciafarina River at three separate spots, all west of the Mexican
batteries on Independence and Federation Hills. From there, the force
maneuvers itself to positions from
where it can assault the western side
of Federation Hill.

The Mexicans begin to bolt from
a redoubt that is also on the western

Bishop's Palace Monterey.

side of the hill, about 400 feet above the Saltillo Road. The task becomes more complicated as the hill is extremely steep and the Americans find themselves facing 500 Mexican troops along with their artillery. The Texas Rangers draw the bulk of the enemy's fire, but this also permits the 5th and 7th Regiments to drive against the Gateway South.

The 5th ascends the hill on the northern flank (left) of the fortification and the Mexican line breaks. The troops withdraw to Fort Soldado on the other side of the hill; however, they depart in such a hurry that they fail to take their artillery pieces. The Americans charge after the Mexicans as they retreat. The Mexicans in the eastern fort abandon it and haphazardly speed toward the Santa Catarina River, where they reach Independence Hill.

In the meantime, General Anastasio Torrejon's cavalry attempts to out-flank the American position, but by that time, Duncan and Mackall's batteries commence fire and it is effective. The Mexican cavalry is unable to form. In addition, the remainder of General Worth's force is able to repel several attempts by General Anastasio Torrejon's cavalry. Throughout the day, General Worth's force sustains only one killed and several wounded. Meanwhile, on the eastern side of Monterrey, General Zachary Taylor is not meeting with the same success.

Taylor's men consolidate their foothold around La Teneria and prepare to renew the attack. The action begins at 0300 on 22 September when Worth dispatches a handpicked detachment of Texas Rangers, artillerymen, and men from the 8th Infantry to launch a surprise attack against Fort Libertad on the western summit of Independence Hill. The troops climb nearly nine hundred feet and are a mere one hundred yards from the Mexican positions before a sentry spots them. Caught off guard, the Mexicans cannot react in time. After firing a fierce volley into the enemy position, the Americans fix bayonets and charge. The Mexican line becomes disoriented. They flee east toward the Obispado (Bishop's Palace).

Some of the artillerymen, having pulled a 12-pounder howitzer up the hillside, place it within the captured fort, then begin to bash the sides of the Obispado with effective fire. The 5th and 7th Infantry speed to the high ground and join in the assault. At about 1500, the Mexicans lose their hold on the Obispado. The Americans are quick to haul the Mexican flag down and hoist Old Glory up the staff to fly the flag above the fort.

General Worth, at about noon, completes his task. He directs four companies of the 4th Artillery, along with six companies of Texas riflemen, commanded by Major Mike Chevalier under the command of Charles Ferguson Smith, to secure the batteries on Federation Hill. Smith moves along the San Juan River until he arrives at a crossing point. He jumps into the water with his force following him. In the meantime, General Worth discerns that the Mexicans would raise determined resistance. He directs the 7th Regiment, commanded by Captain Miles, to support General Scott's contingent. Captain Miles, upon orders, makes no secret about his intentions. He crosses the river and forms at the base of the mountain. Meanwhile, from their positions above, the Mexicans pound the regiment with a combination of grape and round shot as well as musket fire. Nevertheless, the regiment escapes harm and sustains no injuries. Captain Miles remains totally unprotected until General C.F. Smith arrives at the base of the mountain.

Lieutenants Garrett, Gardner and Little, leading small parties, ascended the mountainside. The Mexican guns seemingly silence the American contingents. However, Captain Smith arrives. He begins to take the point and by doing so, he sustains heavy fire. His contingent moves about and continues to ascend the mountain. General Worth is able to observe the ascent. He sends the 5th Infantry under Major Scott and the Louisiana troops under Blanchard to support the assault. The reinforcements bolt across the river, then from the base of the mountain, they ascend and carry the first fort. Afterward, they continue their assault until the second fort falls. By now, the regiments are working together to gain final victory. The 5th and the 7th accelerate their pace. The Mexicans are unable to match the ferocity of the Americans. They fight with vengeance, but they are compelled to withdraw a step at a time.

Blanchard's troops are the first to fire with great effectiveness, which opens the way toward Soledad. The Mexican standard is brought down and the flag of the 5th Regiment is seen flying from the mountain. The 7th Regiment soon after unfurls its flag. General C. F. Smith is to hold the ground taken by his troops, while Captain Miles with his 7th Regiment remains at El Soledad. Major Smith, commanding the 5th Regiment, back-tracks down the mountain and heads toward the city of Monterrey.

The morning of the 22nd begins with the Americans preparing to storm the Bishop's Palace. Lieutenant Colonel Thomas Childs commands the assault party, composed of three companies of the 8th Infantry, commanded by Captain Screven, 200 Texan riflemen under Colonels Hays and Walker, and three companies of the artillery battalion under Captain Vinton. The attack is led by Captain John Sanders and Lieutenant Meade, both topographical engineers.

Colonel Childs is spotted by Mexicans as he ascends the mountain. They fire upon him from their positions on the mountain. Others join in and fired wildly, but the attack party keeps coming. The Mexicans are compelled to retreat to their breastworks. All the while, the Mexicans continue to offer opposition; however, the charging Americans do not stop. They charge to the fort, then the Texans use their rifles as clubs and the regulars make excellent use of their bayonets. The Mexicans run down the mountain toward the Bishop's Palace. Once at the palace, the Mexicans see that their pursuers are small in number.

They mount a cavalry charge that stuns the attackers, but worse, another large group that was concealed behind the hill charges. When they get close the Americans fall back. Thinking it is a retreat, the Mexicans continue forward. Just as the Mexicans get to a point away from the walls of the palace, the concealed columns advance up the mountain-side. At nearly the same time, the column which had retreated stands its ground and delivers a devastating blow. Nevertheless, the Mexicans keep rushing forward. Then suddenly, they discover that other Americans had arrived and are attempting to surround them. The Mexicans turn their horses and bolt back toward the palace, with Americans in pursuit.

The Americans are entering the palace at the same time as the Mexicans. Soon the Americans displace the enemy. And then a huge series of explosions is heard as the guns of the castle and the fort mix with the roar of small arms. The Bishop's Palace is won. Lieutenant George Ayres replaces the Mexican standard with Old Glory. The guns of the Mexicans are turned and aimed at Monterrey.

The American losses due to this charge amounted to only one man, Captain McKavett of the 8th Infantry. Prior to the battle, he was asked if he would like in recognition of his meritorious service at Resaca de la Palma to "retire from further combat." He responds: "I have too much fighting Irish blood in me to withdraw!" Shortly thereafter, Captain James Duncan arrives. He posts his artillery to the front of the palace and commences fire against the barricades, which are below them. Mexicans still in the barricades quickly depart. The forts and other strongholds of the Mexicans on the western end of the city have been captured by General William Jenkins Worth.

Participants at this battle include Lewis Henry Little (later Confederate general); William Whann Mackall (later Confederate general); Lieutenant William Thomas Harbaugh Brooks (later Union general), who is brevetted captain for his gallantry; and John James Peck (later Union general), who is praised by his commanding officer, Captain Duncan: "It affords me the liveliest gratification and pleasure, to bear testimony to the coolness, gallantry and judgment with which the officers associated with me, First Lieutenant J.F. Roland, Second Lieutenants W. Hays and J.J. Peck, discharged their respective duties on both these glorious days; the steadiness and bravery of my men is beyond all praise; their work was done in the presence of the whole army, and they may with pride appeal to their comrades us to the manner in which it was performed." John Pope (later Union general) participates at this battle and in the Battle of Resaca de la Palma.

September 20–25 in Mexico, BATTLE OF MONTERREY At 0600 on the 20th, General Zachary Taylor hears gunfire as it roars across the town of Monterrey. It signals that General Worth is engaging the Mexicans on the west. General Taylor then deploys his 1st and 3rd Divisions on the plain north of Monterrey. He intends to hold the Mexicans there in their fortifications and to prevent General de Ampudia from reinforcing the west. The Mexicans, however, totally ignore Taylor's move, giving him the opportunity to launch his attack against the northeastern corner of Monterrey.

Five hundred yards of flat open ground stands between the American attack force and the city. And it is further protected by thirty guns located in the Citadel and La Teneria. Taylor decides that his 1st and 3rd Regiments (1st Division) and the District of Columbia and Maryland Volunteers would be the first to enter Monterrey. General David Twiggs is too ill to command, so Taylor places Lieutenant Colonel John Garland in temporary command of the 1st Division. He is to lead the assault.

General David Twiggs (Wilcox, *History of the Mexican War*).

The mortar commanded by Captain George Douglas Ramsay (later Union general) and the 24-pounder howitzer commanded by Captain Lucian B. Webster commences fire upon Monterrey. The Mexican batteries respond. Garland groups his troops slightly beyond the artillery of the Mexicans. Afterward, in a coordinated effort, the regiments speed across open ground toward Monterrey. The incoming artillery fire inflicts heavy casualties, causing the regiments to break into smaller units. However, the Maryland and D.C. units continue to take high casualties, particularly when the troops get too close to the artillery of La Teneria. The result of the fire is devastating. Those who are able run for the rear, which leaves only Colonel William H. Watson, battalion commander, with about 70 troops to continue the advance. Those who make it into the city become isolated. They are unable to remain cohesive. General William Butler is wounded during the attack against La Teneria from the east.

Colonel John Garland attempts to concentrate his troops inside the town and waits for directions from Major Joseph King Fenno Mansfield (later Union general); however, they are not accustomed to urban warfare. Mansfield, after he reconnoiters the area, determines that no Mexican troops are in the area where Garland's troops are holding. Major Mansfield urges Garland to move through the city to capture the Mexican fortifications that protect the northeastern section of Monterrey.

Complications develop due to the narrowness of the streets. It is extremely difficult to maneuver due to the stone houses that obscure the view from one street to the other. While Garland's troops move the streets essentially become mazes. In addition, Major Mansfield had misses the point that the Mexicans had built loopholes in the flat roofs of the city. The Mexicans lie prone out of sight, giving them the ability to fire at the passing Americans units.

The unexpected Mexican fire causes much confusion in the American ranks. While they press forward in column formation, they come under fire from a hidden battery. Major Mansfield and Captain W. G. Williams are among the first to get hit. Mansfield, although wounded, continues to direct his troops. Suddenly, other concealed batteries join in the fight. The results are more devastating and the casualty list grows even more. The Americans are pinned down by the Mexican guns and the snipers on the rooftops.

In the meantime, the 1st Infantry Regiment secures a foothold in the rear of La Teneria; however, they do not have the troops to progress further and capture the position. However, Mansfield and Garland are not apprised of the situation at La Teneria.

General Taylor hears the sounds of gunfire from the inner city. It is a signal to him that things are not going well. Taylor directs reinforcements to speed into the city. Bragg's battery is rushed to the city to counter the Mexican guns. General John A. Quitman's brigade — composed of the 3rd Division, 4th Division, the 1st Ohio and the 1st Mississippi

Rifles — is sent against the obstacle at La Teneria.

The 1st and 3rd Infantry fight from house to house and from street to street. Major W. W. Lear, in command of the 3rd, is hit with a ball that goes through his neck. He falls after being mortally wounded. Colonel William Watson arrives and is told that the Baltimore battalion would be required to support the regulars. Watson rides off and at that moment his horse is shot from under him. He jumps up and proclaims that he is unhurt. Then, while urging his men to attack, he is hit in the jugular vein. Watson dies nearly instantly.

Captain Brackus (1st Infantry), leading his company and some of the others, succeeds by using bayonets to gain possession of a shed that stands about 120 yards from the rear of the northeast battery. From there, Backus heads south and takes possession of a distillery that is heavily defended. In the meantime, the volunteer divisions led by General Quitman, preceded by two companies of the 4th Division, gain possession of the front of the redoubt. However, Lieutenant Richard H. Graham is mortally wounded. Lieutenant Charles Hoskins and Lieutenant J. S. Woods are both killed. Hoskins is hit in the heart. Captain Brackus, by that time, ceases fire. He repositions his troops on the roof of the distillery and on the roof of the shed, then orders them to commence fire upon the fort. The Mexicans see the Volunteer Division approaching their position and this prompts them to quit firing their artillery.

Bragg's artillery arrives to bolster the infantry. After firing some rounds, it becomes obvious that his 6-pounders are ineffective. The rounds bounce off the stone walls of the city's buildings and then exploding harmlessly. An identical effect was felt when Bragg's batteries fired upon the concealed Mexican batteries.

All the while, the Mexican batteries continue to fire. Colonel Garland and Major Mansfield are compelled to order a general retreat. The operative troops begin to retrace their steps to get out of harm's way. Nevertheless, they were unable to get Bragg's guns out of the way. The infantry is forced to literally lift the 880-pound guns and rotate them 180 degrees to permit the remainder of the troops to escape.

About half of Garland's men are wounded and Bragg lost ten of his artillerymen and twelve horses. General John A. Quitman had gained success at La Teneria, but his losses in the 4th Infantry were also high. The three companies of the 4th Regiment lost about 33 percent of their officers and men while assaulting La Teneria. After about three minutes, the unit retreated. General William Butler, commander of the 3rd Division, is wounded (shot below the knee) during the assault. He is replaced by Brigadier General Thomas L. Hamer. In addition, Colonel Alexander M. Mitchell, commander of the regiment, is shot from his horse and seriously wounded. The regiment is ordered into the suburbs of the city where it is not exposed to the fire, but yet it is in a more practical place from which it could pinpoint the positions of the enemy. It takes cover along a fence.

General Taylor, who observes the entire ordeal of the Ohio regiment, orders Captain Braxton Bragg (later Confederate general) and Captain Miller of the 1st Infantry to advance in support of the Ohioans. Bragg turns his guns upon the Mexican cavalry and compels them to retreat hurriedly toward the Citadel.

In the meantime, General Quitman's other forces, the 1st Tennessee and the 1st Mississippi Rifles, are able to evade much of the Mexican fire. They charge La Teneria's perimeter and by noon, following about one hour of combat, La Teneria is captured by the 1st Mississippi Rifles. Lt. Colonel Alexander McClung is up on the parapet with his regiment just behind. A Mexican officer presents his sword to McClung, but in transferring it, McClung is seriously wounded in the thigh. His men, reacting instantly, kill him on the spot. Meanwhile, Colonel Campbell's regiment, which had secured the left, hoists the American flag on the wall of Monterrey. La Teneria is the first foothold seized along the eastern front, but it is soon contested. Sniper fire originating in the nearby rooftops begins immediately.

The American artillerymen under Captain Ridgely take over the Mexican artillery and turn it against the Mexicans who are defending Fort Diablo and the Citadel. With the support of Ridgely's artillery fire, General Taylor reforms his forces and they begin to take out the other positions. The 1st Ohio crosses the Ojo de Agua at a point below La Purisima. Once across, they attack Fort Diablo. However, the troops are un-able to penetrate the Mexican defenses. They are compelled to withdraw.

To the right, Colonel Garland's brigade assaults the fort, but it too is halted short of its objective. Mexican lancers threaten the 1st Ohio during its advance and appear on the plains north of city again in the late afternoon, but each time, guns from Bragg's battery drive off the horsemen. Although unsuccessful inside Monterrey, the light artillery again proves its usefulness in the open. By nightfall on 21 September, General William J. Worth controls Federation Hill in the west, while Taylor keeps his hold on La Teneria.

During the night of the 22nd–23rd, after midnight, General de Ampudia abandons his outer defenses and concentrates on defending the city from its Citadel and other defenses. On the night of the 22nd, Fort Diablo is abandoned, but this is not discovered until the following morning. Once Taylor is informed, he directs General Quitman to occupy it. Elements of the 1st Mississippi and Tennessee Regiments occupy the fort; however, the Mexicans have taken their artillery, leaving nothing of value for the Americans. After the Americans occupy the fort, the Mexicans who still hold positions in the vicinity begin firing into the it. The Americans are then tasked with driving them out of their hiding places.

The Mexicans are reported to be on the retreat down the Caderita Road. General Henderson is directed to give pursuit with his 2nd Texas Regiment. In the meantime, General Twiggs' division, Hamer's brigade of volunteers, Bragg's artillery and May's dragoons are ordered to march upon the city.

At about the same time that General John A. Quitman takes possession of the fort, General Taylor arrives at the scene. He orders Quitman to advance toward a strong point (horn work) and if possible to occupy it. Quitman dispatches a contingent of riflemen under Lieutenant Groves, which is bolstered by one company of Tennessee volunteers, commanded by Captain McMurray. Afterward, General Quitman directs four additional companies (two from Mississippi and two from Tennessee), commanded by Colonel Jefferson Davis. The troops advance using the houses for cover. They rush to the redoubts, driving them from there. They take up new positions in the fortified houses, from where they pour effective fire into the redoubts. The Americans are soon reinforced as the battle becomes more general.

Meanwhile, General Henderson returns after finding no enemy troops along the Caderita Road. General Taylor directs Henderson to dismount and participate along with General Quitman's brigade. The Americans are once again compelled to engage in the street-by-street fighting to seize their objectives.

During the early morning hours of the 23rd, the Americans begin their assault. General Worth assaults from the east while General Taylor pounds against the west. The movement is designed to drive the Mexicans to the center of the city.

The Americans are taught a valuable lesson during the fighting on the 21st. Rather than forming in columns and trying to navigate the narrow streets, where they are the direct targets of the snipers and the batteries, this time, they move from house to house. Using axes, battering rams, sledge hammers, and when necessary, 8-inch artillery shells, they plow through the houses. The tactic seemingly works well, except that it is extremely difficult to take the time to clear the roofs and buildings.

The Texans are led by General Henderson and Colonel Woods. They are incited to battle by Colonel Woods, who tells them to "remember the cruelties of Mier, Goliad and the massacre of Fannin's men." The caution works. The Texans, led by Lt. Colonel Mirabeau Lamar, charge down the street and after breaking into the houses, they go to the roofs. In the event a Mexican appears, he is killed. They continued unabated until they reached General Quitman.

The Mexicans slowly abandon their positions and as expected, they retreat to the large cathedral, while U.S. troops begin to flank them. When the Americans advance to within two blocks of the city's central plaza, Taylor orders them to withdraw. Taylor seemingly is concerned about the number of civilians who seek protection near the cathedral. General Taylor is aware a huge cache of ammunition is stored there. Taylor transfers his only 10-inch mortar to General William Worth and directs him to fire it every twenty minutes into the plaza. Afterward, D. Franco D.P. Morales, the governor (civil magistrate) of Nuevo Leon, seeks to gain permission for civilians to evacuate the city.

At 8 A.M., he sends the following message to General Taylor:

> As you are resolved to occupy the place by force of arms, and the Mexican general-in-chief resolved to defend it at every cost, as his honor and duty require him to do, thousands of victims who, from indigence and want of means, find themselves now in the theatre of war, and who would be uselessly sacrificed, claim the rights which in all times and in all countries humanity extends. As governor of the state, and a legitimate representative of the people, I state their case to you, and hope, from your civilization and refinement, that whatever may be the event of the present contest, you will issue orders that families shall be respected, or will grant a reasonable time for them to leave the capital. I have the honor to salute you, general-in-chief of the army of occupation of the United States, and to assure you of my highest consideration. God and Liberty. Franco De P. Morales.

General Taylor declines Morales' request.

At about 9 P.M. on the 22nd, General de Ampudia suggests to General Taylor that he will abandon Monterrey and his troops will retain their arms. At 0700 on the following day, General Taylor responds to General de Ampudia. He informs the Mexican general that all arms are to be forfeited. Afterward, General de Ampudia replies by asking Taylor to convene an armistice commission, which he does. General William J. Worth, General Henderson and Colonel Jefferson Davis represent the United

States. Those representing Mexico are General J. M. Ortega, General T. Requena and the governor of New Leon, Manuel M. Llano. The commissioners arrive at a compromise following negotiations, which had broken down without a conclusion. General de Ampudia receives one week to abandon the city and gains permission for his troops to retain their personal weapons and one 6-gun battery. The commission also sets up an eight-week cease fire. For the duration of the cease fire, General Taylor agrees that he will not advance beyond the town of Linares, which stands about fifty miles south.

The American commissioners agree to those terms due to the condition of their own troops. General David Twiggs' division and General Butler's have both been badly hurt and General Worth and the Texas regiment are both exhausted. General Taylor is aware that if he is to continue the operation to seize Monterrey, he will incur more casualties. He is also aware that his supplies are low and his manpower is extremely low. Consequently, he decides that time is needed to allow him to refurbish his supplies and receive reinforcements.

General de Ampudia keeps his end of the bargain. He surrenders before the seven-day deadline. However, General Taylor has come upon the unintended consequences for his part in the agreement. President Polk concludes that Taylor is not the officer to finish out the war. The president decides to give General Scott a command.

The Americans lose 120 killed, 368

wounded, and 43 missing. Officially, the Mexicans record their losses as 367 men killed and wounded.

After General de Ampudia evacuates Monterrey, the Americans care for the wounded from both sides. Captain Nathan S. Jarvis uses confiscated buildings as hospitals. The setting is much improved over the conditions that existed before the buildings are confiscated. Amputations are done on field blankets. Nonetheless, the conditions remain poor and problems like malaria, gangrene and infections spread fast among the wounded.

The victory at Monterrey represents yet another success for the U.S. Army. It was the third time in less than four months that it faced a superior numbered army and come out with a victory. However, at Palo Alto and Resaca de la Palma, the Americans sustained lower casualties.

Second Lieutenant Franklin Gardner (later Confederate general) participates at this battle. He is brevetted to first lieutenant for gallantry. Later he participates at Vera Cruz, Churubusco, and Molino del Rey. He is again brevetted to captain in the latter battles. Also, 2nd Lieutenant William Montgomery Gardner (later Confederate general), 1st U.S. Infantry arrives at Monterrey during the afternoon following the battle. He remains at Monterrey until the regulars are ordered to Tampico to join with General Scott's command.

Second Lieutenant Richard Caswell Gatlin (later Confederate general), 7th Infantry, is wounded at this battle. Daniel Harvey Hill also participates in the capture of Monterrey.

Afterward, he participates with General Scott at Vera Cruz and Cerro Gordo. He also leads storming parties at Padierna and at Chupultepec. Colonel Albert Sidney Johnston (later Confederate general), 1st Texas Rifle Volunteers, participates at this battle. Another Mississippian, Evander McNair (later Confederate general) serves with Company E, 1st Mississippi Rifles. William Read Scurry (later Confederate general) serves as a private in the 2nd Texas Regiment. He takes part in the battle for Monterrey and afterward musters out as a major.

William Bowen Campbell (later Union general) participates at this battle as colonel of the 1st Tennessee. Afterward, he takes part at Vera Cruz and Cerro Gordo. Lieutenant Charles Griffin (later Union general), an artillery officer, participates at this battle. August Valentine Kautz (later Union general) is in the war as a member of the 1st Ohio Regiment. John Reese Kenly (later Union general) takes part at this battle.

September 21   American troops attack and secure the road to Saltillo, Mexico, removing it as an obstacle from the path of capturing Monterrey. The cost, 394 dead or wounded.

September 22–30   In California, Mexican Californians commanded by General Jose Maria Flores rebel against the United States, capturing a vast portion of Southern California, including Los Angeles and San Diego. Americans capture Independence Hill, overlooking the heavily fortified palace at Monterey. The Mexicans assault the position, but they are repulsed. The

Americans pursue the retreating attackers, capturing their artillery and overrunning the palace, raising the Stars and Stripes.

In other activity, General Kearny publishes a set of laws that become known as the "Kearny Code." General Kearny also appoints Charles Bent as governor of the territory. He names Donaciano Vigil as secretary, Richard Dillon as sheriff, and Francis Blair as U.S. district attorney.

September 23   In Mexico, General Pedro de Ampudia sends a peace proposal to the Americans. General Taylor responds: "Unconditional surrender." Negotiations continue and an armistice of 8 weeks is signed, allowing Mexican troops to withdraw from the city.

In California, at the post at Los Angeles, Captain Archibald Gillespie and his Marines successfully repulse a Mexican attack on the small American garrison at Los Angeles at 3 A.M. Gillespie states: "We were not wholly surprised, and with 21 rifles, we beat them back." However, they are forced to surrender when overrun by more than 500 Mexicans on September 30 after a bitter siege. Captain Gillespie is permitted to leave. He is to depart from California from San Pedro. Nevertheless, during the siege, Gillespie is able to sneak through the lines and reach Captain William Mervine, U.S. Navy, at Monterey.

Also, Gillespie dispatches Juan Flaco to Monterey with word for Commodore Robert Stockton. He puts nothing in writing in case the messenger is caught. Instead, Gillespie hands Flaco a pack of cigarettes. He writes on the cigarette wrappers "Believe the bearer" and then stamps them with his seal. Mexicans shoot Flaco's horse from under him, but he is unhurt. He receives another horse following his escape from the pickets on foot.

Finally, on 29 September, Juan Flaco locates Commodore Stockton in San Francisco. In the meantime, Gillespie's situation is becoming worse. On the same day, the Mexicans issue another and final ultimatum to Captain Gillespie. They promise him that if he surrenders, his force will have its safety guaranteed.

Gillespie does not keep the agreement. He marches out of the fort with the drums beating and the colors flying, along with two artillery pieces. Gillespie is to give his cannon to the Mexicans before boarding the ship. Before departing the post he spikes all of the guns, and those that he takes to the ship, he tosses into the bay.

September 24   In Mexico at Monterrey, a rider, Colonel Moreno, arrives at the upper forts. He is carrying a letter from General Pedro de Ampudia to General Taylor. He is met by Lieutenant Colonel Rogers, who escorts him to the headquarters of General Hamer at La Teneria. He is then taken to the headquarters of General Taylor at San Domingo.

September 25   In Mexico, Mexicans evacuate Monterrey. Taylor takes command of the city, including the almost invincible Citadel, at little cost. General Winfield Scott remarks, "Three glorious days."

The commissioners designated by

General Taylor again meet with their Mexican counterparts. The Mexicans want the word "capitulation" exchanged for "surrender." It is suggested that the word "stipulation" be used instead of "capitulation." In the meantime, General Pedro de Ampudia, in the presence of his commissioners, destroys the Spanish copy of the capitulation, which he had signed. However, the citizens of Monterrey are not to be held back. Rather than wait for the official word, they rush to the quarters of the Americans to sell them food. The Americans are quick to purchase from them; they are nearly starved due to the last couple of days of being exposed to the elements.

General Persifor Smith is directed to occupy the Citadel. Also, General de Ampudia, after leaving the city, moves to Saltillo. John Wolcott Phelps (later Union general) participates at this battle. Subsequently, he participates at Vera Cruz and at the capture of Mexico City. Stewart Van Vliet (later Union general) takes part in this battle. Later Van Vliet participates at Vera Cruz.

In other activity, General Kearny begins a forced march to California with 300 men. American Colonel Sterling Price takes command of Sante Fe three days after Colonel Kearny's departure. William Yarnel Slack (later Confederate general) serves as captain of the 2nd Missouri Volunteers under Price. A small group of engineers who carry two small howitzers, led by Lieutenant William H. Emory, and hunters and guides led by Antoine Robidoux and Jean Charbonneau also accompany Kearny.

September 26–27   In California, at Isaac Williams' Rancho Santa Ana del Chino, close to Chino, a detachment of 24 Americans under Benjamin D. Wilson are gathered. Californians had doubted that the Americans would remain loyal. Later that night the house is surrounded. At dawn on the following day, the two sides exchange gunfire. It ends with one Californian dead and two others wounded. In addition, three Americans are wounded. The Californians begin to set the house afire, but at that time, Wilson surrenders to Varela. The Californians march their prisoners to Boyle Heights, the principal camp of the Californians. Initially, the prisoners are to be executed in retaliation for the death Carlos Ballesteros, the man killed at the ranch. However, the prisoners are eventually taken to the Rancho los Cerritos, in the vicinity of Long Beach, California, where they are eventually released. The incident is remembered as the Battle of Chino.

September–October   In naval activity, the United States keeps pressure against the Mexicans on the sea as well as on land. The American Navy is much superior to the Mexican Navy, allowing little chance of defeat. In September, the Mexicans lose 12 vessels to the American Navy, including the brigantine *Susana* and the sloop *Salita*. During October, the Americans continue to capitalize on their naval strength. The *Cyane* seizes 12 Mexican ships without support of other American vessels.

October   In Mexico, Admiral Matthew Perry leads an expedition that includes a 200-man contingent of Marines commanded by Captain Alvin Edson. They capture Frontera and San Juan Bautista, but they do not occupy either city.

Elsewhere, headquarters for the regiment of mounted riflemen is established at Jefferson Barracks, Missouri. The various companies are formed at Jefferson Barracks and at Fort McHenry in Maryland and in Columbus, Ohio. The unit, which was to head for Oregon, instead is ordered to join with General Scott's forces in Mexico. While crossing the Gulf of Mexico from New Orleans to Point Isabel, a violent storm strikes. The horses are all lost in the storm, being washed overboard. The regiment, except for two companies that are able to mount Mexican horses, is compelled to fight as infantry. U.S. Marines aboard the USS *Cyane* participate in the capture of twelve Mexican vessels off the coast of lower California.

October 6   In California, General Stephen Kearny continues his trip to the desert. He encounters a group of riders yelling and screaming like Indians. The riders are 19 horsemen escorting Kit Carson, who is carrying a message from Washington to Commodore Robert Stockton. Seemingly, the contest for California had ended and Stockton had raised the flag in San Diego's harbor. Carson then acts as Kearny's guide to California for the balance of the route.

In naval activity, Captain William Mervine arrives at San Pedro this day aboard the USS *Savannah*.

October 7–8 BATTLE OF DOMINQUEZ RANCHO   In California, Captain

Gillespie, along with Captain William Mervine (U.S. Navy), initiate their march on Los Angeles with about 225 Marines and sailors who are attached to the USS *Savannah*, which is at San Pedro. En route the Americans encounter about 125 Mexicans led by Jose Antonio Carrillo. The American contingent has no artillery, but they insist on capturing the gun of the Californians. They attack three separate times, but after losing 12 men, Captain Mervine calls off the attack. He retreats to San Diego under cover fire from Gillespie's men. Mervine buries his dead on an island in San Pedro Bay. It is commonly known as Deadman's Bay, but the official name is Isla de los Muertos.

October 11   President Polk receives word on the Battle of Monterrey, Mexico, and on the armistice. Polk orders the armistice to end. Polk also condemns General Taylor for permitting the Mexican army to escape.

October 15   U.S. Marines participate in the second expedition against Alvarado, Mexico. Commodore David Conner withdraws after shelling enemy positions.

October 23   U.S. Marines attached to Commodore Perry's squadron participate in the expedition up the Tabasco River. The Marines land and capture Frontera, California.

October 24   The steamship *McKim* arrives at Galveston, Texas, from Brazos Santiago. The *McKim*, which has sustained some damage to its machinery, is transporting General A. S. Johnston (later Confederate general) and Texas volunteers.

October 24–25 In Mexico, U.S. Marines attached to Perry's squadron land at a spot on the Tabasco River below Fort Accachappa, then advance and capture the fort. Afterward, they re-embark and the expedition continues up the river. Later that day, the Marines land at San Juan Bautista and capture that place. The town of Tabasco receives an intense bombardment from the American Gulf Squadron, commanded by Commodore Perry. Perry's troops capture or destroy all vessels in the harbor. Midshipman Charles Kinnard Graham (later Union general) is attached to this squadron.

October 27 U.S. Marines participate in the landing and capture of the town of San Pedro, California.

November 13 In Mexico, General Zachary Taylor dispatches a contingent of about 1,000 troops from Monterrey to occupy Saltillo, which stands about 65 or 70 miles to the southwest. Saltillo is the primary city that dominates the only road leading to Mexico City from the north. The road is practical for the movement of guns and wagons.

November 14 U.S. Marines and seamen attached to Commodore David Conner's squadron capture Tampico, Mexico, without opposition. Afterward, a garrison is established. John Sanford Mason (later Union general) is stationed here on garrison duty.

November 15 *In naval activity,* the USS *Boston* is wrecked on Eleuthera Island in the Bahamas. The ship is lost, but all hands are saved. The commanding officer, Commander George Frederick Pearson, is subsequently tried at Norfolk, Virginia, for losing

his ship. He is found guilty and sentenced to a one year suspension. The same court tries Commander Carpenter for the loss of the USS *Truxton.* He is sentenced to being cashiered; however, the president modifies his sentence, knocking it down to a one year suspension.

In other activity, a contingent of about 150 Mexican troops attacks a 10-man detachment commanded by Lieutenant Talbot at Santa Barbara. The Americans had been staying at a home surrounded by Mexicans who demanded surrender. Talbot, an officer in Captain Frémont's command, rejected the ultimatum. Instead, he and the others walked out of the house and withdrew to the hills to the rear of the mission. The Mexicans never fired a shot. The ten Americans halted on a hill and the Mexicans started a fire that encircled them. Talbot marched his small command through the fire and afterward, they crossed the mountains and from there they continued to advance to Monterrey, where the party arrived in a few days.

November 16 In California, an American force commanded by Captain Charles Burrass (or Burroughs) and Bluford K. Thompson (General Taylor's command) engage Californians commanded by Manuel de Jesus Castro in the vicinity of Saltillo in northern California in the Salinas valley. Each side sustains a few men killed and wounded. Nevertheless, Saltillo is captured.

November 18 Elements of the Mormon battalion depart from Santa Fe, New Mexico, en route for California.

Colonel Doniphan directs that about 100 men and 23 women are sent back to Fort Puebla, a trappers' post on the Arkansas River. Doniphan decides that the winter weather was too great for them to complete the advance.

November 19 U.S. Marines and seamen attached to Commodore Conner's squadron land and seize Panuco, Mexico.

November 22 Navajo Indians sign a peace treaty with the United States at Ojo or Bear Spring.

General Winfield Scott (Frost, *The History of Mexico and Its Wars*).

November 23   In Washington, D.C., General Winfield Scott on or about this day receives orders to move to the Rio Grande to assume command of the army there. Scott receives a letter dated this day from the War Department that states, "The President, several days since, communicated in person to you his orders to repair to Mexico, to take the command of the forces there assembled, and particularly to organize and set on foot an expedition to operate on the Gulf coast, if, on arriving at the theatre of action, you shall deem it to be practicable." General Scott writes to the president that "the enemy in front is not half so much to be feared as an attack from the rear."

Also, the secretary of war writes to General Scott:

Sir — The President, several days since, communicated in person to you his orders to repair to Mexico, to take the command of the forces there assembled, and particularly to organize and set on foot an expedition to operate on the Gulf coast, if, on arriving at the theatre of action, you shall deem it to be practicable. It is not proposed to control your operations by definite and positive instructions, but you are left to prosecute them as your judgment, under a full view of all the circumstances, shall dictate. The work is before you, and the means provided, or to be provided, for accomplishing it, are committed to you, in the full confidence that you will use them to the best advantage.

The objects which it is desirable to obtain have been indicated, and it is hoped that you will have the requisite force to accomplish them.

Of this you must be the judge, when preparations are made, and the time for action arrived.

Very respectfully, Your obedient servant W.L. MARCY, SECRETARY OF WAR.

In related activity, General Winfield Scott issues orders to General Taylor to dispatch the core of his army to points at the mouth of the Rio Grande and Tampico, where they are to await transport to Scott's invasion staging area. Also, Benjamin Huger (later Confederate general) is appointed chief of ordnance for General Scott. He participates at Vera Cruz, Molino del Rey and Chapultepec. John Gray Foster (later Union general) accompanies General Scott on his expedition to capture Mexico City. He is brevetted twice for gallantry. Also, Captain Michael Kelly Lawler (later Union general), 3rd Illinois Regiment, participates in General Scott's campaign to seize Mexico City. Lieutenant George Brinton McClellan, Corps of Engineers, accompanies General Scott on the campaign to seize Mexico City. Charles Pomeroy Stone (later Union general) participates at this battle. Also, Lieutenant Thomas Williams (later Union general) serves as aide-de-camp to General Scott. He is brevetted captain and major for gallantry.

November 24   The Mormon Battalion, commanded by Colonel Philip St.

George Cooke (later Union general), stands at Los Playna, Sonora, about 350 miles from Santa Fe, New Mexico. The unit is en route to California. Water is scarce.

November 26   *In naval activity,* the USS *Somers,* a brigantine commanded by Ralph Semmes, while on blockade duty in the Gulf of Mexico spots a blockade runner, the schooner *Criolla,* which manages to get into the port of Vera Cruz. Semmes launches a boat from which a party boards the ship. The winds, however, are unfavorable and the party cannot get its prize to sea. The party sets the *Criolla* afire and returns to the *Somers* with seven prisoners. The *Criolla* turned out to be a spy ship operating under the authority of Commodore David Conner.

November 30   General Winfield Scott leaves New York for the Rio Grande.

Commodore David Conner (Frost, ***The History of Mexico and Its Wars).***

He is thoroughly confident that his government is acting in good faith and that it will provide everything necessary to prosecute the war. He has no thoughts that his government would attempt to dishonor him by declaring him unfit for the position to which he had just been appointed. But unknown to him, U.S. President James Polk, who had named him commander-in-chief, was preparing to end his career.

Elsewhere, Albion Parris Howe (later Union general) participates with General Scott during his campaign to capture Mexico City. Lieutenant Henry Jackson Hunt (later Union general), artillery officer, participates with General Scott during the campaign to seize Mexico City. He is brevetted for gallantry at Contreras, Churubusco and Chapultepec.

December   In Pennsylvania, the 1st Regiment of Pennsylvania Volunteers is raised. It departs from Pittsburgh on 23 December and arrives in New Orleans about the latter part of February. A second regiment is afterward raised and it leaves for Texas via New Orleans. Lieutenant Alexander Hayes (later Union general) serves during the war with the Pennsylvania units and he is brevetted for his gallantry.

In other activity, the Palmetto Regiment from South Carolina arrives in Texas. It is accompanied by graduates of the Citadel, also in South Carolina. James Cantey (later Confederate general) serves as an officer with the regiment. He participates with the regiment until he is wounded in Mexico; then he returns to South Carolina.

December 5   Captain Archibald Gillespie, U.S. Marine Corps, and his detachment of 35 men join up with General Kearny, who is en route to San Pasqual, California. In other activity, Midshipman R. Clay Rogers, a seaman of the USS *Somers,* Doctor J.W. Wright and John G. Fox go ashore to examine the Mexican's magazines to determine if it can be destroyed. After the trio makes its way from the boat, they are surrounded by a party of seven Mexican soldiers. Doctor Wright manages to escape, but the remaining two are sent to Perote, where they are confined.

December 6 BATTLE OF SAN PASQUAL In California, General Stephen Kearny sends Edward Stokes, an Englishman, ahead to inform Commodore Robert Stockton at San Diego that he had annexed New Mexico and established a civilian government there before moving to San Diego. Stockton is quick to act. Stockton dispatches Lieutenant Archibald Gillespie, a Marine, and 37 riflemen, along with one field gun.

Lieutenant Gillespie informs Kearny that a large band of rebels is encamped about five to six miles away at San Pasqual. The insurgents are led by Andres Pico, the brother of Mexican Governor Pio Pico. Kearny is intent on engaging the Californians despite a torrential downpour. He calls for a council of war, and he also plans a reconnaissance of their camp before attacking it on the following morning.

One man, Captain Benjamin Moore, is against his plan. He attempts to persuade Kearny that he is underestimating his opponents. Moore tries to persuade Kearny to

Battle of San Pasqual (Frost, *The History of Mexico and Its Wars*).

launch a surprise attack against the camp before the Californians could mount their horses. Nevertheless, Kearny is confident that he is going to attack in the morning.

In the meantime, Lieutenant Gillespie suggests to Kearny that his "mountain men" could get into and out of the enemy camp without being discovered. Kearney turns down Gillespie. He is confident that the task can be handled by his aide-de-camp, Lieutenant Thomas Hammond, six dragoons and the Californian deserter Rafael Machado. Machado leads the detachment into the valley of San Pasqual.

Machado moves to about one-half mile from an Indian encampment, where he is informed that Pico's men are sleeping. Nevertheless, Hammond decides that Machado is taking too long. He rides into the camp with his force. Their swords are all banging, which gets the dogs to barking. The noise alerts Pico's men, about 100 in number, and shortly thereafter, Pico's men are up and prepared to mount their horses.

Hammond has inadvertently blown Kearny's surprise. Pico's men are mounted and they ride toward Hammond's force, which is on the retreat. Pico, however, is convinced that Hammond's group is only a scouting party. Pico directs his troops to round up their horses so they can abandon their camp.

Meanwhile, Hammond returns to Kearny's camp to inform him that Pico had been alerted to the presence of the Americans. Kearny then decided that the attack must be made immediately, despite a pouring rain. The weather had become inclement and extremely cold. Kearney's force had seen their ammunition drenched in the rain, but did not check it. Meanwhile, Pico is concerned only with abandoning his camp. Kearney is convinced that Pico's men are blocking the road to San Diego.

Kearny is aware of the health of his mules and intends to seize horses from the Californians. Kearny is also still convinced that the Californians would run from battle once his force encounters them. Kearny initiates his attack. His force arrives at a ridge between San Pasqual and Santa Maria. Kearny tries to tell them that their government is anticipating that they will charge "with the point of the saber." Kearny instructs his troops to encircle Pico's camp. Just afterward, his troops descended the ridge, but the force gets stuck in some low clouds as well as fog.

Kearny takes note of the conditions and orders his force to initiate a trot; however, the order is misinterpreted by Captain Abraham R. Johnston's command. Despite being about 1,000 yards from the camp, Johnston's detachment thought he said "Charge." From that command everything goes downhill. Kearny, having heard the order to charge said: "Oh heavens! I did not mean that!" About forty men are out in front of the others, at least by one and a half miles from the main body.

Meanwhile, the Californians see the charge as well as the condition of their mounts, including near dead horses and mules. Kearny's force loses its cohesion as the advance guard under Johnston breaks away from the others. Kearny is far back in the pack. Johnston drives directly into Pico's camp; he is instantly killed. At the tail end, Lieutenant Gillespie and his volunteers are moving forward.

Captain Benjamin Moore orders his troops to charge. He pushes his horse to the limits in an attempt to cut off the Californians. Moore passes the point on his right and with dawn approaching, he can see the Californians down the road. Moore halts, then looks to his rear and realizes that he is the only American who has cleared the point. Moore remains where he is and suddenly notices that all of the Californians had not gone down the road. In front of him, there are about 70 Californians with Andres Pico. Captain Moore is in a precarious position with few options. He can either head back around the point to join his soldiers or he can charge the enemy.

Captain Moore chooses to charge the Californians with intent to kill the man in the center. The Californians watch in amazement as the American officer gallops toward Pico. The Californians do not take notice of a second American officer, Lieutenant Thomas C. Hammond, who had come around the bend.

Moore, at a full gallop, fires his pistol at Pico but misses. In an instant, Moore raises his sword and makes a second pass at Pico. Two

Californians, Leandro Osuna and Dionisio Alipas, intercept Captain Moore and both stick him with their lances. Afterward, other Californians come up and dispense their lances into Captain Moore. Pico then comes over to Moore and stabs him.

Captain Benjamin Moore's body falls off his horse as the Californians retrieved their spears. Pablo Apis, an Indian, comes up to Moore and he also runs his lance into his body. Moore is lanced up to eight times. Thomas Sanchez then rides his horse over to Moore and shoots him in the head.

Lieutenant Thomas C. Hammond hears the shot and sees the Californians gathered around Captain Moore's body. Hammond rides over to try to save his brother-in-law, but the Californians kill Hammond by their lances.

Suddenly, the Californians halt and turn their horses around to charge the Americans. The Americans try to fire their weapons but their ammunition is too wet to ignite.

Kearny finally arrives at the scene, but it is too late for him to take command and too late to yell any coherent command. It is a very chaotic situation. Then Kearny himself is struck in the back by a lance. The Californians had turned toward Lieutenant Gillespie's "mountain men." Gillespie is wounded a few times, including a lance that misses his heart. Despite being wounded multiple times, Gillespie, gets back to the guns which had arrived. He and a naval midshipman, James Duncan, bring them into action.

The Californians capture one of the guns. They drag it off the field, break off the engagement and ride away. The encounter is especially short, but also extremely severe. About fifty Americans had entered the fray and of those, 21 troops are killed and seventeen are wounded, including Kearny.

Captains Johnston and Moore, Lieutenant Hammond, along with two sergeants and a corporal are killed by lance thrusts. General Stephen Kearny and Captains William H. Warner (topographical engineers), Archibald Gillespie and Samuel Gibson were all seriously wounded, along with Antoine Robidoux.

December 7   General Stephen Kearny positions his battle weary troops in a defensive posture along the San Bernardo River in California to await reinforcements from Commodore Robert Stockton.

December 7–14   Company A, 2nd Mississippi Regiment, is formed at Columbus, Mississippi. It is mustered in at Vicksburg on 5 January 1847. Then on 12 January 1847, the company and the remainder of the regiment depart Vicksburg aboard the vessel *Sam Dole*. It arrives in New Orleans on the 14th.

December 8   *In naval activity,* the USS *Somers* (brigantine) operating in the Gulf of Mexico, is struck by a sudden storm and capsizes within a matter of minutes, with a loss of two officers and 39 enlisted men.

In Mexico, General Zachary Taylor is set to depart from Tamaulipas with the bulk of the troops, including the Baltimore battalion and the volunteers from Georgia, Mississippi and Tennessee, all of the regulars, except one company of artillery, and about two companies of the 7th Infantry. It will take Taylor about eight or ten days to begin this move. Taylor is to advance about 200 miles to Victoria, where he is to leave a garrison of about 1,000 troops. He is also expected to hook up with General Robert Patterson there. Also, General John Ellis Wool's division is encamped at Parras, where he is to establish a depot. The 1st and 2nd Regiments, Indiana Volunteers, are on their way from Camargo to join him. General William J. Worth is at Saltillo with a force of about 1,500 troops and General William O. Butler commands at Monterrey with about 2,000 troops. Generals David Twiggs and Persiphor Frazer Smith are both at Victoria and General John Quitman departs Monterrey for Victoria on 14 December. General James Shields (later Union general) is in command at Victoria.

Also, Alfred Iverson, Jr. (later Confederate general), the son of Senator Alfred Iverson, Sr., is sworn in as second lieutenant with the Georgia volunteers, a regiment raised by his father. Henry Root Jackson (later Confederate general) serves as colonel of the 1st Georgia Volunteer Regiment. Lorenzo Thomas (later Union general) serves for the duration as General William O. Butler's chief of staff. Lewis "Lew" Wallace (later Union general and author of *Ben Hur: A Tale of the Christ*) joins the service as first lieutenant of the 1st Indiana.

December 10 Beleaguered American troops under General Stephen Kearny are attacked by Mexicans. The

General John A. Quitman (Frost, *The History of Mexico and Its Wars*).

Mexicans even attempt to stampede horses to break the American lines. However, the Americans stand fast and the Army of the West repulses the Mexican attack. One hundred sailors and eighty Marines arrive to reinforce the Americans.

In other activity, American General John E. Wool moves his troops to reinforce Taylor's Army at Saltillo. Lieutenant Irvin McDowell serves during the war as an aide-de-camp to General Scott. He later participates at the battle of Buena Vista and is brevetted captain.

December 12 **In California,** General Stephen Kearny's troops arrive. The USS *Portsmouth* and the USS *Congress* are there to greet them. As Kearny's men enter San Diego they see "Old Glory" flying, hoisted by the U.S. fleet.

In other activity, Colonel Alexander Doniphan's troops depart from Valverde en route to El Paso, by way of the treacherous Jornada del Muerto (Journey of the Dead) route, arriving at El Brazio, 30 miles outside of El Paso, on Christmas Day.

December 14   Major William Gilpin leaves Valverde with 300 men heading for El Paso.

December 19   Colonel Alexander W. Doniphan, a lawyer from Missouri, leaves with the remaining 356 troops through the Jornada del Muerto. His total attack force arrives at the village of Santa Anna, 60 miles outside of El Paso del Norte. Mosby Monroe Parsons (later Confederate general) raises a company of mounted volunteers, the Cole County Dragoons, which becomes Company F, 1st Missouri Mounted Volunteers, and takes part in the Sante Fe expedition. Captain Parsons participates at Brazito, Chihuahua, and Sacramento. He returns to St. Louis, Missouri, and arrives there on 30 June 1847.

December 20   In Mexico, Commodore Matthew C. Perry, aboard the USS *Mississippi*, along with the USS *Bonita*, *Petrel* and *Vixen*, seize Laguna in Tobasco. Marines and seamen debark and destroy the guns and ammunition in the fort and town. Commander Sands is left in command. The *Petrel* and *Vixen* remain in charge of the town. The *Bonita* moves out to hold the mouth of the Tobasco River.

December 21   *In naval activity,* U.S. vessels attached to Commodore Matthew C. Perry's Squadron debark Marines and seamen at the Mexican stronghold of Carmen, and after meeting some opposition, seize and occupy the town. Perry's squadron will seize two Mexican ships off Alvarado on the 27th.

December 23   In Louisiana, General Winfield Scott departs New Orleans aboard the steamer *Alabama*. The ship arrives at Brazos Santiago, from where it heads for Tampico.

December 24   In South Carolina at Charleston, Mayor Thomas L. Hutchinson presents the Palmetto Regiment its first flag. The flag is described as "being made of Blue Silk, with the Coat of Arms of the State of South Carolina upon one side, and the United States Arms and a Palmetto Tree upon the other side, with the Inscription 'Presented by the City of Charleston.'" The flag is also reported to have the motto "Not for ourselves we conquer, but our country." The flag is carried by the regiment throughout the war. Also, Joseph Brevard Kershaw (later Confederate general) serves as lieutenant in the Palmetto Regiment. He is struck by a fever and sent home after serving for one year.

December 25 BATTLE OF EL BRAZITO (BATTLE OF TEMASCALITOS)   In New Mexico, about a half mile from Colonel Doniphan's troops, there are 1,200 Mexican dragoons, infantry and militia, commanded by Lt. Colonel Antonio Ponce de Leon. The Mexican commander sends an officer summoning the Americans to send Doniphan to the Mexicans or they will take him themselves. Doniphan responds: "Charge and be damned." In a short while, Doniphan, while playing cards, is informed of the enemy's advance on

U.S. cavalry at El Brazito (Frost, *The History of Mexico and Its Wars*).

the American positions and responds: "Boys, I now hold an invincible hand, but I'll be damned if I don't have to play it out in steel now."

American troops under Doniphan engage this contingent of Mexicans outside of El Paso, devastating them without suffering any fatal casualties, through accurate deadly rifle fire at close range, scattering the Mexicans in full retreat. This battle is remembered as the Battle of El Brazito (Battle of Temascalitos). It was fought in the vicinity of Las Cruces, New Mexico. The victory by the Americans opens the route to El Paso, which is seized on the following day.

December 26   In Texas, the city of El Paso surrenders to the United States.

Colonel Doniphan's troops occupy the city the following day.

In other activity, Montgomery D. Corse (later Confederate general) is commissioned as captain, Company B, First Regiment of the Virginia Volunteer Infantry. David Addison Weisiger (later Confederate general) serves with this regiment as second lieutenant. General William Gates, with about 1,000 troops, commands at Tampico. Captain James Lawson Kemper of Virginia (later Confederate general) is captain of Virginia volunteers. He is mustered into the service too late to take part in any battles.

December 27   In Mexico, U.S. Marines attached to Commodore Matthew C. Perry's squadron participate in the capture of the *Amelia*, a Mexican schooner off Alvarado. The Spanish schooner *Isabel* is also captured.

In **Texas**, Colonel Doniphan, at El Paso, sends a dispatch requesting reinforcements. Major Clarke sends Captain Weightman along with his six pieces of artillery and 45 Laclede rangers and 65 others. They move out and complete the 350 mile march in late January. Major Clarke follows and passes him en route.

December 28   Iowa is admitted to the Union as the 29th state.

December 29   General Stephen Kearny and Commodore Robert Stockton depart San Diego storming toward Los Angeles with a force of approximately 500. The U.S. Marines attached to the USS *Congress*, USS *Portsmouth* and the USS *Cyane* are assigned to the 1st Division under command of Captain Zeillin. In other activity, Brigadier General John A. Quitman's force arrives at and occupies Victoria, Mexico. A defending force of about 1,500 cavalry is at Victoria, but it abandons its positions at the approach of Quitman. On 4 January, General Taylor arrives with the division of General David Twiggs.

1847

January   The 5th Regiment is ordered to move to the mouth of the Rio Grande, from where it is to be transferred to General Scott's command. Elsewhere, Captain Robert Hall Chilton, 1st Kentucky Rifles, and his patrol are captured by Mexicans. They are taken to Mexico City and detained until a prisoner exchange is held. Lieutenant John Hunt Morgan (later Confederate general) is attached to the 1st Kentucky, but he is not on this patrol.

In other activity, Richard Stoddert Ewell (later Confederate general) at about this time is assigned to General Scott's command. He participates in the Battles of Vera Cruz, Cerro Gordo, Contreras, Churubusco and Mexico City. In late August he is promoted to brevet captain.

January 1   In **Texas**, General Winfield Scott arrives at the Rio Grande

on or about this day. It became obvious during the early part of January that the U.S. government was not prepared to carry out the attack on Vera Cruz. The ten additional regiments to be raised for the attack did not come about. Instead, the Congress did not act until the final days of its session. In the meantime, Santa Anna was at San Luis Potosi with a force of about 22,000 troops. San Luis Potosi is a fortified city that contains about 60,000 inhabitants. General Scott dispatches Lieutenant Ritchie with the plan of attack on Vera Cruz for General Taylor, but he is intercepted and killed by Mexicans. Santa Anna comes upon the plan, which ensures that he is aware of Scott's plan.

General Scott leaves about 10,000 volunteers and a few companies of artillery of the regular army with General Taylor. He directs Taylor that if necessary, he is to focus his attention on Monterrey. Taylor, however, is able to maintain all posts that are under his jurisdiction. In addition, with about one-half of his force, he achieves the huge victory at Buena Vista (February 22–23).

January 2 THE BATTLE OF SANTA CLARA The only battle fought between the forces of the U.S. and Californians in the Northern district of California is the Battle of Santa Clara. The fighting takes place on an open plain about three miles from the Mission Santa Clara.

The Americans come out of the woods onto the plain. Upon their entrance they spot rancheros closing against them. The American cannon are stuck in the mud, which causes the advance to halt. The two sides exchange fire, but no casualties occur. The rancheros return toward their camp, permitting the Americans to resume their march toward the mission.

January 4   In Mexico, General Zachary Taylor arrives at Victoria. Earlier he had decided to modify his strategy. Taylor also decided to abolish the Volunteer Division, which is composed of the Ohio and Kentucky regiments (William O. Butler) and the Georgia, Mississippi, and 1st Tennessee regiments in another brigade (John A. Quitman). Taylor took General David Twiggs' division, including John Quitman's brigade and the Baltimore Battalion. In addition, he leaves General William Jenkins Worth's division at Saltillo, John Ellis Wool at Parras, and William Butler at Monterrey. General Butler, senior officer, is placed in command of the troops left behind. General Robert Patterson, at Matamoros, later joins General Taylor at Victoria.

The 2nd Infantry and the 2nd Tennessee hook up with Taylor at Montemorelos on the way to Victoria and joins the march to Victoria. However, Taylor does not remain in Victoria. He returns to Monterrey on the 14th after hearing that Washington had decided that most of his army was going to be transferred to General Scott's army. Also, Benjamin Franklin Cheatham (later Confederate general) serves as captain with the 1st Tennessee. Later he becomes captain of the 3rd Tennessee.

January 8 THE BATTLE OF RIO SAN GABRIEL American troops — about 600 under the command of General Kearny, and the reinforcements, including Marines, under Commodore Robert Stockton — encounter a force of mounted Mexicans on the San Gabriel River. The Americans form into a square defense, with each of the four divisions facing outward from a side. After they began to cross the river, they are hit by fire from two of the Californians' artillery pieces. At about the same time, the Californian lancers charge toward the left side of the square. Inspired by the battle cry "New Orleans!" the Americans fight tenaciously, defeating the enemy overwhelmingly and doing it on the same day Andrew Jackson won the battle of New Orleans 32 years before. Once they cross the river, the Americans set up their artillery and return fire; the Mexicans retreat and pull their guns back. The Americans resume their advance.

In the meantime, the Mexican cavalry circles the American square and launches another charge against its rear face; however, Gillespie's division is posted there and they repel the charge. The Americans, after moving about one-half mile, again are hit by the Californians' guns, but the Americans return fire and their superior firepower compels the Mexicans to withdraw. The Americans resume their advance the next morning, but they yet again encounter the Californians at a spot at La Mesa, south of the city of Los Angeles. The Californians charge the Americans as they had the day before, but yet again, the American artillery duplicates its superior firepower and drives the Californians back. On 10 January, the Americans reach Los Angeles and Gillespie raises Old Glory, where he had been compelled to take it down the previous September. The Marines commanded by Captain Zeilin participate in this battle.

In other activity, the Mexican Congress authorizes the raising of 15 million dollars to continue the war against the United States. The method used to raise the funds: "by mortgage upon or the sale of the property of the clergy."

January 9   In California, Commodore Robert Stockton's force, which includes Marines, engages the Californians in the Battle of La Mesa at present-day Vernon. Stockton's force, including Marines, is traveling on foot, but they are able to defeat the mounted Californians. The Californians initiate a charge and try to outflank the Americans, but to no avail. They are forced to withdraw and regroup at Pasadena. The Californians are exhausted, which compels them to give Stockton's force the city of Los Angeles. The Californians sustain 15 dead and about 25 wounded. Mexican General Flores returns to Mexico after the contest.

January 10   In California, General Stephen Kearny recaptures Los Angeles and in effect ends Mexican Rebel opposition. The Mexicans within a few days sign the Treaty of Cahuenga. This treaty ends most opposition between the Mexicans and the United

Colonel Stephen Kearny (Wilcox, *History of the Mexican War*).

States in California. Americans raise Old Glory where Captain Gillespie of the U.S. Marines was forced to surrender three months earlier.

In Mexico, General Jose Heredia, with about 700 troops, departs from Durango for Chihuahua. When he arrives at Cuencame, in the northern portion of the state of Durango, he is informed of the action near El Paso. From there, General Heredia moves on to Chihuahua where he intends to assume command of the forces there.

January 11   In California, Colonel John Frémont, a few miles above San Fernando, receives a message from General Stephen Kearny that informs him that the Californians had been defeated and that the city of Los Angeles had been captured. Frémont afterward makes camp in the vicinity of the mission at San Fernando and dispatches Jesus Pico, a cousin to General Pico, to locate the California army in order to open negotiations. Pico finds the advance guard of the Californians encamped at the Verdugo Ranch. While he is detained there, he tells the primary generals that Colonel Fremont had arrived with his army and that they could receive better terms if they surrender to Frémont than they could receive from Commodore Robert Stockton. General Flores had departed from the encampment earlier in the day, but before he left he named General Andres Pico as commander of the Mexican army.

January 13   In California, Lieutenant Colonel John C. Frémont and Mexican General Andres Pico at the abandoned ranch house of Tomas

Feliz (Campo de Cahuenga) sign the Treaty of Cahuenga (Capitulation of Cahuenga). The treaty essentially leads to California becoming a state. It also terminates hostilities in California for the duration of the war.

The treaty reads:

> To All Who These Presents Shall Come, Greeting: Know Ye, that in consequence of propositions of peace, or cessation of hostilities, being submitted to me, as Commandant of the California Battalion of the United States forces, which have so far been acceded to by me as to cause me to appoint a board of commissioners to confer with a similar board appointed by the Californians, and it requiring a little time to close the negotiations; it is agreed upon and ordered by me that an entire cessation of hostilities shall take place until to-morrow afternoon (January 13), and that the said Californians be permitted to bring in their wounded to the mission of San Fernando, where, also, if they choose, they can move their camp to facilitate said negotiations.
>
> Given under my hand and seal this 12th day of January, 1847. J.C. Fremont, Lieutenant-Colonel U.S.A., and Military Commandant of California.
>
> ARTICLES OF CAPITULATION made and entered into at the Rancho of Couenga, this thirteenth day of January, Anno Domini, eighteen hundred and forty-seven, between P.B. Reading, Major; Louis Mclane, Jr., Commanding Artillery; Wm. H. Russell, Ordnance Officer; commissioners appointed by J.C. Fremont, Lieutenant-Colonel United States Army and Military Commandant of the territory of California; and Jose

Antonio Carrillo, Commandante de Esquadron, Agustin Olivera, Diputado, commissioners appointed by Don Andres Pico, Commander-in-Chief of the California forces under the Mexican flag.

ARTICLE I.— The Commissioners on the part of the Californians agree that their entire force shall, on presentation of themselves to Lieutenant-Colonel Fremont, deliver up their artillery and public arms, and they shall return peaceably to their homes, conforming to the laws and regulations of the United States, and not again take up arms during the war between the United States and Mexico, but will assist in placing the country in a state of peace and tranquillity.

ART. II.— The Commissioners on the part of Lieutenant-Colonel Fremont agree to and bind themselves on the fulfillment of the first article by the Californians, that they shall be guaranteed protection of life and property, whether on parole or otherwise.

ART. III — That until a treaty of peace be made and signed between the United States of North American and the Republic of Mexico, no Californian or other Mexican citizen shall be bound to take the oath of allegiance.

ART. IV.— That any Californian or other citizen of Mexico desiring, is permitted by this capitulation to leave the country without let or hindrance.

ART. V — That in virtue of the aforesaid articles, equal rights and privileges are vouchsafed to every citizen of California as are enjoyed by the citizens of the United States of North America.

ART. VI — All officers, citizens, foreigners or others shall receive the protection guaranteed by the second article.

ART. VII.— This capitulation is intended to be no bar in effecting such arrangements as may in future be in justice required by both parties.

January 14 General Zachary Taylor returns to Monterrey. He is informed that the Polk administration had decided that most of his army, including volunteers and regulars, are to be transferred to General Winfield Scott's expedition into Mexico. In other activity, the steamboat *Sam Dole* arrives in New Orleans. It has delivered the 2nd Mississippi Regiment, commanded by Colonel Charles Smith (later Union general). The regiment encamps on the battleground and remains there until 30 January.

January 17 The *American*, a transport ship, departs New York. It is transporting surf boats and arrives at Brazos on 6 February. About 30 other transports are lying off the Brazos bar. Many others are well within the bar. They are loading and embarking troops. In other activity, Lieutenant Gershom Mott (later Union general) is appointed at about this time in the 10th U.S. Infantry, but the regiment does not see any foreign service. Also, Joseph Anthony Mower (later Union general) joins the army as a private at about this time. George William Taylor (later Union general) serves with the regiment.

January 19 A company (55 troops) of infantry that was ordered from Fort Snelling to Mexico departs from the post on this day. The commanding officers are Captain Joseph B. Plummer (later Union general), Lieutenant Gordon Granger and Lieutenant Donham. While en route to the Rio Grande, Private Richard Monohan falls overboard from the transport *Tioga* and drowns. During the voyage, the temperature drops drastically causing some in the company to have their hands, feet, and ears become frozen.

January 23   In Mexico, Mexican General Minion's forces capture two parties under Major Solon Borland and Major Gaines at a point about 60 miles from Saltillo. A Texan, Captain Henrie, and a Mexican guide are also captured. Minion, before the Americans surrender, gives his word that Henrie would be treated as a prisoner of war and that the Mexican guide would receive a fair trial. Nevertheless, shortly after they surrender, the Mexican guide is executed. Captain Henrie decides that he might receive the same treatment. On the following day, the prisoners are taken to San Luis Potosi under a guard of 200 troops. One of the men with General Minon, Manuel Sanchez, recognizes Captain Henrie and says to him: "Well, sir, I suppose you will visit the city of Mexico a second time." Henrie replies: "That is very doubtful."

During the evening, Henrie, who had told some of the other prisoners about his plan to escape, somehow winds up on Major Gaines' horse and Gaines' pistols are still in their holsters. Henrie spots a hole in the line and gallops through it. One guard takes off in pursuit, but his horse is no match for the Kentucky horse.

Henrie is out of range when shots are fired at him.

On the 28th, Henrie, having lost his horse, which expires from a lack of water, arrives at a road. He follows it until about one hour after dusk, then spots a detachment of riders, but they are not distinguishable. Finally, he notices that they are friendly and from the state of Arkansas. He shouts to them and they come up to him. They place the nearly helpless Henrie on a horse and take him to an American outpost at Agua Nueva. Captain Pike, commander at the post, said that Henrie "was the most miserable looking being he ever saw. His shoes were worn out, his pantaloons cut in rags, his head was bare, and his hair and beard matted, his hands, feet, and legs were filled with thorns from the prickly pear, and his shin was parched and withered with privation, exposure, and exertion. He had tasted no water for four days, and seemed almost famished for want of it."

January 24   In New Mexico, Colonel Sterling Price (later Confederate general) defeats a band of insurgents at Taos, New Mexico. It is only a minor action at what is known as the Battle of Canada; however, Price is able to get a promotion to brigadier general out of it.

January 25–31   In Texas, Major Clark passes Captain Weightman's command, speeds to El Paso and learns from Colonel Doniphan that the city expects an attack that night. Clarke sends back an express with 28 mules and information concerning the attack. Captain Weightman, just as he is finishing his march across the Jornada del Muerto, meets with the express. He speeds on to Dona Ana and explains the situation to his command. He leaves his baggage on January 30 and carries only ammunition and cooked food. After crossing the Rio Grande three separate times they finally enter El Paso on 31 January. Soon after their arrival the reinforcements are told that the attack was a false alarm.

January 27 In Mexico, General Santa Anna, at San Luis Potosi, addresses his force:

The operations of the enemy demand that we should move precipitately upon his principal line, and we go to execute it. The independence, the honor, and the destiny of the nation depend at this moment on your decisions. Soldiers! The entire world observes us, and will expect our sets to be as heroic as necessary. Privations of all kinds surround us in consequence of the neglect shown toward us, for more than a month, by those who should provide your pay and provisions. But when has misery debilitated your spirits or weakened your enthusiasm! The Mexican soldier is well known for his frugality and patience under suffering — never wanting magazines for marches across the deserts, and always counting upon the resources of the enemy to provide for his wants. To-day we shall undertake to march over a desert country without succor or provisions. But be assured that we will immediately provided from those of the enemy, and with them you will be sufficiently remembered. My friends we go to open the campaign. What days of glory await us! What flattering future for our country! How satisfactorily when we contemplate that we have saved its independence! How the world will admire us! And when in the bosoms of our families we shall relate the risks and fatigues which we have endured, the combats with and triumphs over a daring and presumptuous enemy, and hereafter, when telling our children that we have saved our country a second time, the jubilee will be complete, and the sacrifices will appear to us to be nothing. Soldiers! Hurry forth in the defense of your country. The cause we sustain is a holy one; never have we struggled with more justice, because we fight for honor and religion of our wives and children! What sacrifice, then, can be too great for objects so dear? Let our motto be, "CONQUER OR DIE!" Let us answer before the great Eternal that we will not want an instant in purging our soil of the stranger who has dared to profess it with his presence. No treaty, nothing which may not be heroic and proud.

January 28 In Mexico, Santa Anna, this self-designated Napoleon of the west, leaves San Luis Potosi with an Army of between 15,000 and 18,000 men to destroy General Zachary Taylor's forces. The Mexicans under Santa Anna advance toward Fanque de in Vaea. The units include three infantry regiments, one brigade of cavalry, and an artillery contingent. Two days later, another division advances in the same direction.

January 29 In New Mexico, after fighting at the Battle of Canada, the

Pueblo Indians and New Mexicans withdraw to Embudo, in the vicinity of present-day Dixon. There, they decide to make yet another stand, in a canyon south of the town. In the meantime, Colonel Sterling Price discovers the road through Embudo is not suited for the wagons and artillery. Colonel Price detaches three companies, commanded by Captain John H.K. Burgwin, Captain Ceran St. Vrain and Lieutenant B.F. White, to engage the rebels. The Americans easily overcome the rebels. The defenders lose about 20 killed and 60 wounded. The Americans lose one man killed and one wounded. Sterling Price's official report of the battle states:

General Sterling Price (Wilcox, *History of the Mexican War*).

The rapid slopes of the mountains rendered the enemy's position very strong, and its strength was increased by the dense masses of cedar and large fragments of rock which everywhere offered shelter. The action was commenced by Captain Ceran St. Vrain, who, dismounting his men, ascended the mountain on the left doing much execution. Flanking parties were thrown out on either side, commanded respectively by Lieutenant White, 2d Regiment Missouri Mounted Volunteers, and by Lieutenants Mellvaine and Taylor, 1st Dragoons. These parties ascended the hill rapidly, and the enemy soon began to retire in the direction of Embudo, bounding along the steep and rugged sides of the mountains with a speed that defied pursuit. The firing at the pass of Embudo had been heard at La Joya [now called Velarde], and Captain William Y. Slack, with twenty-five mounted men had been immediately dispatched thither. He now arrived, and rendered excellent service by relieving Lieutenant White, whose men were much fatigued. Lieutenants Mellvaine and Taylor were also recalled; and Lieutenant Rufus Ingalls was directed to lead a flanking party on the right slope, while Captain Slack performed the same duty on the left. The enemy having by this time retreated beyond our reach, Captain John Burgwin marched through the defile and debouched into the open valley in which Embudo is situated, recalled the flanking parties, and entered that town without opposition, several persons meeting him with a white flag.

January 30   In Louisiana, the 2nd Mississippi Regiment departs from New Orleans aboard ship and it arrives at Lobos Island on 18 February. On the 24th, General Winfield Scott orders the regiment to St. Lago. The regiment, commanded by Colonel Charles Clark, receives new orders to move to Matamoros, where it arrives on 5 March. Once there the regiment is ordered to Camargo and from there it is ordered to Monterrey, where it arrived on 6 April. General Taylor then orders the regiment to march to Saltillo. The 2nd Mississippi Regiment arrives at Camp Taylor at Buena Vista on 30 May 1847.

February 1   In Mexico, Mexican General Parodi with the 12th Regiment and the battalion of the national guard of Jalico depart from San Luis. They advance toward Monterrey. In other activity, General Zachary Taylor and his staff departs from Monterrey en route to Saltillo. Braxton Bragg's battery and George Thomas's battery, the 1st Mississippi Rifles and Lieutenant Colonel May's squadron of dragoons accompany him. The batteries of Captain John Washington and Captain Lucien B. Webster are at Saltillo. After the troops depart from Monterrey, only about 500 troops (Indiana and Ohio volunteers under

Colonel William P. Rogers) remain; however, those troops man the citadel or Black Fort, and it is believed that they can hold the city. The Mexicans are aware that Monterrey cannot be taken without artillery. In addition, the 2nd Dragoons under Captain Ripley Allen Arnold are called up from the mouth of the Rio Grande to reinforce the city.

In other activity about this time, President Polk appoints Thomas Alger Rowley (later Union General) as second lieutenant in the regulars. He participates in the battles of Vera Cruz, Jalapa, Cerro Gordo and Mexico City.

February 2   In Mexico, Santa Anna begins moving north. He arrives at Agua Nueva, about 35 miles from General Zachary Taylor's headquarters on the 21st. Taylor, however, decides that his positions at Agua Nuesta are not defensible. He retires to the Buena Vista ranch. Taylor's force of about 4,800 is able to dig in and hold formidable positions.

February 3–5   THE SIEGE OF PUEBLA DE TAOS   In New Mexico, Colonel Sterling Price arrives at Taos and discovers that the rebels (Mexicans, Taos and Apache Indians) have entrenched themselves at the Pueblo. Price decides to bombard the enemy; however, the artillery does not inflict much damage because the walls of the pueblo are too strong. Price changes tactics. He surrounds Taos and attacks. The Americans engage the rebels for nearly four hours before penetrating the town. The rebels are driven to the mountains, but they are pursued by dragoons. The entire rebel force is compelled to surrender by February 5. Second Lieutenant Franz Hassendeubel, of Battery B, 1st Battalion, Missouri Light Artillery, enters the pueblo. He demands and receives the surrender of the garrison.

Colonel Price sustains 7 killed, including Captain John Burgwin. He also sustains about 45 wounded. The Mexicans, Taos and Apache Indians sustain about 51 killed during the pursuit that follows. The fighting at Pueblo de Taos ends the rebellion. Its two instigators, Pablo Montoya and Tomas Romero, who are captured during the struggle, are put in jail. Romero is murdered by a dragoon before his trial and Montoya is convicted of treason and hanged on 7 February at the Plaza de Don Fernando. Subsequent trials brought about 21 public hangings. The battle is the final one of the Taos Rebellion.

February 4   Colonel Louis de Russy and his Louisiana regiment arrive at Tampico in Mexico following a forced march. They had been recently shipwrecked opposite Lobos Island while aboard the transport *Ondiake* along the Mexican coast.

February 7   The arrival of General Winfield Scott is anticipated at Lobos Island in Mexico. Six companies of Louisiana and South Carolina troops arrived on 3 March, but about 7,000 more are due to arrive from Tampico.

February 8   **In Texas,** the forces (about 924 troops) of Colonel Alexander Doniphan depart from El Paso del Norte. They are escorting a merchant train of about 315 wagons to the city of Chihuahua. The contingent continues toward its destination, but on the 25th, Doniphan's spies inform him that about 1,500 Mexicans are at the town of Inseneas.

February 12   A giant snowstorm hits San Luis, Mexico.

February 13   **In Mexico,** General William Jenkins Worth at Saltillo continues as weather permits to forward troops, munitions and supplies to Lobos. Weather has been terrible and has greatly interfered with Worth's operation. In other activity, General Winfield Scott embarks on this day for Brazos. The 1st Pennsylvania volunteer Regiment arrives off Brazos on or about this day.

February 18   Charles Thomas Campbell (later Union general) is appointed second lieutenant in the 8th U.S. Infantry Regiment. Campbell served for the duration of the Mexican War. He is promoted to captain during August 1847. He is mustered out of the service in August 1848.

February 19   **In Mexico,** General Winfield Scott, aboard the USS *Massachusetts,* arrives at Tampico. On the following morning, he arrives at General Robert Patterson's headquarters. He discovers that about 9,000 men are waiting to embark for Vera Cruz. Four brigades — under General David Twiggs, Gideon Johnson Pillow, James Shields and John Quitman — are to embark on the 20th and the 21st.

In other activity, Santa Anna is on the fringes of the desert, about 35 miles from Agua Nueva. He has amassed about 15,000 troops.

February 20   **In Mexico,** General Taylor dispatches a small contingent of Texas spies commanded by Major Benjamin McCulloch (later Confederate general) to the hacienda of Encarnacion, about 30 miles distant. The contingent reports back that there is a commanding Mexican cavalry force there, but it cannot determine the size of the force. Also on the 20th, Lieutenant Colonel Charles A. May is dispatched to the hacienda of Hecliondo. Elsewhere, Mexican General Santa Anna begins his advance at about noon. He halts at the front of the hacienda of Buena Vista.

Also, William Polk Hardeman (later Confederate general) participates at this incident and afterward fights at Buena Vista. Henry Eustace McCullogh (later Confederate general), the brother of Benjamin, takes a post on the frontier that helps to contain the Indians. Samuel Davis Sturgis (later Union general), who graduated from West Point in 1846, is captured close to Buena Vista while he is on a reconnaissance mission. He is held for about eight days.

February 21   In Mexico, General Scott, aboard the USS *Mississippi*, arrives on Lobos Island, 7 miles outside of Tampico, to plan and initiate the siege on Vera Cruz. In other activity, General Taylor is informed that Santa Anna is advancing with his army and that it has cavalry as the vanguard. The Mexican cavalry is moving east to block the road running between Agua Nueva and Saltillo. On the same day, General Taylor orders some of his force to withdraw up the Saltillo Road, where they will hold more practical positions close to the hacienda Buena Vista. Afterward, General Taylor moves

back to Saltillo, while General John Ellis Wool remains to deploy his troops.

In other activity, William Nelson (later Union general and naval officer) serves in the fleet that carries General Scott's invasion of Vera Cruz. Joseph Gilbert Totten (later Union general) one of the first men to graduate from West Point (1806), serves as General Scott's chief engineer; he is brevetted as brigadier general on 29 March 1847. Zealous Bates Tower (later Union general) participates at Buena Vista; he serves on General Scott's staff and is brevetted captain and major for his gallantry.

February 22–23 BATTLE OF BUENA VISTA   In Mexico, General Taylor is informed that the Mexican army is in sight. Taylor's forces are in position and are holding strong positions. The road upon which the Mexican cavalry is advancing and the valley on the right is not practical for artillery and the left is inundated with a series of ridges and ravines that keep the cavalry from taking advantage of its superiority. Meanwhile, the Mexican artillery cannot be properly utilized. Consequently, the infantry is also greatly restricted.

Captain Washington's battery (4th Artillery) is deployed to hold the road. Colonel Hardin's 1st Regiment, Colonel William Henry Bissell's 2nd Illinois Regiment, the Texas volunteers under Captain Patrick E. Conner, and the 2nd Kentucky under Colonel Hugh McKee hold the ridges on the left and to the rear. Colonel Archibald Yell's Arkansas regiment and Colonel H. Marshall's Kentucky regiment of cavalry (1st Kentucky

Bragg's battery (Tomes, *Battles of America by Sea and Land*).

Cavalry) are deployed on the far left close to the foothills of the mountain. Other units are the Indiana Brigade (2nd and 3rd Regiments) commanded by Colonel William Bowles and Colonel James Henry Lane; the Mississippi Regiment commanded by Colonel Jefferson Davis; the 1st and 2nd Dragoons, commanded by Captain Enoch Steen (Steene) and Lieutenant Colonel Charles A. May; and the light batteries of Captains William T. Sherman and Braxton Bragg. The 3rd Artillery, commanded by Brigadier General Lane, was held in reserve. At about eleven A.M. General Santa Anna demanded that Taylor surrender. Taylor replied, "Tell Santa Anna to go to hell. Put it in Spanish and send it back by this Dutchman."

Meanwhile, the Mexican columns, which were recognizable to Taylor's lookouts, were spotted when they moved onto the field. The U.S. 2nd Kentucky Regiment, along with a detachment of artillery on the American right, were detached. Meanwhile, the Mexican light infantry had engaged on the far left parts of the Kentucky and Arkansas cavalry, dismounted, and a rifle battalion from the Indiana brigade under Major Gorman, the whole commanded by Colonel Marshall. The Mexicans maintained steady fire while they ascended the mountain in an attempt to turn the flank.

Several pieces of Captain John W. Washington's battery are detached to the left. They receive support from

Jeff Davis' infantry defeats the Mexican cavalry (Frost, *The History of Mexico and Its Wars*).

the 2nd Indiana Regiment. The Mexicans plant an occasional shell into this part of the line; however, no casualties are taken. The Mexican light troops continue to skirmish with the Americans until about dark. They inflict only slight casualties upon the Americans. The wounded are taken to Saltillo.

Once Taylor discerns that no strong attack would be launched before the following morning, he moves to Saltillo with the Mississippi regiment and the Second Dragoons. The troops bivouac without fires. Meanwhile, a large contingent of cavalry is visible throughout the day in the rear of the town. It is commanded by General Minion and is deployed to harass the American retreat. However, the Americans do not retreat. The city is occu-pied by four companies of Illinois volunteers, commanded by Major Warren (1st Regiment). In addition, the 1st Artillery's two 24-pounders deploy from where it can command the approaches. The train and head-quarters camp is protected by two companies of Mississippi riflemen, under Captain Rogers, and one field piece, commanded by Captain William H. Shover, 3rd Artillery.

Taylor, having taken the steps to protect his rear, moves back to Buena Vista on the morning of the 23rd. Meanwhile, during the night of the 22nd, the Mexican light troops ascend the mountainside in an attempt to turn the American flank. During the early morning hours of the 23rd, the action begins. American rifle-men — commanded by Colonel Humphrey Marshall, reinforced by three companies of the 2nd Illinois, commanded by Major H. T. Trail — are able to hold their ground against a much larger force of Mexicans. The American fire is devastating. General Lane directs the 2nd Indiana and his artillery to move forward. The artillery is pushed up to within musket range, but still, it is unable to hold back the infantry. Meanwhile, the infantry is ordered up to support the artillery, but it is pushed back in disorder. In addition, a Mexican battery on the left is able to fire a cross-fire of grape and canister.

Captain John Paul Jones O'Brien is unable to hold his position, without support. He is able only to withdraw his three artillery pieces while under attack by General Francisco and General Manuel M. Lombardi. The 2nd Indiana misinterprets the pullback to be a general retreat. The regiment in turn begins to take flight toward the Buena Vista Ranch. The horses and cannoneers of the third piece are either killed or disabled. The 2nd Indiana Regiment, under Colonel Bowles, is unable to rally. It does not participate in the remainder of the battle. However, a small group of troops under Colonel Bowles, including Captain Nathan Kimball (later Union general), disgusted with the 2nd Indiana, joins with the Mississippi regiment and serves well.

That portion of the line gives way while the Mexicans begin to appear in large numbers against the left line. The 2nd Indiana is unable to regroup. Meanwhile, to the left, Arkansas riflemen fight viciously to hold the high ground. They are supported by the artillery of Lieutenant George Thomas and Samuel French, but they too are forced back.

General John Wool shifts Bragg's battery, the 1st Illinois and the 2nd Kentucky to fill the hole. Combined fire inflicts

General John Ellis Wool (*Late Mexican War*).

huge losses and brings a halt to part of the attack. Just as this fighting was unfolding, the Jalisco Lancers and the Mexican 4th Cavalry, commanded by General Julian Juvera, swings through the field and heads for Buena Vista.

At about the same time, General Zachary Taylor returns to the area. The Mississippi Regiment, commanded by Jefferson Davis, had been ordered to the left and comes in contact with the Mexican infantry, which had turned the American left. The 2nd Kentucky under Colonel McKee and its supporting artillery under Captain Braxton Bragg had earlier been ordered from its position to bolster the left. That regiment and a contingent of the 1st Illinois under Colonel Hardin drives the Mexicans back and recovers part of the ground that was earlier lost. Colonel Hardin captures an enemy flag before he is killed. He also kills a Mexican with his pistol while lying on his back. As a last request before he dies, Colonel Hardin asks that the flag be sent to his wife.

The batteries of Captain Sherman and Captain Bragg are positioned on the plateau. They take out much of the infantry in the front and in the back as well. The Mexicans pounce upon the Mississippi Regiment, but the 3rd Indiana Regiment, commanded by Colonel Lane, is hurriedly rushed to its aid. At about the same time, Lieutenant Kilburn, with a piece of Bragg's artillery, is ordered to bolster the infantry that is engaged. The Mexicans' infantry and cavalry are repulsed repeatedly as they try to penetrate the line.

Taylor orders the regular cavalry and Captain Pike's Arkansas squadron, under Lieutenant Colonel Charles A. May, to check the Mexican cavalry, which is advancing in the rear, along the foothills of the mountain. The Kentucky cavalry and the Arkansas cavalry assist in this action.

Meanwhile, the left continues to be threatened by a superior force bolstered by a contingent of Bragg's artillery, along with more aid from Captain Sherman's battery. The artillery has a debilitating effect on the enemy along the base of the mountain. Meanwhile, the two regiments that oppose the Mexicans create some confusion in their ranks. The combination of artillery fire and the two regiments thrown against them prompts some of the attackers to retreat.

The squadron of the 1st Dragoons, commanded by Lieutenant Rucker, is ordered up a deep ravine to intercept and disperse Mexicans who are attempting to retreat. The dragoons are unable to accomplish the task due to a Mexican battery established to cover the retreat. Another huge column of the enemy is spotted on the far left. It appears as if the column is poised to drive down upon Buena Vista.

Lieutenant Colonel May is ordered to provide support to that point. He is to receive two pieces of artillery from Captain Sherman's battery, commanded by Lieutenant Reynolds. At about the same time, the commands of Major Trail and Major Gorman, which is organized by the chief of artillery, Major Munroe, are posted in Buena Vista to defend the baggage and the trains.

The Mexicans attack before Colonel May arrives at the hacienda, but they are met by the Kentucky and Arkansas cavalry commanded by Colonel Marshall and Colonel Yell. The Mexican column immediately divides, one portion sweeping by the depot, where it receives a destructive fire from the force which had collected there, and then gaining the mountain opposite, under a fire from Lieutenant Reynolds' section, the remaining portion regaining the base of the mountain on the Americans' left.

In the meantime, Lt. Colonel May and his squadron of the 1st Dragoons and contingents of the Arkansas and Indiana troops, commanded by Lieutenant Colonel Roane and Major Gorman, check the Mexican cavalry at the base of the mountain. Colonel Archibald Yell of the Arkansas cavalry is killed while leading his regiment. His horse becomes uncontrollable and its bridle breaks. After going into the lines of the Mexicans, he is lanced in the head and dies. The Mexicans are jammed into the ravines and slim gorges, but the American artillery is riveting the area with frightful results.

Santa Anna sends a message to Taylor asking what he wants. Taylor dispatches General Wool to the Mexican lines. Taylor orders a cease fire. Meanwhile, General Wool is unable to hook up with Santa Anna. He is also unable to get the Mexicans to cease their fire. In the meantime, on the far right of the line, the Mexicans continue their retreat. Despite the American effort, they are able to join with the rest of their army, which is also at the base of the mountain. Earlier in the day, the cavalry under General Minion had ascended the

Death of Colonel Yell (Frost, *The History of Mexico and Its Wars*).

elevated plain above Saltillo. It occupies the road that runs from the city to the field of battle.

When they close against the town, Captain Webster commences fire with his artillery. Afterward, while Webster is pulling back from his redoubt returning to Buena Vista, Captain Shover moves up with his artillery piece. Shover is supported by mounted volunteers. The piece opens fire with good effect. The Mexicans are driven into the ravines that connect to the lower valley, followed closely behind by Shover's troops. The Mexicans charge the artillery once or twice; however, they are repelled in grand fashion. The Mexicans are compelled to retreat in confusion. They make no future appearance on the plain. It appears as if the Mexicans had partially ceased fire on the main field of battle and were focusing their efforts on protecting their artillery.

In the meantime, General Taylor is called away from the field, but he is gone only a short time when he hears lots of musket fire. Upon his return, Taylor discovers the 1st Illinois and the 2nd Kentucky are engaging a superior force that is overrunning the Americans. Captain O'Brien has two pieces of artillery holding off the attackers until he runs out of ammunition. Lacking infantry support, because they are routed, O'Brien is compelled to abandon his guns.

Taylor acts quickly. He sends Braxton Bragg's battery in as support and its fire, using double canister, is effective. At about the same time, Jefferson Davis' troops and dragoons arrive to give more support. Washington's guns also arrive and they drive off the Mexicans and rescue the 1st Illinois from the ravine in which they had sought shelter.

Captain Bragg, who arrived from the left, is ordered to commence firing. Bragg has no infantry to support his battery, which is endangered. Bragg begins to fire when the enemy is only several yards from his guns. Suddenly, the first cannonade compels the Mexicans to pause. The second and third blasts are sufficient to compel the Mexicans to retreat haphazardly. Bragg's actions save the day.

Meanwhile, the 2nd Kentucky Regiment advances too far to support Bragg. It is attacked by the enemy and driven back. The Mexicans press the attack and drive the American regiment into a ravine, which leads to Captain Washington's artillery battery. The Mexicans continue into the ravine and are hit by the artillery fire. The fire causes them to withdraw.

In the meantime, the remainder of the American artillery had been repositioned on the plateau. It is supported by the Mississippi and 3rd Indiana Regiments. The troops of the Mississippi Regiment reach the ground and pour fire upon the enemy. Afterward, the Mexicans make no moves to attack the American lines. With night approaching, the Americans are able to tend to their wounded. They also have time for the troops to take some rest.

The troops sleep through the night without fires. During the pause in the fighting, the Americans make preparations to receive the Mexicans if they renew their attack. They take their

Colonel Henry Clay (Frost, *The History of Mexico and Its Wars*).

wounded to Saltillo. In addition, seven fresh companies are brought up to reinforce the troops. Close by is Colonel Marshall with Kentucky cavalry and four heavy guns, commanded by Captain Prentiss, First Artillery.

During the night, scouts discover that the Mexicans had abandoned the field. Scouts also determine that they had moved back to Agua Nueva. However, the Americans are too exhausted to follow them.

The next morning an officer is sent to General Santa Anna to negotiate an exchange of prisoners, and on the following day, it is completed. The Americans collect their dead and see to their burial. The Mexicans had left many wounded on the field. They are

delivered to Saltillo where medical aid is given to them.

The Kentucky 2nd Rifles, the 2nd and 3rd Indiana and the 3rd Ohio Volunteer Regiments participate at this battle. American casualties are 264 dead, 450 wounded and 26 missing. Mexican casualties are 2,000 killed or wounded. Those killed include Colonel Hardin, 1st Illinois; Colonel Hugh W. McKee and Lieutenant Colonel Henry Clay, Jr., 2nd Kentucky Regiment; and Colonel Archibald Yell. Taylor is hit by two Mexican bullets but is unhurt and remains on his horse, "Old Whitey," all day. Colonel Jefferson Davis is seriously wounded during the fighting. He is removed from the field by Captain Robert Hall Chilton (later Confederate general). During the Battle of Buena Vista, Colonel Jefferson Davis' troops open fire, devastating the Mexican charge. General Taylor remarks, "Well done Jeff! Hurrah for Mississippi."

Among prisoners seized are two deserters who had been under the command of General Taylor. They are taken before him, and he says: "Such rascals ... might do for Santa Anna — they would not suit him and it would be wasting powder and shot to shoot them." Both men were drummed out of the army to the music of "Rogue's March."

Lieutenant James Fleming Fagan (later Confederate general) serves in Colonel Yell's command. Also, 2nd Lieutenant Samuel Gibbs French, 3rd Artillery (later Confederate general) is wounded at this battle. Elkanah Brackin Greer (later Confederate general) had joined the 1st Mississippi

1847

Rifles as a private during 1845. He participates in the battles of Monterey and Buena Vista. First Lieutenant Richard Griffith (later Confederate general) of Philadelphia, Pennsylvania, had enlisted in the 1st Mississippi Rifles. He serves in the regiment for the duration. Humphrey Marshall (later Confederate general) takes part in this clash. Carnot Posey (later Confederate general) is slightly wounded at this battle. John Selden Roane (later Confederate general) serves as lieutenant colonel of Colonel Yell's Arkansas regiment. Upon the death of Colonel Yell, Roane assumes command. Also, Captain Albert Pike (later Confederate general) takes part in this battle. Later, Roane and Pike engage in a duel regarding the regiment's actions at Buena Vista. Neither man is injured at the duel.

Samuel Beatty (later Union general) participates at this battle as first lieutenant with the 3rd Ohio Regiment. Also, Henry Washington Benham (later Union general) is wounded in this action. Captain James Henry Carleton (later Union general), who serves on General Wool's staff, also takes part. He is brevetted as major for his gallantry. Second Lieutenant Jefferson Columbus Davis (later Union general) participates as a member of the 3rd Indiana Regiment. In 1848, on 17 June, he is commissioned into the regular army as a first lieutenant, 1st Artillery Regiment.

Captain Amos Beebe Eaton (later Union general) serves at this battle as General Taylor's chief commissary. He is brevetted major for his gallantry at Buena Vista. Lieutenant William Buel Franklin (later Union general)

is brevetted for gallantry in this clash. Speed Smith Fry (later Union general) had raised a company of the 2nd Kentucky Infantry, which he commands. Willis Arnold Gorman (later Union general) serves as major of the 3rd Indiana and takes part in this battle. Subsequent to the expiration of his regiment's service, Gorman recruits the 4th Indiana. Second Lieutenant Gordon Granger (later Union general) participates at this battle. He also participates in the campaign to seize Mexico City. Also, Colonel John J. Hardin, a cousin of Mary Todd Lincoln, is killed at this battle. His grandson, Martin Davis Hardin, graduates West Point 1859 and becomes a Union general during the Civil War.

Lieutenant Henry Hobson (later Union general) takes part in this clash and is promoted to first lieutenant for his gallantry. Captain Nathan Kimball (later Union general) serves as a member of the 2nd Indiana Volunteers. Captain James Dada Morgan (later Union general) participates at this battle as a member of the 1st Illinois Regiment. Benjamin Mayberry Prentiss (later Union general) takes part. He had raised and commanded a company of the 1st Illinois Regiment. The next year, he musters out and returns to Illinois, where he takes up the study of law.

John Fulton Reynolds (later Union general) who graduated from West Point in 1841, participates with General Zachary Taylor for the duration of the war. He participates at Monterey and at this battle. James Brewerton Ricketts (later Union general) participates at this battle and at Monterey. Captain Lowell Harrison Rousseau (later Union general) is another participant. Captain Henry Rucker (later Union general) is brevetted major for his gallantry in this conflict.

Lieutenant Thomas West Sherman (later Union general), 2nd Regiment, is brevetted major for his gallantry at Buena Vista. Alfred Sully (later Union general), participates. In 1848, the 2nd Regiment is sent to California. Captain John Blair Smith Todd (later Union general) participates at this battle. Thomas Welsh (later Union general) serves with the 2nd Kentucky Regiment. He is wounded at Buena Vista. After he recuperates, he transfers to General Scott's command, where he serves as second lieutenant of the 11th Infantry Regiment. Lieutenant John Wood (later Union general) is brevetted for his gallantry at this clash. Initially, he served in the corps of topographical engineers, but in 1846, he transferred to the cavalry. William Henry Lamb Wallace (later Union general) volunteers to serve in the 1st Illinois Regiment; he participates at this and other battles.

February 23 William Booth Taliaferro is commissioned as captain in the U.S. Army. He is assigned to the 9th U.S. Infantry Regiment. He is mustered out of the service at the end of the Mexican War as a major.

February 24 In Texas, the 2nd Mississippi Infantry arrives at the mouth of the Rio Grande. Thomas Carmichael Hindman (later Confederate general) also arrives. He serves as a second lieutenant with the regiment. Thomas' older brother, Robert, serves as a private. The regiment later arrives

at Buena Vista, where it is assigned guard duty. The next month, Hindman is appointed as acting adjutant; however, he does not participate in any major combat during his time in service. Also, Mark Perrin Lowrey (later Confederate general) serves with the 2nd Mississippi volunteers as a private, but he does not see any action.

February 25 In Mexico, near Buena Vista, Colonel William Selby Harney (later Union general) moves out with a squadron of the 2nd Dragoons (Thornton's) which is commanded by Major Edwin V. Sumner. The force is bolstered by 50 dragoons under Captain Ker. They are en route to the Medelin River, where it has been reported that a large force of Mexican cavalry has gathered. The contingent arrives at the Morena River with two artillery pieces and about 2,000 men. Once the dragoons of Captain Ker approach the bridge, they are met with heavy fire that kills one corporal and wounds two others.

Colonel William Selby Harney, after determining that the bridge is heavily defended, orders his troops to withdraw. He also sends an urgent request for two artillery pieces. In the meantime, Captain William J. Hardee, who is back at the beach unloading horses, is informed of the fighting at the bridge. He collects men on the beach and while moving through the camp, he gathers some additional troops, numbering about 40. He leads the troops on foot to the bridge to support the Americans.

Colonel William T. Haskell, 2nd Tennessee Regiment, and Captain

Colonel Harney's dragoons (Frost, *The History of Mexico and Its Wars*).

Benjamin F. Cheatham, 1st Tennessee, also form to fight with the dragoons. Shortly afterward, Lieutenant Judd and Lieutenant H. Brown, 3rd Artillery, arrive with the two artillery pieces that had been requested. The entire reinforcing team speeds toward the bridge.

Captain Ker deploys the Tennesseans to the left of the bridge. He directs Captain Hardee and Lieutenant Hill to bolster the guns, but orders them to be prepared to charge the bridge. Major Edwin V. Sumner, who remains with the wounded, is held in reserve. In the meantime, Lieutenant Judd, with the artillery, slowly approaches the bridge. After he arrives at a distance of about fifty yards, the Mexicans open fire. Americans to the left and right of the bridge commence their fire to draw

attention from Judd's artillery, which delivers six or eight potent rounds into the enemy positions and prompts the Mexicans to seek better cover.

While the Mexicans are in retreat from the artillery rounds, Cheatham, Hardee and Haskell charge the bridge, causing the Mexicans to withdraw and reform farther back. Colonel William Selby Harney orders the obstacles to be cleared, while Major Summer's force gallops across the bridge. The Mexicans, upon seeing the horses on the charge, retreat into the chaparral, but Mexican cavalry intercepts the American cavalry.

The American cavalry overwhelms the Mexicans. One detachment of about thirty lancers are pursued by Lieutenant Lowry, Lieutenant Oakes and several others. The Mexicans in the party are either dismounted or sabered. Pursuit continues until they reach Medelin, about six miles distant. Once they arrive another party of Mexican lancers is spotted as it retreats. Lieutenant Lewis Neill, 2nd Dragoons, and three others give chase. Other dragoons are sent, but before they can catch Lieutenant Neill, he is found fighting two of the lancers and they are able to lance him twice, in the arm and chest. Lieutenant Neill falls from his horse. Nevertheless, the pursuit continues until dark.

On the following morning, Major General Robert Patterson arrives at the bridge, accompanied by Colonel Campbell's regiment. Colonel Selby Harney's command loses two killed and nine wounded, but the number of casualties of Lieutenant Judd's detachment remains unknown. The Mexican casualties are unknown, however, it was more than fifty men killed or wounded.

February 26   In Mexico, General Zachary Taylor issues Order No. 2, Headquarters, Army of Occupation, Buena Vista, 26 February 1847.

1. The commanding general has the grateful task of congratulating the troops upon the brilliant success which attended their arms in the conflicts of the 22d and 23d. Confident in the immense superiority of numbers, and stimulated by their presence of a distinguished leader, the Mexican troops were yet repulsed in every effort to force our lines, and finally withdrew with immense loss from the field.

2. The general would express his obligations to the officers and men engaged for the cordial support which they rendered throughout the action. It will be his highest pride to bring to the notice of the government the conspicuous gallantry of particular officers and corps, whose unwavering steadiness more than once saved the fortunes of the day. He would also express his high satisfaction with the conduct of the small command left to hold Saltillo. Though not so seriously engaged as their comrades, their services were very important and efficiently rendered. While bestowing this just tribute to the good conduct of the troops, the general deeply regrets to say that there were not a few exceptions. He trusts that those who fled ingloriously to Buena Vista, and even to Saltillo, will seek an opportunity to retrieve their reputation and to emulate the bravery of their comrades, who bore the brunt of the battle, and sustained against fearful odds the honor of the flag.

The exultation of success is checked by the heavy sacrifice of life which it has cost, embracing many officers of high rank and rare merit. While the sympathies of a grateful country will be given to the bereaved families and friends of those who nobly fell their illustrious example will remain for the benefit and admiration of the army.

By order of Major General Taylor; W.W.S. BLISS, ASS'T ADJ'T GEN.

February 26 to March 27   In Mexico, five National Guard regiments, led by General Matías Pena y Barragan, revolt. The leaders of the revolution issue a thirteen article plan that declares the anti-clerical January law null and void. It also calls for the resignation of Santa Anna and Gomez

Farias. The five units are filled with the sons of doctors, lawyers and merchants. Gomez offers them amnesty, but it is declined. The five units continue fighting in Mexico City until Santa Anna returns from Buena Vista. He is able to bring about a peace settlement with the leaders of the revolution. The Mexican Congress eliminates the position of vice president, which essentially removes Gomez Farias from his office. Santa Anna also agrees to repeal the law of January 11 in exchange for a donation of 1.5 million pesos from the church to fund the war.

February 27   In California, Colonel Alexander Doniphan is informed by his spies that the Mexicans had established strong resistance at the pass of the Sacramento River, about 15 miles distant. The pass of the river is formed by a point of the mountains on the right and a deep and dry sandy channel of a creek on the left. Between these two points, the plain rises to a height of about 60 feet. They also tell him that no water is available from the point where they stand and the river. The Mexicans deploy a battery of four guns on the right side of the mountain. To the left, the Mexicans deploy another battery. In addition, they have three entrenchments that each contain two 6-pounders, and on the crest, they have 27 redoubts that permit them to deploy their infantry. The Mexicans then place their cavalry to the front of the redoubts and in them in an effort to mask them. Due to intelligence he receives, Doniphan calls a halt to his advance until the following morning.

In other activity, an express reaches headquarters from Colonel George W. Morgan, 2nd Ohio Regiment, who reports that his train had come under attack on the 21st near Marin. Three companies of the 1st Ohio Regiment are immediately dispatched to relieve the party. A woman, Miss Burns, who is with the train, reports that she was in the third wagon and remained there until she saw her father, who was shot. She left the wagon to help her father, but upon checking on him, she determined that he was dead. She tried to escape, but after running for several hundred yards she was captured. Mexicans took her to a ranchero where the women there took care of her. Later, she was released and went to Monterrey.

William Haines Lytle (later Union general) participates in the war as 2nd lieutenant of the 2nd Ohio Regiment, but he musters out as a captain on 25 July 1848. George Francis McGinnis (later Union general) serves in the war as 2nd lieutenant of the 2nd Ohio Regiment; he also musters out on 25 July 1848. Robert Byington Mitchell (later Union general) serves in the war as a lieutenant in the 2nd Ohio Regiment.

February 28 BATTLE OF RIO SACRAMENTO   The Americans under Colonel Alexander Doniphan are awakened at the break of dawn. The entire train, composed of about 315 wagons, is separated into four columns. Doniphan also intermixes his force by placing it and the artillery between the wagons. After arriving at a point several miles from the Mexicans, Doniphan initiates a reconnaissance of his position and shortly thereafter, his train advances. Doniphan decides that with Mexican guns on his right that he will advance his wagons and his cavalry in quick fashion.

The cavalry charges up the elevation, bringing four pieces of artillery behind. The Mexicans spot the cavalry and move to intercept it. One thousand troops bringing four pieces of artillery with them speed to cut off the Americans; however, the Americans make the ascent and re-form before the enemy arrives. The Mexicans halt, while the Americans advance the head of their column to within 1,200 yards of their position. Meanwhile, the wagons gain the elevation and form into a defensive position.

At that point, the Americans commence fire from their battery while the Mexicans do the same. One of the Mexican guns is knocked out of commission and about 15 gunners are killed. While the Mexicans begin to retreat to positions in the rear of their works, the Americans resume their march. They remain to the right to avoid the Mexican battery that is on the left (Mexican right) as well as their most formidable redoubts, which are positioned on the left, near where the road passes. The Americans advance but halt before coming under the range of the Mexican battery on the right.

Captain Weightman (artillery) receives orders to charge with two 12-pound howitzers. He is to be supported by cavalry under Captains Reid, Hudson and Parsons. The howitzers charge forward and get the support of Reed, but the order to the

remaining two companies does not arrive. At that time, Captain Parsons requests permission from Colonel Doniphan to attack the redoubt to the left of Weightman. Permission is granted and Parsons charges the positions. The remainder of the two battalions, 1st Regiment, are dismounted, but they follow closely behind the cavalry. They direct their fire upon the Mexicans, which compels them to pull back. Major Clarke, commanding the remainder of the battery, also advances. They encounter a contingent of cavalry that tries to pass them on the left to get to the wagons and the rear. However, they are repelled and compelled to fall back.

The American riflemen, supported by the cavalry and the howitzers, clear the remainder of the obstacles. Afterward, the Americans rush to the redoubts and with their bayonets and sabers, they complete their task. Nevertheless, the battery on the right remains active. It had poured fire upon the Americans since the attack had begun. And now, it is holding about 500 troops.

Major Clarke is ordered to commence firing upon the battery. In the meantime, Lieutenant Colonel Mitchell and Lieutenant Colonel Jackson, in command of the 1st Battalion, are ordered to remount their horses and charge the battery on the left. Major Gilpin is ordered to pass through the 2nd Battalion on foot, then to ascend the mountain on its opposite side. In the meantime, the American battery knocks the Mexican battery out of commission. The Americans in the meantime rush up the mountain. The column pushes forward and the Mexicans take flight over the mountain.

Colonel Doniphan with his victory at Sacramento names several officers for their service. He praises Captain Thompson (1st Dragoons), who acts as his aide. Lieutenant Wooster, U.S. Army, and Major Campbell of Springfield, Missouri, are also included in his praise.

The Mexican army at the battle of Sacramento includes 1,200 cavalry from Durango, the Vera Cruz dragoons, 1,200 infantry from Chihuahua, about 300 artillerists and 1,420 rancheros. These forces were commanded by Major General Heredia, Brigadier General Garcia Conde, General Uguerte and Brigadier General Trias (governor). American participants number 924, excluding about 100 who were detailed with holding the horses and the driving teams.

The Americans soundly defeat the Mexicans at Rio Sacramento, causing them to lose all artillery, wagons and supplies. Americans suffer 1 killed and 1 mortally wounded and a few wounded; the Mexicans sustain more than 300 killed and about 300 wounded, along with 40 prisoners.

March 1 Lt. Col. D. Mitchell marches into Chihuahua, Mexico, with an advance guard of 150 men. The remainder under Colonel Doniphan follows.

March 2 In Mexico, victorious American troops capture the city of Chihuahua. General Kearny had ordered them to report to General John E. Wool; however, Doniphan believes that General Wool is presently at Saltillo and surrounded by the Mexicans. Doniphan proposes that he will force

his way to Saltillo. Marsena Rudolph Patrick (later Union general), General Wool's commissary, participates in the battle. He is brevetted major during this campaign.

March 3 George Washington Morgan, colonel of the 2nd Ohio, is commissioned colonel of the 15th U.S. Infantry Regiment. He had been serving under General Zachary Taylor, but by now he is under General Winfield Scott. Colonel George Morgan later participates at Contreras and Churubusco, where he is wounded twice and is brevetted brigadier general.

March 4 Orders come from the War Department, adjutant general's office, in Washington, D.C. on March 4, 1847:

1. The regiment authorized to be raised under the "approved February 11th, 1847" will be recruited, armed and equipped for active duty in the field without delay; and the several officers appointed in each will report for orders and recruiting instructions to their respective colonels, who will establish their recruiting headquarters at some central position and report to the adjutant general. Colonels are charged with superintending the recruiting of their respective regiments; and will assign the lieutenant colonel and majors to such sub-recruiting districts as may be found expedient. When two or more companies and raised and sent to any depots, or ordered to the seat of war, a field officer should be assigned to the command.

2. The established recruiting regulations will be strictly observed by all officers, and the required returns, muster, and descriptive rolls, re-

ports, &c. will be regularly made and transmitted through the proper officer to the adjutant general and other chiefs of staff, in strict conformity with the rules of service and the blanks with which they have been furnished. The attention of recruiting officers is specially directed to the prompt rendition of the recruiting accounts, and the abstract of contingent expenses, required for the second auditor, and the colonel as superintendent, which must be forwarded within three days after the expiration of each month or semi-monthly when called for. See paragraphs 50, 51, and &c. revised recruiting regulations, 1847.

3. As soon as eighty men shall be enlisted by a captain and two subalterns, they will be inspected, mustered, armed, and equipped as a company, and be considered ready to take the field. The final assignment of the subalterns, and the permanent designation of companies by the letters of the alphabet, will be made by the colonel at the proper time. See paragraph 43 "General Regulations for the Army."

4. The attention of recruiting officers and commanders of posts is directed to paragraph 73 of General regulations. Recruits must be drilled in the school of the soldier, as far as practical, from the moment of enlistment, even when there may be no arms at the rendezvous, until sent to join their companies or regiments.

5. The officers of the new regiment (infantry and dragoons) will furnish themselves with the prescribed infantry tactics (See Scott's system). Cavalry tactics will not be furnished until the regiment is sup-

plied with horses, until which time the dragoon officers and men will be well drilled as foot soldiers.

6. The officers appointed, and the ten companies to be recruited in the States of Maine, 4; New Hampshire, 2; Vermont, 1; Rhode Island; 1; and Connecticut, 2; will constitute the "ninth regiment of infantry" to be commanded by Colonel —; headquarters established for the present at Boston. Fort Constitution and Fort Adams, RI will be used as recruiting depots for the regiment and the concentration of companies, preparatory to their immediate embarkation for the rest of the war.

7. The officers appointed, and the ten companies of infantry to be recruited in New York, 7; and New Jersey, 3; will constitute "the tenth regiment of infantry," under Colonel Robert E. Temple; headquarters at New York. Fort Hamilton and Lafayette will be the receiving depots for this regiment.

8. The officers appointed, and the ten companies of infantry to be recruited in Pennsylvania, 6; Delaware, 1; and Virginia, 3; will constitute "the eleventh regiment of infantry" Under Col. Albert C. Ramsey; headquarters at Baltimore. The companies to be raised in the interior of Pennsylvania for the regiment will proceed to Point Isabel, under their respective captains, via the Ohio River, and embark at Pittsburgh or Wheeling, as may be most convenient; and those recruited in Philadelphia and Delaware will rendezvous at Fort Mill, preparatory to immediate embarkation for the same point; the companies raised in eastern Virginia will be sent to New Orleans, and then to Point Isabel, with

the least practicable delay, where the regiment will be concentrated.

9. The officers appointed, and the ten companies of infantry to be recruited in North Carolina, 2; S. Carolina, 2; Texas, 2; Arkansas, 2; and Missouri, 2; will constitute the "twelfth regiment of infantry" under Colonel Louis D. Wilson; headquarters at New Orleans. The companies will be raised in North and South Carolina will rendezvous at Fort Moultrie, SC, preparatory to their immediate departure for Point Isabel; and the companies to be recruited in Texas, Arkansas, and Missouri will proceed, as soon as organized, under their respective captains, via New Orleans, to Point Isabel.

10. The officers appointed, and the ten companies of infantry to be raised in Virginia, 1; Georgia, 4; Alabama, 4; and Florida, 1; will constitute the "thirteenth regiment of infantry" under Colonel Robert M. Echols; headquarters at New Orleans.

11. The officers appointed and the ten companies of infantry to be raised in Louisiana, 5; Tennessee, 4; and Illinois, 1; will constitute the "fourteenth regiment of infantry" under Colonel Wm. Trousdale; headquarters at New Orleans.

12. The officers appointed, and the ten companies of infantry to be raised in Ohio, 5; Michigan, 3; Iowa, 1; and Wisconsin, 1; Mexican-American War and the Media will constitute the "fifteenth regiment of infantry" under Colonel George W. Morgan; headquarters at Cincinnati.

13. The officers appointed, and the ten companies of infantry to be raised in Kentucky, 4; Indiana, 4; and Illinois, 2; will constitute the "sixteenth regiment of infantry"

under Colonel J.W. Tibbatis; headquarters at Newport, KY.

14. As soon as any company to be recruited for the 13th, 14th, 15th, or 16th regiments shall be raised and organized; it will proceed without further delay to Point Isabel, under the captain, by the most expedient route, unless otherwise ordered, where these regiments will be concentrated.

15. The officers appointed and the ten companies of infantry raised in Pennsylvania, 2; Maryland, 3; Virginia, 2; Miss., 1; Georgia, 1; and Kentucky 1; will constitute the "regiment of volunteers" under Colonel T.P. Andrews; headquarters for the present at Washington, D.C. The companies recruited in Pennsylvania, Maryland, and Virginia will be concentrated at Fort Monroe, preparatory to their immediate embarkation for the seat of war; and those to be raised in Mississippi, Georgia, and Kentucky will proceed direct to Mexico, under their respective captains, as soon as organized.

16. "The third regiment of dragoons" is to be raised in the following states: Michigan, New York, Pennsylvania, Maryland, North Carolina, South Carolina, Alabama, Louisiana, Kentucky, and Indiana— in each company, Colonel Edward G. W. Butler; headquarters at New Orleans. As soon as raised and organized, the companies will proceed direct, under their respective captains, without loss of time to Point Isabel.

17. The foregoing arrangement of regiments and assignment of companies are made for the present with a view to expedite the recruiting service — subject hereafter to

such revisions and modifications as the good of the service may require.

18. The president expects that the new regiments will be raised and brought into the field in the shortest practicable time. The public interest require that the recruiting service be pushed with the greatest vigor by every officer employed in it; and, at the same time, the strictest economy is enjoined in all expenditures and arrangements, &c. Efforts must not be limited to one rendezvous or neighborhood, but auxiliary stations, within a convenient range, should be temporarily established by the same officer, according to the facilities of intercourse and the chances of success, &c.

BY order, R. Jones, Adjt. General

March 7 *In naval activity,* General Scott, in the steamer *Secretary* with Commodore David Conner, recon-

noiters the city of Vera Cruz looking for the best place to land his troops. They select a spot west of the island Sacrificios. Vera Cruz is protected by three forts, Fort Santiago, Fort Concepcion and the strongest, Fort San Juan de Ulua, which possesses 128 guns. Scott decides to avoid the guns of the city by landing southeast of the city at Collado Beach.

On March 9, after the troops had been transferred to the ships of war, the fleet, with General Scott aboard the USS *Massachusetts,* sets sail for the objective. The ships that are to attack Vera Cruz are the USS *Ohio,* Captain Stringham, 74 guns; USS *Potomac,* Captain Aulic, 44 guns; USS *Raritan,* Captain Forrest, 44 guns; *John Adams,* Captain McCluney, 20 guns; *St. Mary's,* Captain Saunders, 20 guns; *Albany,* Captain Breese, 20 guns; *Decatur,* Commander Pinckney, 16 guns;

Bombardment of Vera Cruz (*The Military Services of Lt. General Winfield Scott*).

Porpoise, 10 guns; *Perry,* 10 guns; *Bonita,* 1 gun; *Reefer,* 1 gun; *Petre,* Lieutenant Shaw, 1 gun; *Tampico,* Midshipman Perry, 1 gun; *Nonata,* Midshipman Smith, 1 gun; *Mississippi,* Commander Perry, 1 gun; *Princeton,* Captain Engle, 9 guns; *Spitfire,* Captain Tattnall, 3 guns; *Vixen,* Captain Sands, 3 guns; *McLean,* Captain Howard, 3 guns; *Union,* Captain Rudd, 4 guns; *Alleghany,* Captain Hunter, 10 guns; *Hunter,* Lieutenant McLaughlin, 6 guns; *Petrila,* 6 guns; *Scorpion,* Commodore Bigelow, 1 gun; *Scourge,* Lieutenant Hunter, 1 gun; *Relief,* 6 guns; *Supply,* 2 guns; *Fredonia,* 2 guns; the bomb ketches *Stromboli,* Commander Walker, 1 gun; *Aetna,* Commander Van Brunt, 1 gun; *Vesuvius,* 2 guns; *Hecla,* 1 gun; *Electra,* 1 gun; sloop *Marmer,* 1 gun; and the cutter *Forward,* Capt *Nones,* 6 guns. The total number of guns is 333.

In other activity, Gustavus Adolphus de Russy is commissioned as first lieutenant, 4th Artillery Regiment, on this day. During the war with Mexico he participates at Contreras and at Churubusco, where he is brevetted as first lieutenant for his gallantry. Soon he is brevetted as captain for his gallantry at Chapultepec. On August 17, 1847, he attains full rank of captain.

March 9   In Mexico, General Scott's forces hit the beach three miles southeast of Vera Cruz near Sacrificios under cover of U.S. naval gunfire. The landing is covered by two steamers and five gunboats. Five thousand five hundred troops head for shore in 67 surf-boats from Commodore Conner's squadron once the signal gun is fired.

The boats, rowed by seamen, rush to the beach, with every man anxious to be the first to hit it. Conner's lighter vessels flank the boats in an effort to protect the boats from a crossfire from the beach. However, opposition is not raised. The entire operation is executed without any mistakes. Outside of the city, there are hills of loose sand that are irregular, ranging from twenty to about 250 feet in height, and the terrain is also inundated with chaparral. Unfortunately, the carts and 115 draught horses have not arrived from Tampico, nor have the 300 pack mules, which are needed to carry the supplies and ordnance. General William Jenkins Worth's brigade of regulars leads the descent. He is followed by U.S. volunteers under Major General Robert Patterson and Brigadier General David Twiggs' reserve. The troops trek through the sand hills with Old Glory in the lead.

From their positions, the city of Vera Cruz and the castle of San Juan de Ulua and its 128 guns are in full view. The docks are consumed with the ships of foreign nations and their decks are permeated with the crews, who are peering at the astonishing sight. The first division of troops had landed a little before dawn, with the second and third following closely behind. By 10 A.M. the entire army composed of about 10,000 troops had landed and without the loss of a single life. This is the first amphibious landing for the United States Army. The Mexican army offers no direct opposition to the landing, however, the guns of the castle are able to bombard the landing force with constant firing of round shot and thirteen-inch shells.

Scott's information from his topographical engineers exposes the dangers of the landing and they did a masterful job. Everything they had examined was correctly done. Scott's invasion of Vera Cruz is impeccable in its execution. No lives are lost and no accidents occur. Nevertheless, there are some Mexican forces that advance against the Americans, but they only impede the operation slightly. By the 12th, the entire army is able to land and occupy its positions. However, most of the wagons, horses and the mules had not yet arrived.

U.S. Marines, attached to the Army's 1st Division, participate in the struggle for Vera Cruz. Also, during the siege, the U.S. is hit with a yellow fever epidemic. During the fighting, Lieutenant Colonel James Polk Dickerson (Palmetto Regiment) is wounded in the chest on the 10th. Captain Alburtis, 2nd Infantry, has his head shot off by a 52 pound cannon ball on the 11th. Bushrod Rust Johnson (later Confederate general) participates at this battle. Second Lieutenant George Earl Maney (later Confederate general), 1st Tennessee Regiment, had enlisted for three months. When his enlistment expired, he joined the U.S. Army as first lieutenant, 3rd U.S. Dragoons. He participates with General Scott during his advance on Mexico City. Captain Henry Hopkins Sibley (later

Confederate general) who was engaged in recruiting duty during the initial part of the war, takes part in this battle. Subsequently, he participates at all major battles, and on 16 February 1747, he is brevetted captain and again after Vera Cruz, he is brevetted as major.

Joseph K. Barnes (later Union general), who first joined with the occupation army and crossed the Rio Grande under General Taylor, participates at this battle. He continues with General Scott until the capture of Mexico City. John Haskell King (later Union general) participates at this battle. Captain James Nagle (later Union general), who formed the Washington Artillery, takes part in this clash as a captain of the 1st Pennsyl-

General Robert Patterson (Frost, *The History of Mexico and Its Wars*).

vania Regiment. James Scott Negley (later Union general) also accompanies the regiment. He serves as a private in the regiment. Also, Captain Thomas Algeo Rowley (later Union General) serves (1847–1848) with a company (Jackson Blues) as a member of the Pennsylvania volunteers.

March 11 The Mexican schooner *Jose Eliza* has the misfortune of encountering the USS *Portsmouth* in waters near Mazatlan and is quickly captured.

March 13 On or about this day, the bomb ketches USS *Etna* commanded by Captains G. J. Van Brunt and the USS *Stromboli* commanded by Captain W. S. Walker are scheduled to depart Boston en route to the Gulf of Mexico in several days. In other activity, the Mexicans at the castle and within the city continue to fire at the Americans invading Vera Cruz; however, the guns are not very effective. In related activity, a storm which has interrupted the operation of the Americans ceases on this day. This permits the Americans to unload heavy armaments. The Americans are still waiting for the arrival of the pack mules.

March 15 American forces take possession of Chihuahua after defeating the Mexicans that defended it.

March 17–24 THE BATTLE OF VERA CRUZ At Vera Cruz, Mexico, American troops carry their provisions and military supplies on their backs through chaparral under the horrid rays of the tropical sun. The lines of siege extend about five miles.

Meanwhile, a strong storm overtakes the area, making it impossible to land any heavy equipment. The storm subsides on the 17th and the Americans debark 10 mortars and four 24-pound guns, along with howitzers. On the 18th, during the night, the trenches are opened. With the engineers, miners and sappers leading the way, the army approaches the city.

On 22 March, seven of the 10-inch mortars are placed in their battery and General Scott demands that Vera Cruz surrender. The governor of Vera Cruz, General Morales, however, rejects the demand for the castle as well as the city. Once the demand is rejected, a mortar battery that stands about 800 yards from the city opens fire that continues unabated. By the 24th, the batteries are reinforced with 24-pounders and Paixhans guns. On the following day, the batteries are all participating in the bombardment. After darkness falls, the sky is illuminated by the shells that are crashing through the night air. The devastating artillery fire is also responsible for setting fires among the various buildings in the city.

All the while, the guns of the castle are returning fire. During the days of the siege, while General Scott is walking around the lines, he has to tell the men "to get Down — down men. Don't expose yourselves." One of the troops responds: "But General, you are exposed." Scott retorts: "Oh! *Generals* now-a-days can be made out of anybody, but men cannot be had."

Lieutenant Colonel D.S. Miles, U.S. Army, is given command of the troops in Vera Cruz as well as the cavalry and infantry that remain outside the city. During the battle for Vera

Cruz, the U.S. sustains about 80 casualties. The Mexicans sustain about 180 killed or wounded. About one-half of the Mexican casualties are civilian. First Lieutenant Edward Johnson (later Confederate general) participates at this battle. He also participates at Cerro Gordo, Churubusco, Molino del Rey, and Chapultepec. Johnson received two brevet promotions, to captain and major, during the war.

March 19 The USS *Orpheus* departs Governor's Island, New York, en route for Tampico, Mexico. The vessel is transporting about 400 troops of the 3rd and 4th U.S. Infantry Regiments to Tampico. They are commanded by Lieutenant Schuyler Hamilton. Another vessel, the USS *Lewis*, is transporting about 120 men commanded by Lieutenant J. H. Potter, 7th Infantry. The troops are to join the 1st and 2nd Artillery Regiment under General Taylor at Saltillo.

March 20 The USS *Smyrna* departs from Boston. It is transporting the last two companies of the Massachusetts volunteer regiment, commanded by Captain Nicholas and Captain Walsh. Captain Cushing will leave for Texas in the next couple of days.

March 21 Commodore Matthew Perry relieves Commodore Conner as commander of the Home Squadron.

March 22 Working at a furious pace, Americans have now managed to seal off the fortress city, Vera Cruz, and General Scott demands their surrender. The Mexicans refuse to surrender and General Scott immediately commences bombardment of the city of Vera Cruz, leveling Fort Santa Barbara.

In other activity, Commodore Joseph Hull's squadron operating off Monterey, California, spots the British blockade runner *William*. The Marines attached to the squadron capture it.

March 24–25 General Winfield Scott requests heavy naval guns be put ashore to assist in capturing Vera Cruz. Commodore Matthew Perry replies to the request with the words "Certainly General, but I must fight them." The guns are landed under the protection of gunboats commanded by Josiah Tattnall. These naval cannon, supported by army ordnance and navy gunboats, commence firing with precise accuracy, crumbling sections of the city's walls. After less than two days of incessant bombardment, the shaken Mexican defenders run up the white flag and request terms for surrender.

March 25 **In Mexico,** at Vera Cruz, the foreign consuls of the European powers request that General Scott grant a truce that they could get their women and children to safety. Scott replies that only the governor could be granted a truce if he were going to surrender. Scott reminds the consuls that the foreign consuls had already been forewarned and refused to act.

March 26–27 **In Mexico,** Mexican General Landero begins surrender negotiations with the United States in Vera Cruz. General Scott postpones his invasion. General William J. Worth, General Gideon Pillow and Colonel Joseph Totten (engineer corps) are appointed commissioners for the Amer-

ican army. The Mexican commissioners are supplied by the governor of
Vera Cruz. On the night of the 26th,
the articles of capitulation are signed.

In other activity, Commodore Perry
writes to Secretary of the Navy John
Y. Mason: "I am writing in the midst
of one of the heaviest northers I ever
experienced. Twenty-three merchant
vessels have already gone ashore since
morning, many of them with army
stores and munitions. The vessels of
the squadron have so far held on.—
The loss of life I fear will be great.
This is the third norther we have had
since I took command, five days since,
and we have had thirty wrecks." Lieutenant David Rumph Jones (later
Confederate general), 2nd Infantry,
participated at this battle. James Longstreet (later Confederate general) also
takes part. Afterward, he participates
at the Battles of Contreras, Churubusco, Molino del Rey and Chapultepec.

Captain William Thomas Harbaugh
Brooks participates at this battle.
Later he takes part at Cerro Gordo,
Contreras, and Churubusco. On 29
August 1847 he is brevetted as major
for his gallant and meritorious actions
at Contreras and Churubusco. Major
Brooks also is involved with the capture of Mexico City. Also, Charles
Champion Gilbert (later Union general) participates at this battle. Following the battle, he is posted there
as lieutenant in the 1st Infantry Regiment on garrison duty.

March 27   Ships lost off Vera Cruz
during the two northers include the
barque *Mopang*; brigantines *Caroline,
Mary Ann, Ellen* and *Clara, Othello,*

Colonel Joseph Totten (Frost, *The
History of Mexico and Its Wars*).

Orion, and *Will*; schooners *Sear Sutler,
Enterprise, Phebe Eliza, Louisa, Elea-
nor, Sea Nymph, Monitor, Blanch E.
Sayre, Harriet Smith, Corinne, Ella,
Oscar Jones, Orion, H. Walker, A.J.
Horton, Teconic, Mary Priam, Pacific,
Volesco* and the American ship *Dia-
dem.*

March 29   **In Mexico,** the Mexicans
at Vera Cruz lay down their arms and
United States forces raise Old Glory
over the city of True Cross. General
Scott announces that the flag is flying
over Vera Cruz and the castle of San
Juan de Ulua. At 10 A.M., the Mexicans fire a salute and then lower their
colors. Americans suffer fewer than
100 casualties during the entire campaign to capture Vera Cruz. American
casualties: 19 fatal, including Captain

Alburtis and Captain Robert Vinton, and 57 wounded. Captain Vinton's son, Francis Laurens Vinton, later becomes a Union general. General William J. Worth is appointed temporary governor of Vera Cruz. Eliakim Parker Scammon (later Union general) is appointed to General Scott's staff at Vera Cruz.

March 30 The USS *Portsmouth's* contingent of Marines supported by sailors, lands at San Jose, Mexico, seizing it.

March 31   In Mexico, General John A. Quitman departs from Vera Cruz for Alverado. He is leading the Alabama, Georgia and South Carolina regiments and Steptoe's battery. Quitman is tasked with opening a road that will handle mules, horses and supplies for the army.

In other activity, General David Twiggs departs and heads for Puente Nacional. General William Jenkins Worth, the governor of Vera Cruz, departs from it with another division within a few days. Also, Edward Lloyd Thomas (later Confederate general) of Georgia serves as a private with the Georgia Mounted Volunteers. He participates at Vera Cruz and at the capture of Mexico City. For his gallantry he is promoted to lieutenant.

March–April   In California, the 1st Regiment, New York Volunteers, begins to arrive in San Francisco. Lt. Colonel Henry Burton, U.S. Army, is the commanding officer. The regiment is to reinforce Navy and Marine forces in the region.

April 1 The USS *Portsmouth*, patrolling off Alvarado, debarks its contingent of Marines with sailor support troops which devastate the Mexican fortifications in the area. The crew of the *Portsmouth* cruises farther and seizes several more Mexican towns during the remainder of the month, including La Paz on the 13th.

April 5 Santa Anna sets up headquarters at Encero, Mexico.

In other activity, Theophilus Toulin Garrard (later Union general) of Kentucky serves with the 16th U.S. Regiment, commanded by Colonel W. Tibbats. The regiment departs on 25 April for Newport, Kentucky, where it musters into federal service. Afterward it sails for New Orleans and from there to Brazos Island, where it is ordered to Camargo on the San Juan River. Six companies of the regiment are then ordered to Monterrey, Mexico. Later, during August 1847, Company E and three other companies are ordered to Cerralvo, which is commanded by Lt. Colonel Webb. After about nine months at Cerralvo, the company is ordered to Monterrey and it is there when peace is announced.

April 7 Marines attached to the USS *Portsmouth* capture the American ship *Admittance* off San Jose in lower California.

April 8   In Mexico, Winfield Scott begins the march on Mexico City. However, the wagons, horses and mules needed to haul the ammunition and supplies are not available. They remain back in the United States. They do arrive, but slowly, as they come into Mexico from the Ohio and Mississippi Rivers. On 8 April, ten days after the surrender of Vera Cruz, General David Twiggs sets out on the Jalapa Road. The rest of the divisions follow.

April 9 Jones Mitchell Withers (later Confederate general) is appointed colonel of the 13th U.S. Infantry. On 13 September, he is promoted to colonel of the 9th U.S. Infantry. In 1846, he joins the regiment in which he is attached to Captain W. E. Martin's company in Mobile. However, only a part of the regiment makes it to New Orleans and the government declines accepting it.

April 12 **In Mexico,** American forces reach the town of Plana del Rio, in the vicinity of Cerro Gordo. General David Twiggs reconnoiters the region and afterward, he decides to attack the Mexicans on the following morning. However, he delays the attack until the arrival of General Scott. In the meantime, General Robert Patterson arrives with additional troops.

April 14 **In Mexico,** American forces under Major General Robert Patterson stall at Plana del Rio, and are joined by General Scott. Scott decides to make a new reconnaissance and determines that the batteries defending the place are too strong. Scott orders that a road be cut to the right of the American army and to the left of Cerro Gordo. The troops begin the task and the Mexicans fail to discover the work for three days. The road actually winds around the mountain and then ascends to the rear of the Mexican forts before it reconnects with the Jalapa Road.

April 17 **In Mexico,** General Scott issues General Order No. 111. Plana del Rio, April 17, 1847:

The enemy's whole line of intrenchments and batteries will be attacked in front, and at the same time turned, early in the day to-morrow — probably before ten o'clock, A.M.

The Second Division (Twiggs') of regulars is already advanced within easy turning distance toward the enemy's left. That division has instructions to move forward before daylight to-morrow, and take up a position across the National road in the enemy's rear, so as to cut off a retreat toward Xalapa.

It may be reinforced to-day, if unexpectedly attacked in force, by regiments — one or two taken from Shields' brigade of volunteers. If not, the two volunteer regiments will march for that purpose at daylight to-morrow morning, under Brig. General Shields, who will report to Brigadier General David Twiggs, on getting up with him, or the general-in-chief, if he be in advance. The remaining regiment of that volunteer brigade will receive instructions in the course of this day. The first division of regulars (Worth's) will follow the movement against the enemy's left at sunrise to-morrow morning.

As already arranged, Brig. General Pillow's brigade will march at six o'clock tomorrow morning along the route he has carefully reconnoitered, and stand ready as soon as he hears the report of arms on our right, or sooner if circumstances should favor him, to pierce the enemy's line of batteries at such point — the nearer the river the better — as he may select. Once in the rear of that line, he will turn to the right or left, or both, and attack the batteries in reverse; or, if abandoned, he will pursue the enemy with vigor until further orders.

Wall's field battery and the cavalry will be held in reserve on the National road, a little out of view and range of the enemy's batteries. They will take up that position at nine o'clock in the morning.

The enemy's batteries being carried or abandoned, all our divisions and corps will pursue with vigor.

This pursuit may be continued many miles, until stopped by darkness or fortified positions toward Xalapa. Consequently, the body of the army will not return to this encampment, but be followed tomorrow afternoon, or early the next morning, by the baggage trains of the several corps. For this purpose, the feebler officers and men of each corps will be left to guard its camp and effects, and to load up the latter in the wagons of the corps. A commander of the present encampment will be designated in the course of this day.

As soon as it shall be known that the enemy's works have been carried, or that the general pursuit has been commenced, one wagon for each regiment and one for the cavalry will follow the movement, to receive under the directions of medical officers, the wounded and disabled, who will be brought back to this place for treatment in general hospital.

The Surgeon-general will organize this important service and designate that hospital, as well as the medical officers to be left at it.

Every man who marches out to attack or pursue the enemy will take the usual allowance of ammunition,

and subsistence for at least two days. By command of Maj. Gen. Scott, H. L. SCOTT, A. A. A. GENERAL."

In other activity, the Americans (1,000 strong) implant a battery on a hill that was seized below Cerro Gordo. An 18-pounder and two 24-pound howitzers are taken up the hill. The night is stone darkness and the hill is high. The task takes from 7 P.M. until 3 A.M. In the meantime, the troops, exhausted from the ordeal, are sleeping under the stars. The battery is now in a location that commands all of the Mexican positions except for Cerro Gordo.

April 18 BATTLE OF CERRO GORDO
At dawn on this day, as the sun begins to peek over the horizon, the troops at the newly planted battery can see the Mexicans as they move out for reveille. The lancers are finely dressed and the infantry is in uniform of the day. And they are joined by a column of artillerymen. As the Mexicans form for their muster, they have no idea that the American batteries are prepared to commence fire.

General Gideon Pillow launches his attack against the hills upon which the Mexicans had placed their batteries. However, the attack gets snarled by the batteries, which pour an enfilade upon them. The Americans maintain their assault, but the batteries continue to pound the attackers. Nevertheless, General La Vega's corps is compelled to try to halt the Americans. His corps remains active until the place finally falls, at which time he surrenders about 3,000 troops.

Meanwhile, General Twiggs' troops have been awakened at dawn. They

Colonel William S. Harney (Frost, *The History of Mexico and Its Wars*).

General Gideon Pillow (Wilcox, *History of the Mexican War*).

are up and ready to take on their foe. Their artillery is activated and it pounds the Mexican batteries. Meanwhile, Twiggs' troops ascend the hill, while General James Shields' troops are speeding down the Jalapa Road to the rear of Santa Anna.

The Mexican batteries open their fire upon the advancing troops of General David Twiggs. They are ascending the hill under an enfilade of fire. Attacking are the 1st Artillery, the 7th Infantry, followed closely by the 2nd and 3rd Infantries, along with the 4th Artillery. Colonel Selby Harney is leading the assault. The Mexican fire remains devastating as the troops continue their ascent, but the Americans are not deterred. They maintain their progress until the hill is taken. Suddenly, the hill is gained. Mexican General Vasquez is killed in the fortress and the flags of the 1st Artillery and the 7th Infantry are hoisted on the Mexican batteries. In the meantime, Sergeant Henry pulls down the Mexican flag.

Back on the Jalapa Road, the volunteers under General James Shields rush a fort and they capture it and the road. Shields is shot in the lung. Santa Anna and about 8,000 of his troops escape. The Mexicans leave their baggage behind as the army flees down the Jalapa Road.

Dragoons under Colonel Harney continue the pursuit. Someone who was there describes it:

Passing down the ravine where the National Guard had three times attempted to dislodge the mounted riflemen, who, supported by the howitzer battery, literally rained death among their ranks, I was obliged to turn back and retrace my steps. The gorge was choked up with the mangled bodies of the flower of the Mexican army. The wolf-dog and the buzzard howled and screamed as I rode by, and the stench was too sickening to be endured. Returning to the National road we passed a large number of cannon taken by our troops, and saw piles of muskets charred with fire in heaps, where they had been heaped and burned.

All along the road were the bodies of Mexican lancers and their horses, cut down by Colonel William Selby Harney's 2nd Dragoons when these fire-eaters chased Santa Anna and his retreating troops into and beyond Jalapa. Almost every man's skull was literally split open with the sabres of our horsemen. and they lay stretched upon the ground in ghastly groups.

During the charge, Captain Patten, 3rd Infantry, was wounded. He lost part of his left hand. In addition, General Scott had witnessed the charge by Harney. Afterward, Scott approached Harney and said: "Colonel Harney, I cannot now adequately express my admiration of your gallant achievement, but at the proper time I shall take great pleasure in thanking you in proper terms." Harney claimed the praise was due to his officers and men.

General Worth's reserve division moves up the road and zooms past General Twiggs. He continues the

General James Shields (Wilcox, *History of the Mexican War*).

race to intercept Santa Anna's fleeing Mexican Army, which has seemingly acquired angels' wings. Nonetheless, General Worth is compelled to halt his pursuit when he sees Jalapa in the distance. It is only about 12:00 P.M. and the Americans are victorious.

The Mexicans under Santa Anna are thoroughly thrashed by the Americans commanded by General Twiggs under General Scott's command. The Americans seize approximately 3,000 prisoners, 5,000 stands of arms and over 40 pieces of artillery. Jalapa falls to the Americans on the following day and then Scott's force moves closer to Mexico City. They seize Puebla in mid–May.

General Scott, in a letter to the war Department dated 19 April, states that he was "embarrassed by the results of the victory.... Three thousand prisoners, forty-three pieces of bronze artillery manufactured at Seville, five thousand stand of arms, five generals, with the munitions and materials of an army, captured in a single battle, are the fruits of victory, and demand the earnest care of the conquering general! The men must be paroled; the small arms must be destroyed; we have not the men to take care of them."

General Scott visits all of the wounded at Cerro Gordo. He later makes sure that each of them is transferred into the town of Jalapa, where they will become more comfortable. One of those visited is General Shields. His wounds are severe and the medical personnel have grave doubts about his survival. Nevertheless, Shields proved all of his detractors wrong. He did in fact survive

and later, in about ten weeks, he is back in the saddle. They capture the town.

In other activity, an American force composed of Marines and seamen, numbering about 1,500 troops, is landed in the Tuxpan region. They encounter and engage about 400 Anishinabe soldiers and defeat them. The U.S. force sustains three killed and 11 wounded. The Anishinabe casualties remain unknown. Also, second lieutenant Barnard Bee (later Confederate general) is wounded at this battle. He is brevetted first lieutenant for gallantry. Bee's gallantry is continued as he participates in the Battles of Contreras, Churubusco, Chapultepec and the City of Mexico. He is awarded the brevet of captain for his services and he receives a sword of honor from his home state, South Carolina. In addition, the 2nd Kentucky Rifles participate at this battle.

Also, Lieutenant Daniel Frost Marsh (later Confederate general) takes part in this clash. Joseph Eggleston Johnston (topographical engineer, later Confederate general) participates. He is wounded twice while on a reconnaissance mission. In addition, he participates at the Battles of Vera Cruz, Contreras, Churubusco, Molino del Rey, Chapultepec and Mexico City. He receives three brevets for gallant and meritorious service. Lieutenant John Porter McCown (later Confederate general) participates at this battle; he is brevetted for his gallantry. Dabney Herndon Maury (later Confederate general), is brevetted first lieutenant at this action, where a ball from a musket shatters his arm. Gustavus Woodson

Smith (later Confederate general), who leads a company of miners, sappers and pontoniers, is brevetted to captain for his gallantry at Cerro Gordo and Contreras. After the war, he returns to West Point as principal assistant professor of engineering.

Captain Robert Allen (later Union General) participates at this battle; he is brevetted as major for his gallantry. Lieutenant Napoleon Jackson Tecumseh Dana (later Union general) participates at this battle with the 7th Infantry. He is left for dead on the battlefield but survives. Also, James William Denver (later Union general) had raised a company of Missouri volunteers. Afterward, he participates in General Scott's campaign to take Mexico City. Lieutenant Alfred Gibbs (later Union general) is slightly wounded in this action.

George Henry Gordon (later Union general) participates in this battle. He also participated at Vera Cruz and the capture of Mexico City. He was twice wounded during the campaign and was promoted to first lieutenant for his gallantry at Cerro Gordo. Major Edwin Vose Sumner (later Union general) participates at this battle. He earns the nickname "Bull Head" due to a story from the War of 1812 that a musket ball bounced off his head. He is brevetted lieutenant colonel for his gallantry in this clash. Later, at the Battle of Molino del Rey, he is again brevetted colonel for his gallantry. On 23 June 1848, he is promoted to colonel of the 1st Dragoons. In 1851 he is named military governor of the New Mexican Territory. George Sykes (later Union general) participates at this

battle and is brevetted captain for his gallantry.

April 18 to June   Commodore Perry's Mosquito Fleet lands Marines and seamen in Mexico. An American force composed of Marines and seamen, numbering about 1,500 troops, is landed in the Tuxpan region. They encounter and engage about 400 Anishinabe soldiers and defeat them. The U.S. force sustains three killed and 11 wounded. The Anishinabe casualties remain unknown.

April 19–22   The American Army under General Scott enters Jalapa, Mexico. Also, on or about this day, La Hoya is abandoned. The Mexicans leave 54 pieces of artillery and mortars (bronze and iron), 11,000 cannon balls, 14,000 bombs and 500 muskets. General Worth enters the town on the 22nd and occupies the castle in Perote.

April 22   The U.S. 5th Infantry, as part of the army, enters the city of Perote, Mexico. It captures all of the Mexican supplies and armaments, which includes 54 guns and mortars, and 500 muskets. The captured items are seized at the Castle of Perote, on the crest of the Eastern Cordilleras, about 50 miles from Jalapa, Mexico.

April   Alexander Doniphan is ordered back to General Taylor's headquarters in Monterrey, then to New Orleans, finally mustering out of the Army in July 1847.

April–May   The Texas 2nd Regiment is formed at San Antonio. It is commanded by Colonel John C. Hays. It is mustered into service of the United States for 12 months or the duration of the war. Also, Joseph Lewis Hogg (later Confederate general) serves as a private in Captain William F. Sparks' Company E, 2nd Regiment, Texas Mounted Rangers.

May 5   Colonel James McIntosh (5th Infantry) departs from Vera Cruz with a force of 800 men. They are attacked at Passo de Ovejas and halted, but within a few days, they are joined by General George Cadwalader (later Union general), who brings with him about 600 troops and six howitzers.

May 8   Santa Anna resigns from office: "I this day, terminate forever, my public career."

Santa Anna (Frost, *The History of Mexico and Its Wars*).

May 9   Marines attached to the USS *Independence*, a razee, participate in the capture of the Mexican vessel *Correo* in the Pacific Ocean.

May 11   **In Mexico,** at Jalapa, General Scott issues a proclamation:

I will not believe that the Mexicans of the present day are wanting in courage to confess errors which do not dishonor them, and to adopt a system of true liberty, of peace and union with their brethren and neighbors of the north; neither will I believe that they are ignorant of the falsity of the calumnies of the press, intended to excite hostility. No! public sentiment is not to be created or animated by falsehood. We have not profaned your temples, nor abused your women, nor seized your property, as they would have you believe.

We say this with pride, and we confirm it by your own bishops, and by the clergy of Tampico, Tuspan, Matamoros, Monterey, Vera Cruz, and Jalapa, and by all the authorities, civil and religious, and the inhabitants of every town we have occupied. We adore the same God and a large portion of our army, as well as of the population of the United States, are Catholics, like yourselves. We punish crime wherever we find it, and reward merit and virtue.

The army of the United States respects, and will always respect, private property of every description, and the property of the Mexican Church.

Mexicans! the past cannot be remedied, but the future may be provided for. Repeatedly have I shown you that the government and people of the United States desire peace, desire your sincere friendship.

Abandon, then, rancorous prejudices, cease to be the sport of individual ambition, and conduct yourselves like a great American nation; leave oft at once colonial habits, and learn to be truly free, truly republican, and you will become prosperous and happy, for you possess all the elements to be so. Remember that you are Americans, and that your happiness is not to come from Europe.

May 14 THE AFFAIR AT AMOZOQUE General Santa Anna had arrived at Puebla, Mexico, with his army that was gathered at Orizaba. On this day he advances to Amozoque, but he keeps his cavalry out of sight. His intention is to pass General William J. Worth and attack General John Quitman, but to his surprise, Worth is at Amozoque. A skirmish erupts and the Americans prevail. The Mexicans reportedly lose about 80 troops, but it is most probably an exaggerated number, while the Americans sustain no casualties.

Lieutenant Charles Pomeroy Stone (later Union general) participates at this skirmish. He had also participated at Vera Cruz under Captain Benjamin Huger (later Confederate general). Afterward, he participates at Contreras, Molino del Rey and Chapultepec, where he is brevetted captain for his gallantry. Also, while in Mexico, Stone ascends Popocatepetl, a volcano, and plants Old Glory on its summit. Stone also participates in the attack upon and capture of Mexico City.

May 15   In Mexico, General Worth's force encounters sporadic resistance at Puebla. After dismissing the opposition, he enters the city. From 12 March to the 15 May, the American Army had seized Vera Cruz. The castle of San Juan Ulua and Cerro Gordo had fallen

into American hands. Afterward, the towns of Jalapa and Puebla were occupied. The Americans had also seized about 10,000 prisoners, 700 cannon, 10,000 stands of arms and 30,000 shot and shells had been confiscated from the Mexican Army. General Scott, his army reduced to about 5,000 men, is compelled to remain in Puebla. The army has been reduced due to sickness and leaving garrisons at conquered places.

In Washington, D.C., there is a desire for peace. The American government is concerned about Mexico in the event that it is conquered in its entirety. How would the U.S. cope with the population? The U.S. is attempting to get Mexico to surrender without invading the heartland of its southern neighbor. The U.S. sends Nicholas P. Trist to Mexico; however, he is not an envoy because an envoy would be used only in peacetime. Nevertheless, he is authorized to bring about peace. Trist arrives in Jalapa just before Scott is scheduled to depart for Puebla.

In other activity, Marines attached to the USS *Mississippi* participate in the landing in which Carmen, Mexico, is captured. Major Willis Arnold Gorman (later Union general) participates at the battle of Puebla with the 4th Indiana Regiment. After the war, Gorman is named second governor of the Minnesota Territory.

May 17   General Pillow departs from Vera Cruz with a force of about 1,000 men. Later, General Pierce leaves with about 2,500 troops. At Jalapa, the American Army is divided up with its bulk going to the main army under General Scott.

May 18 The Mormon battalion in New Mexico receives orders to march to California. They load the wagons at Pueblo and the command advances. It crosses the Arkansas River on 24 May.

May 21 The secretary of the Navy orders the formation of a Marine regiment to be commanded by Lieutenant Colonel Watson. The regiment is to serve with General Scott.

May 22 Colonel Sowers arrives at Vera Cruz. He is carrying dispatches from General Scott, who is nearing Puebla. Later this day he leaves for Santa Fe to locate Captain Wheat, who is expected to supply reinforcements. Later in company with seven men, he is attacked by Mexican guerrillas. Six men and Sowers are killed; the survivor makes it back to Vera Cruz with the bad news.

May 24 Captain Patrick Edward Connor (later Union general) resigns from the service. He had participated at Palo Alto, Resaca de la Palma and Buena Vista.

May 26–27 After the siege of Pueblo de Taos ends, Major Edmundson departs for the Red River Canyon with a force of about 200 infantry and cavalry. Just they enter the canyon, a New Mexican–Indian force of about 500 attacks them just before dusk. Major Edmundson is compelled to dismount his cavalry because the canyon is thin and full of mud. Once the troops are on foot, they counterattack. The attackers are driven back; however, they begin another attack to crush the Americans. Darkness settles in and the Americans withdraw slightly and re-

deploy on a hill. On the following morning, the Americans return to the canyon to discover that the enemy had retreated. The Americans sustain one man killed and several slightly wounded.

May 30 **In California,** Lieutenant Colonel Henry S. Burton, 1st New York Volunteer Regiment, receives orders to board the USS *Lexington.* Companies A and B of the regiment are to accompany him. He is to capture La Paz, Mexico. Major James Allen Hardie (later Union general), 1st New York Volunteers, accompanies the regiment. Henry Morris Naglee (later Union general) also accompanies the regiment. Captain Nelson Taylor (later Union general) also accompanies the regiment.

June SECOND BATTLE OF TUXPAN Commodore Perry's Mosquito Fleet again lands a force of Marines and seamen. They engage Anishinabe soldiers and once again they defeat them. Later on 30 June, yet again, the enemy attacks, but the Americans prevail.

June 2 Santa Anna rescinds his resignation.

June 4 **In Mexico,** Colonel McIntosh departs from Vera Cruz en route to Puebla with a train of 150 wagons and 600 mules. It is escorted by 800 men. The train also contains $225,000 in specie. On 6 June, the train's advance guard, Captain Ford's Indiana dragoons, is attacked. This causes some confusion and costs the Americans two killed and about five wounded. In less than one hour, another attack is launched against the rear of the train, but before the rear guard gets up to the train, the Mexicans get a large number of wagons and pack mules. Afterward, the Mexicans head into the chaparral, where it is not pragmatic to follow them. Dragoons are posted to the rear of the train and it resumes the advance to Puebla. The Americans lose 30 troops during the march, and about 28 wagons and 200 pack mules are lost. Colonel McIntosh brings his advance to a halt at Paso de Obijas and sends a dispatch to General George Cadwalader at Vera Cruz asking for supplies and reinforcements.

June 8   In Mexico, Captain Bainbridge, 3rd Artillery, departs from Puebla en route to Vera Cruz. His party consists of citizens and disbanded soldiers (150 people). The party receives fire as it approaches Cerro Gordo. Shortly thereafter, Bainbridge is informed that the pass is protected by about four thousand Mexicans. After halting at the pass, Bainbridge reorganizes the train, then continues the advance. They arrive at National Bridge that evening without encountering any resistance. The troops are too fatigued to raise a guard at the bridge. Later, the party learns that Mexicans are barricading the bridge and at about the same time lights are observed on the cliffs and ridges near Cerro Gordo. Some cautions are taken but the night passes without incident. The following morning (9th), the train passed over the

National Bridge (Frost, *The History of Mexico and Its Wars*).

bridge, but it is fired upon by about 25 Mexicans. The wagon master and four others are killed. A contingent of lancers appears on the bridge and prepare to charge, but change their minds when it is determined that Bainbridge's troops are prepared for them. The Mexicans retire. Bainbridge resumes his march and arrives at the pass where Colonel McIntosh is waiting for reinforcements.

On the following day Bainbridge continues his advance to Vera Cruz. Captain Duperu moves with the command of Bainbridge. En route an attack is made upon Duperu's command. The Mexicans are superior in number but Duperu's dragoons prevail. The same day that Captain Bainbridge departs from Colonel McIntosh's encampment, General Cadwalader arrives with about 800 men and two howitzers. Together the two commands move toward the National Bridge. When they pass over the bridge, the Mexicans launch an attack that opens a three hour action. The howitzers are pressed into action and the cavalry charges into the chaparral. After a short while the Mexicans retreat, leaving about 100 men killed and wounded on the field. Americans lose 13 killed and 30 or 40 wounded.

June 14 *In naval activity,* a U.S. squadron consisting of the steamers *Scorpion, Scourge, Spitfire* and *Vixen* pass the bar at the mouth of the Tabasco River en route to capture Frontera. The warships with 40 barges in tow take the town without opposition. The American flotilla moves without opposition and will land nine miles from San Juan Bautista in what becomes the final amphibious assault of the Gulf Squadron. After the successful conclusion of the operation, Commodore Perry remarks: "I was struck as I have often been before with the universal enthusiasm exhibited by the officers and men."

June 15 Colonel Doniphan's troops arrive in New Orleans and receive their first pay in a year.

June 16 The Mosquito Fleet commanded by Commodore Perry captures Villahermosa. It is the final port city along the Mexican Gulf coast.

June 19 Ambrose Powell Hill (later Confederate general) graduates from West Point. He is to join the 1st Artillery Regiment, which is engaged in the Mexican War. However, most of the fighting is over. He is afterward transferred to Fort McHenry in Maryland.

June 24 Tabasco, a Mexican village garrisoned by U.S. Marines, is assaulted by Mexicans attempting to regain the town. The Marines repulse the assault.

June 30 U.S. Marines skirmish with Mexican troops while participating in the expedition to Tamultay, Mexico. In other activity, the strength of the Marine Corps is 1,182 enlisted men of which 75 are officers.

Early July to August 3 **In New Mexico,** Lieutenant Brown and two enlisted men vanish. Their bodies are later discovered close to the village of El Valle, about thirty miles east of Santa Fe. On or about July 6, a contingent of U.S. troops arrives at the village and shortly thereafter, several of the residents are dead. More than 40 men are marched to Santa Fe and charged with the murder of Brown and the two others. A "drumhead court-martial" is convicts six of the men. They are hanged on 3 August 1847.

July 7 In Mexico, Colonel Gates dispatches Colonel De Russy and 128 men from Tampico to Huejutla to seek the release of prisoners. When they arrive at a point about 8 miles from Tantayuca and one mile from the Calabosa River, he receives information from a Mexican Indian that Mexican General Garay is at the river poised to attack the Americans. At about the same time, the Mexicans fire upon the party, killing Captain Boyd and six of his men. The main body of the Americans charges the Mexicans in three separate columns, driving them across the river. The action lasts for about one hour before the Mexicans are driven back. The Americans withdraw to Tantoyuca and engage an enemy force there before entering the town. Once inside Tantoyuca they rearm themselves and destroy provisions they cannot use. At 9 P.M., General Garay issues an ultimatum to surrender. It is refused. It is agreed to meet the general in the plaza at 10 P.M. The party including Captain Wise waits until 12 A.M., without hearing from the general.

In other activity, Joseph Rodman West (later Union general) enters the army as a private in the mounted volunteers. On the 25th he is promoted to captain. Later he is attached to the District of Columbia and Maryland volunteers.

July 9 BATTLE OF CIENEGA CREEK (RED RIVER CANYON) In Mexico, an American contingent of about 31 troops, commanded by Jesse Morin, comes under attack by about 200 New Mexicans and their Pueblo Indian allies. The Americans are compelled to retreat to the banks of the creek. After the retreat, the troops reform and hold until a relief force, commanded by Captain Shepherd, arrives to beat back the enemy. The Americans sustain 5 killed and 9 wounded during the initial contact. The casualty list for the New Mexicans and Pueblos remains unknown.

July 9 In New Mexico, a contingent of about 31 troops, commanded by Captain Jesse Morin, U.S. Army, come under assault by about 200 New Mexicans and allied Pueblo Indians while they are encamped close to Cienega Creek. The Americans are compelled to retreat to positions near the creek, where they were able to retain their positions. The Americans, however, sustain 5 killed acquiring the creek bank position. The New Mexicans and Pueblos launch another fast attack. The remaining twenty-six Americans fight off the assault, killing or wounding many of their enemies, according to reports. Eventually a relief force, a company under Captain Shepherd, arrives and assists Captain Morin's men in defeating the rest of the New Mexican insurgents. The New Mexicans and Pueblos retreat, ending the last battle of the revolt.

It is perhaps known as an "affair" due to the supposed peace between New Mexican insurgents and the Americans which began after the

Siege of Pueblo de Taos. The engagement is the second bloodiest battle for the United States during the revolt in New Mexico. Casualties of the New Mexicans and Pueblos are unknown.

July 12 The Americans depart from their camp at Tantayuca, Mexico, at 2 A.M. They advance to the Panuco Road in a pouring rain. At 10 A.M., a Mexican force attacks them in an action that lasts in a running battle for more than fifty miles. The Americans lose 15 killed, 10 wounded and three missing. Mexican losses are unknown. *See also* 7 **July** 1847.

July 21 Elements of the 1st New York Volunteer Regiment, commanded by Lieutenant E. Gould, arrive at La Paz, Mexico. The unit debarks from the USS *Lexington* and occupies the port town without opposition.

Early August U.S. Marines commanded by Lieutenant Colonel Watson arrive in Puebla to be reformed as a regiment in support of Scott's effort to end the war with Mexico. The Marines form a battalion and will be the portion of Scott's Army that hooks up with a contingent of army troops led by Lieutenant U.S. Grant, which assaults and seizes the San Cosme gate. They are the first troops to enter Mexico City. The army while at Puebla is subjected to discipline and drilling.

August 1 In Mexico, a skirmish develops at San Juan de los Llanos. The Americans prevail. James Morrison Hawes (later Confederate general) is brevetted first lieutenant for his gallantry at this skirmish. Also, Captain John George Walker (later Confederate general), who entered the army during the previous year, is seriously wounded at this battle.

August 5 In Mexico, at Puebla, a war council is held. General Scott lays down his plan of operations. Major Generals Worth, John Quitman, and Gideon Pillow along with Brigadier Generals George Cadwalader, James Shields and David Twiggs are in attendance. In other activity, Lieutenant Colonel Samuel E. Watson and his contingent of Marines arrive at Puebla. Due to a shortage of men, the unit is reformed as a battalion.

August 6 In Mexico, the army under General Winfield Scott is as follows: Puebla, 7,000; General Cadwalder's brigade, 1,400; General Gideon Pillow's, 1,800, General Franklin Pierce's corps, 2,409; garrison at Puebla under Thomas Childs, 1,400. The total which departed Jalapa for Mexico City was just under 11,000 troops. In related activity, General Pierce arrives at Puebla, bringing more than 2,500 reinforcements with him.

August 7 General William Selby Harney's brigade of cavalry, trailed by General David Twiggs' 2nd Division, departs from Puebla en route to Mexico.

August 8 General John Quitman's division of volunteers departs from Puebla en route to Mexico. On the following day, General William J. Worth leaves with the 1st Division. On the 10th, the 3rd Division under General Gideon Pillow departs from Puebla.

August 10 In Mexico, General Winfield Scott, at Puebla, is preparing to

advance against Mexico City. He
leaves about 1,800 soldiers who are
sick under the command of Brevet
Colonel Thomas Childs, 1st U.S. Artillery. The city comes under siege on
14 September.

In other activity, Captain Benjamin Alvord (later Union General),
4th Infantry, participates in the defense of a convoy at Paso de Ovejas.
Lieutenant David Allen Russell (later
Union general) participates at this
skirmish. Two days later, he participates at National Bridge and later he
takes part at Cerro Gordo and Las
Animas. On 15 August, he is promoted to brevet first lieutenant for

his gallantry at these battles. He participates at the affair at Huamantla
before he is posted at East Pascagoula,
Mississippi. Lieutenant Egbert Ludo-
vicus Viele (later Union general),
who graduates West Point in 1847, is
sent to Mexico City, where he is
posted as an infantry officer.

Elsewhere, a detachment of Americans under Major Lally is attacked
close to the National Bridge by Mexican guerrillas. The incident turns
serious with the attack coming from
the front and rear. The Americans
gain the advantage and are able to
prevail, but at a high rate of casualties. The guerrillas keep the region
between Vera Cruz and Puebla
dangerous for travelers. The
most daring of these guerrillas
is a Catholic priest, Father
Jarauta. All chances of capturing him fail for the duration.

August 12 In Mexico, the
rifle regiment and three companies of cavalry reconnoiter the
roads into Mexico City. They
advance to El Penon, a fortified mountain. Afterward, they
swing to the left and come upon
Mexicalcingo, which is protected
by five batteries that command
the road. The reconnaissance
troops then march back and
find themselves under the guns
of El Penon. Nevertheless, they
arrive back at camp at about
midnight.

In other activity, the Mexicans attack a convoy at the
National Bridge (*Puente Nacional*), but it is repelled. Benjamin Alvord (later Union

Colonel Thomas Childs (Frost, *The History
of Mexico and Its Wars*).

general) participates at this skirmish. Later he participates at Cerro Gordo and at Huamantla.

August 13   In Mexico, General David Twiggs' division arrives at Ayotla, which is slightly north of Lake Chalco. General Worth's division is close to the village of Chalco along the southern end of the lake. The divisions of John Quitman and Gideon Johnson Pillow stand close behind.

In other activity, a superior numbered force of Mexicans attacks an American force at Nil Flores, Mexico. Second Lieutenant Schuyler Hamilton (later Union general), the grandson of Alexander Hamilton, is seriously wounded while engaged in hand to hand combat with a Mexican lancer who lances Hamilton through his chest and pierces his lung. Hamilton survives and afterward serves as aide-de-camp to General Scott.

August 15   General William Jenkins Worth advances from his camp at Chalco, Mexico, with the remainder of the divisions trailing. In other activity, General Stephen Kearny marches unopposed into Las Vegas, New Mexico.

August 16   General David Twiggs division departs from Ayotla, Mexico, with the train. General Persifor Smith forms his rear guard. A brief skirmish erupts at Buena Vista, but the Mexicans fled.

August 17   American General William Jenkins Worth occupies San Augustine, Mexico, located along the Acopulco Road. Worth's troops encounter only minor opposition.

August 18   In Mexico, the headquarters of General Worth is at a hacienda along the road to San Antonia. His division is close to the Mexican guns. General Twiggs' division is at rest nearby and the divisions of General Gideon Pillow and John Quitman are also close. General Scott's headquarters is at San Augustine. General Valencia and his army of about 7,000 stand at Contreras, about five miles from San Augustine. In addition, Mexican General Rincon is at Churubusco, where the fortifications are still being worked on. His garrison is composed of the battalions of National Guards (Independencia and Bravo). On the following day and on the 20th, separate batteries arrive to reinforce the city.

August 19   At San Antonio, the Mexican division is reinforced by battalions of the Hidalgo and Victoria. Also, General Santa Anna commands an army of about 12,000 that is deployed in the hills beyond Contreras.

In other activity, General Worth initiates the siege of San Antonia. General Twiggs' division is pushed to the front. At 1 P.M. the division advances from San Juan. The troops have their blankets on their shoulders and two days' supply of bread and beef in their haversacks. The division also brings Magruders' battery and the mountain howitzers.

August 19–20   BATTLE OF CONTRERAS (BATTLE OF PADIERNA)   In Mexico, Captain Mason determines on the 19th that San Antonio could be taken only through the front. The ground to the right is too boggy and to the left, the land is a mass of broken

Contreras (Frost, *The History of Mexico and Its Wars*).

stones and lava. Nevertheless, General Scott is determined to run a road through the obstacles to enable his army to seize San Antonio from the rear. General Worth is ordered to mask, but not assault, San Antonio, while General Pillow's division is to cut the road to Contreras. General Twiggs is to cover General Pillow's division.

General Percival Smith's brigade arrives at the summit of a hill where it encounters General Valencia's battery, which holds 22 pieces of artillery. It dominates the ground that must be gained for the Americans to be able to enter Mexico City. The road continues down the heights and goes through the villages of Contreras, Anselda, and San Angel. In addition, the Mexicans are advancing to support Valencia.

Meanwhile, Captain Magruder's battery — composed of 6-pounders and 12-pounders along with the howitzers of Lieutenant Callender — have been dragged up the mountain, which is permeated with rocks, cactus and the Mexican maguey plant. The mountain also contains patches of corn which conceal the Mexicans and add to the chore of the Americans.

General Scott positions himself on a hill to the front of Contreras at about 4 P.M. on the 19th. He directs his force to get the artillery into play. Nevertheless, the Americans are able to get only three pieces of artillery into the battle. The Mexicans at Contreras have 22 artillery pieces, which pound the American advance. The Americans withstand the barrage for about two hours. When the Mexican artillery fires, the Americans lie down to avoid the iron storm. As soon as it subsides, they are up again, back at their guns. Fifteen of the cannoneers are killed by the artillery fire and about thirteen of the horses are either killed or disabled.

The troops are recalled. The American cavalry is unable to advance because of the ground and the infantry is not able to advance due to the artillery and the Mexican cavalry. The Mexican cavalry charges several times, but the American infantry is not budged. The day's fighting is inconclusive.

During the night of the 19th, General Scott, from his position in the front of Contreras, can see Santa Anna reinforcing Contreras with troops from Mexico. Scott orders contingents into the towns of Contreras and Anselda, which intercept the troops moving along the San Angel road. They will be positioned from where they can also intercept the Mexican army when it retreats. Afterward, the troops will attack General Gabriel Valencia.

By this time, it is early evening and George Cadwalader's brigade had earlier advanced to Contreras. When this succeeds, San Antonio can be turned and attacked in rear as well as in front. Scott directs the 14th Regiment of Infantry commanded by Colonel Morgan to occupy the village. It is soon joined by General Shields' brigade, which is composed of the New York and South Carolina volunteers. The brigades of Smith and Riley advance even farther. Both deploy in the rear of the Mexicans on the hill of Contreras.

Meanwhile, troops of the Mississippi Rifles, the 3rd Infantry and the 1st Artillery battle throughout the day without a decisive result. The night is especially dark and the troops head for their new positions, despite being dispirited and exhausted. The night is so dark and dreary that General Scott sends seven separate officers to get information from Generals Shields and Smith, but only Captain Lee is successful in bringing back the intelligence from General Shields. All the while, the brigades under Ransom, Riley, Shields and Smith sleep during a downpour that causes the water in the road near Contreras and Anselda to flood them out. The wait for dawn is becoming disastrous.

On the 20th at 3 A.M., General Percival Smith commences. He is second in command to General Shields,

General Percival Smith (Wilcox, *History of the Mexican War*).

but he gives way to Smith. Shields is designated to hold the village and intercept the Mexicans who retreat. At 4 A.M., the troops under Generals Cadwalader, Bennet C. Riley, and Percival Smith move into their positions. They pass through a ravine to the west that is covered with orchards and cornfields to gain the rear of the Mexicans, while the Mexicans are focusing on the eastern and southern slopes, where the Americans had earlier attacked and where they anticipate the next assault. Their guns are positioned from where they can dominate the approaches.

The failure of the Mexicans to spot the maneuvering of the Americans spells disaster for them. At 6 A.M., the troops are ready. Riley's brigade sits on the far south and Cadwalader is positioned to his rear. Smith's brigade is to his left.

The signal to attack is given and suddenly, the Americans to the flanks and the rear are up and at them. Riley's brigade is first to commence fire. About 100 rifles fire in unison. The Mexicans turn their guns on the Americans but overshoot them. They spring forward, yelling and firing all the while. They are up and over the crest and into the Mexican entrenchments. The destruction is devastating. Prior to the charge being implemented, a huge force of Mexican lancers is spotted as they come up the road, but they turn around and take flight. The Americans take the batteries and in the process, they also drive the forces under General Gabriel Valencia from their positions. The activity is so quick that it lasts only about seventeen minutes.

Suddenly, the road is consumed with confusion, as the Mexicans had clogged it. The Mexican guns take a high toll on those retreating. Nevertheless, it is unwise for the Americans to fire guns due to the possibility of striking their own men.

Pursuit is begun by the Mississippi Rifles and the 2nd Infantry. While the pursuit is in progress, a huge crowd of Mexicans are spotted along the road. Some are running through the cornfields, but they are headed off by Americans firing upon them. About 500 prisoners are seized by only thirty troops. Of those captured, nearly 100 are officers.

In the meantime, General Shields is ordered to cut off the retreat of General Valencia's corps. His troops fire upon the Mexicans and scatter them. The Americans take about 375 prisoners, of whom about 25 are officers. General Nicholas Mendoza is among the prisoners.

General Scott says in his official report: "Thus was the great victory of *Contreras* achieved; One road to the capital opened; 700 of the enemy killed; 813 prisoners, including, among 88 officers, 4 generals; besides many colors and standards; 22 pieces of brass ordnance, half of large calibre; thousands of small arms and accoutrements; an immense quantity of shot, shells, powder, and cartridges; 700 pack mules, many horses, &c., &c.—all in our hands."

Jose Mariano de Salas, Mendoza, Garcia and Guadalupe are among the chief Mexican generals who were captured. The two brass cannon seized from the Americans in the battle of Buena Vista are recaptured.

The battle is fought and won in such rapid fashion that the divisions of Generals William Jenkins Worth and John Quitman do not arrive in time to join. General Pillow and General Twiggs had achieved the victory and are in hot pursuit of the fleeing Mexicans who are racing down the road to San Angel and Coyohacan, en route to Churubusco. At 8 A.M., only two hours after the battle had commenced, the fighting in the heights ends. It is also over in Contreras. Meanwhile, General Valencia's corps, who escaped capture and death, is taking flight to the main army. The movement which was so decisive severs the enemy's line, but it also opens the road to Churubusco about five miles distant.

Meanwhile, Worth's and Quitman's divisions, which had moved toward Contreras to make a diversion in front, are countermarched. San Antonio, the post that lost the support of Contreras, is the next target. It is assaulted by Colonel Clarke's brigade, Captain Mason (Engineers), commanding, with Lieutenant Hardcasde (Topographical Corps). They attack the left and wind up on the high road to Mexico City.

Meanwhile, the garrison of San Antonio concludes that its position is untenable. The garrison evacuates the post. During the retreat, the troops are caught on the flank by a column of Colonel Clarke and decimated, losing about one-half of the force. The rest, about 2,000, are in fast retreat toward Dolores. The commanding officer is General Bravo.

General Garland's brigade, which is advancing along the causeway, takes possession of San Antonia without opposition. Shortly afterward, the brigades of Clarke and Garland hook up about six hundred yards beyond San Antonia. The brigades move as one in pursuit of the Mexicans, who are heading toward Churubusco.

Mexico, facing total defeat at the hands of the fast-approaching American Army, seeks an armistice. The Americans confidently pummel the Mexicans at both Contreras and Churubusco, with severe casualties to Santa Anna's forces. General Scott's force, half the size of the Mexican defenders, inflicts 33 percent casualties on the Mexicans. Scott then positions his attack force three miles from Mexico City.

Americans suffer 155 killed and 876 wounded. General Franklin Pierce is among the wounded after falling from his horse. The Mexicans suffer 4,000 men dead or wounded and 2,637 captured at Churubusco. At Contreras, American casualties number 60 killed or wounded; Mexican casualties number 700 dead and 800 captured, including four generals. At the Battle of Contreras, U.S. Capt. Simon Drum's 4th Infantry recaptures two brass six pounders, used by Lt. John Paul Jones O'Brien of the same regiment. These cannons are on display at West Point with the following citation: "LOST WITHOUT DISHONOR, RECOVERED WITH GLORY."

Second Lieutenant Franklin Gardner, 2nd U.S. Infantry, subsequent to garrison duty at Vera Cruz and some time at Jalapa, arrives at Contreras. He is wounded in the groin during the battle, but he does not inform the doctors. Daniel Harvey Hill (later Confederate general) participates at this battle. He also participates at Chapultepec. William Henry Talbot Walker (later Confederate general) takes part in this action. Captain Henry Constantine Wayne (later Confederate general) participates at this battle and at Churubusco. He is brevetted major for his gallantry at both. Captain Silas Casey (later Union general) takes part in this action and later at Churubusco, Molino del Rey and Chapultepec. Lieutenant Israel Bush Richardson participates at this battle, at Churubusco and at Chapultepec; he is brevetted as captain and major for his gallantry. Second Lieutenant Thomas Welsh (later Union general), 11th Infantry, participates at this battle and soon after, at the Battle of Churubusco. Captain

Henry Walton Wessels (later Union general), despite being wounded, takes the regimental flag upon the death of the color-sergeant and leads his men against the Mexicans. He is brevetted major for his gallantry.

August 20 THE BATTLE OF CHURU-BUSCO In Mexico, following the decisive victory at Contreras, the Americans push on to Churubusco, which is heavily fortified. The first major obstacle is the Tete du Pont (bridgehead) built along the principal causeway that crosses the Churubusco River. It is composed of two bastions and is further fortified with batteries. The second major obstacle is the convent-church, which is only about 500 yards to the west of the first obstacle and slightly west of the river. The church itself stands out because it is higher

Churubusco (Frost, *The History of Mexico and Its Wars*).

than the high walls. In addition, the outside walls contain two embrasures high enough to dominate the approaches.

General Worth's division becomes the first to encounter the Mexican obstacle at Tete du Pont. Worth's division and Pillow's division advance at about 8 A.M. along the crossroad that leads from San Angel. In the meantime, Quitman's brigade (Pennsylvania volunteers), bolstered by U.S. Marines, is ordered to remain at San Augustine to protect the general depot there.

At 1 P.M. the separate divisions are prepared to attack. The division on the west is to assault the fortified church, while the division under General Worth to the south is designated to assault the Tete du Pont. Mexican General Correra, commander of the artillery, arrives at the road from Coyoacan. He deploys the artillery pieces in a field that surrounds the hacienda at a spot near where the causeway leads to the western gate of the city.

General Perez's brigade is at Portalis, and the remainder of Santa Anna's army is all deployed around Churubusco. The division of General Worth advances along the causeway against Tete du Pont, while General Twiggs is braving heavy fire and attacking the fortified church and its convent. In the meantime, General Shields attacks the Mexican lines on the rear and right. The attack on the church and convent is carried out by the brigades of General Smith and General Riley. The Mississippi Rifles are detached and sent to support the New York and South Carolina vol-

unteers under Shields. And the brigade under Pierce on the left is advancing to assault the Mexican rear and right. This movement on the right is to check the movement on the convent, while it is also to cut off the Mexican retreat to the capital.

The battle for the Tete du Pont is quickly decided. Two columns under Clarke and Garland advance to the front of the works, taking heavy fire from infantry along the line and from several pieces of artillery. The 5th and 8th Infantries, commanded by Lieutenant Colonel Scott and Major Waite, press into the ditch and enter the fort. The Mexicans choose not to defend. They retreat and flee toward Mexico City.

In the meantime, the force under General Twiggs begins its assault on the citadel of Churubusco about one hour before General Twiggs reaches the Tete du Pont. The citadel, composed of the church and convent, is surrounded by several pieces of artillery and a substantial number of troops under Santa Anna. The battle rages for several hours. Mexican General Rimcon is the defending officer. His guns are at the front in San Pablo. The troops of Smith and Riley pound against the defenses and take high casualties.

Two American officers, Captain Larkin Smith and Lieutenant Snelling, both of the 8th Infantry, confiscate a Mexican gun and turn it upon the Mexicans. After about three hours, the citadel is penetrated. Captain Alexander, Captain J.M. Smith and Lieutenant Shepler, along with three companies of the 3rd U.S. Infantry, barge into it. The surrender

Colonel Pierce Butler (Tomes, *Battles of America by Sea and Land*).

of the citadel is accepted by Captain Alexander. He hoists the standard of the 3rd Infantry on the balcony. At the guns, one company of deserters from the American 2nd Infantry, Thomas Riley, commands a company of deserters. They man three guns and fight desperately; often, they tear down the white flag hoisted by the Mexicans.

Santa Anna's army is poised behind the Churubusco River. It is attacked violently by the volunteers from Carolina and New York. They continue to pound against the defenders, taking high casualties. Nevertheless, they maintain the pressure until eventually they conquer. In the meantime, Gen-

eral Pierce faints and has to be removed from the field. The Mexicans retreat toward Mexico City. They waste no time and climb over the dead to get there. The Mexicans are hotly pursued by Captain Kearney, who races to the gates of Mexico City before he reigns in his horse.

The Americans also captured 29 men of the Irish Battalion who are deserters from the American army. They are tried by general court-martial headed by Colonel Riley, 2nd Infantry. All of the men are convicted and sentenced to be hanged. A general order by General Scott on 8 September approves the sentence, except for three who deserted before the war began and two because they were to receive the favor of the court. Four others are also spared. Sixteen of the deserters are executed at San Angel on 10 September.

Colonel Pierce Mason Butler and Lieutenant Colonel James Polk Dickinson of the South Carolina Regiment are both mortally wounded while carrying the flag during the battle. Colonel Dickinson passes the flag to Major Adley Gladden (later Confederate general) who in turn passes it to Lt. Baker of Company A. He carries it until he is forced from illness to hand the flag to Private Patrick Leonard of Company H. Leonard carries it through the remainder of the battle. Colonel Dickinson, Palmetto Regiment of South Carolina, wounded earlier at Vera Cruz, is again wounded in the leg. He seizes the colors from a color bearer and shortly thereafter is hit. Nevertheless, he refuses to have his foot amputated and on 12 September

1847 he dies at age 31. Dickinson's remains are returned to Camden, South Carolina, where he is interred at Monument Square.

Second Lieutenant Franklin Gardner (later Confederate general) participates in the battle of Churubusco. He sustains a severe wound to his chest, but he is able to stagger into a cornfield where he remains until the fight is over. Four troops from his company arrive to place him in a blanket and carry him to safety. The surgeons caring for him are reluctant to search for the bullet which struck him in the chest and lingered in his lung. Afterward, he goes to Mexico City. General Riley, just before departing from the city, appoints Gardner to his personal staff. Lt. Gardner embarks for New Orleans and from there to Jefferson Barracks and then to New York. Also, James Green Martin (later Confederate general) participates at this battle; he loses his arm while leading a charge. William Wing Loring (later Confederate general) takes part in this action. William Steele (later Confederate general) is brevetted captain for his gallantry at Contreras and Churubusco. Captain William Henry Talbot Walker (later Confederate general) is wounded in this action. His gallantry at Contreras and this battle gains for him the brevet of major on 20 August. Captain John Henry Winder (later Confederate general) participates at this battle; he is brevetted major for gallantry. Afterward, he participates at the capture of Mexico City and is brevetted lieutenant colonel for his gallantry there.

Captain Lewis Golding Arnold (later Union general) of New Jersey takes part in this action. Lieutenant Don Carlos Buell (later Union general), 3rd Infantry, is wounded in this battle. He is also brevetted captain and major. Lieutenant William Henry French (later Union general), 1st U.S. Artillery, serves under General Franklin Pierce. He participates at this battle. He had also participated at Cerro Gordo and at Contreras. After the war, he is stationed at various posts along the frontier. In addition, he helps to rewrite the U.S. Army's light artillery textbook. Lieutenant Winfield Scott Hancock (later Union general), 6th U.S. Infantry, is wounded in his knee in this action. He also participated at Contreras. He is promoted to first lieutenant for his gallantry at Churubusco and Contreras. Philip Kearny (later Union general) loses use of his left arm in this battle. Nathaniel Lyon (later Union general) is brevetted captain for his gallantry at this battle and at Contreras. Thomas Jefferson McKean (later Union general) takes part in this battle as an enlisted man and is wounded. In June 1848, he is brevetted second lieutenant of dragoons, but he declines the promotion. Captain Justus McKinstry participates at this battle and at Contreras. He is brevetted major for his gallantry. George Washington Morgan (later Union general) participates at this battle and at Contreras; he is brevetted brigadier general for his gallantry.

Lieutenant John Sedgwick (later Union general) participates at this battle. He had also taken part at the Battle of Contreras, and later, he participates at Chapultepec. He is brevetted as captain for Contreras and Churubusco. At Chapultepec, he is brevetted major. Lieutenant Truman Seymour participates at this battle; he also took part at Contreras. He is brevetted first lieutenant for his gallantry at those two battles. Lieutenant Charles Ferguson Smith (later Union general), 3rd Artillery Regiment, he is brevetted major for his gallantry at this battle. Thomas William Sweeny (later Union general) Company A, 1st New York Regiment, participates at this battle; he loses his right arm. Major Henry Walton Wessels (later Union general) takes part in this action, Vera Cruz, Cerro Gordo and Contreras. Connecticut, his home state, presents him with a jeweled sword for his distinguished service.

August 24   Armistice is agreed upon by General Winfield Scott and General Santa Anna in Mexico.

Late August   An unarmed American wagon supply train enters Mexico City for supplies under the flag of truce, but it is attacked. Santa Anna sends an apology, which is accepted by General Scott.

September 1   Joseph Alexander Cooper (later Union general) joins the 4th Tennessee Infantry Regiment at about this time. He serves as an enlisted man under Colonel Richard Waterhouse.

September 4   The War Department calls for the raising of five new regiments. The call does not include the regiment from Ohio, which is being mustered into federal service. It will depart for Vera Cruz in several days. The new regiments from Kentucky are to rendezvous at Louisville and Smith-

ville. In Tennessee, the new regiments rendezvous at Nashville and Memphis, and the Indiana regiment is to rendezvous at a point along the Ohio River to be designated by the governor. The new regiments are to be raised quickly and then to dispatch to the Rio Grande.

September 6   Mexico rejects the United States' demands for settling the conflict. General Scott writes to Santa Anna that "the 7th and 12th Articles of the Military Convention, which stipulated for a supply of provisions from Mexico had been violated; and that he [General Scott] had good reason for believing, that within twenty-four hours, the 3d Article also had been violated." Scott also informs Santa Anna that he "would allow time for explanation, he would notify him, that if satisfaction on these points was not given by 12 o'clock the next day (7th) the armistice would terminate at that hour."

Santa Anna denies the charges that day and complains that the American army had "in some cities and villages violated temples, plundered the sacred vases and profaned the images venerated by the Mexican people." Santa Anna also states that he is not willing "to sign a treaty which would lessen considerably the territories of the republic." General Scott maintains he went out of his way to ensure that the country's religious articles were not harmed.

September 7   **In Mexico,** the armistice ends at noon, according to the message sent from General Scott to Santa Anna on the previous day. The American Army moves to Tacubaya to

General George Cadwalader (Frost, *The History of Mexico and Its Wars*).

position for a southwestern attack on Mexico City. There are two obstacles in their way, the Castle of Chapultepec and Molino del Rey.

September 7–8 **In Mexico,** the U.S. order of battle is as follows. The 1st Division, commanded by Major General William J. Worth, is composed of the 1st Brigade (Brigadier General John Garland), 4th Infantry, commanded by Major Francis Lee; 2nd Artillery, Captain Horace Brooks; 3rd Artillery, Captain Robert C. Buchanan; and Duncan's Battery, commanded by Colonel James H. Duncan; the 2nd Brigade, commanded by Brevet Brigadier General Newman S. Clarke, is composed of the 5th Infantry (James S. McIntosh), 6th Infantry (Lieutenant Edward Johnson) and the 8th Infantry (Major William R. Montgomery). The 2nd Division, commanded by Major General David

E. Twiggs, is composed of the 1st Brigade, 3rd U.S. Infantry (Colonel James May), the 1st U.S. Artillery (Erastus A. Capron), and Taylor's Battery. The 2nd Brigade, commanded by Brigadier General Bennet Riley, is composed of the 2nd Infantry (Lt. Frederick Steele), 7th U.S. Infantry (Lt. Colonel Dixon S. Miles) and the 4th U.S. Artillery. The 3rd Division, commanded by Major General Gideon Pillow, is composed of the 1st Brigade, commanded by Brigadier General Franklin Pierce, the 9th U.S. Infantry (Colonel Truman B. Ransom), 12th U.S. Infantry, 15th U.S. Infantry (Colonel George Washington Morgan) and Magruder's battery. The 2nd Brigade, commanded by Brigadier General George Cadwalader, is composed of the 11th U.S. Infantry, attached to the 14th U.S. Infantry (Colonel William Trousdale), and Voltigeurs (Colonel Timothy Patrick Andrews and Lt. Colonel Joseph E. Johnston). The 4th Division, commanded by Major General John A. Quitman, is composed of the 1st Brigade, commanded by Brigadier General James Shields, the 2nd New York Infantry (Colonel W. B. Burnett), the 2nd Pennsylvania Regiment (Lt. Colonel John W. Geary); South Carolina Palmetto Infantry (Lt. Colonel James P. Dickinson) and Steptoe's battery, along with the U.S. Marines, commanded by Lt. Colonel Samuel Watson. Also, the infantry is supported by the 1st, 2nd, 3rd U.S. Dragoons and the 4th U.S. Artillery.

September 8 THE BATTLE OF MOLINO DEL REY The attack against Molino del Rey (Kings Mill) is given

Storming of Molino del Rey (Frost, *The History of Mexico and Its Wars*).

to General Worth. The Americans erroneously believe that the facility is manufacturing cannon for the Mexican army. He is to assault the obstacle, capture its artillery and destroy its machinery if it is possible. The strong point is composed of the mill, two reinforced buildings, and the Casa de Mata, a stone structure. However, the Americans have no idea about the defenders. Worth's assault force stands at about 3,000 troops. The Casa de Mata is occupied by about 1,500 Mexicans regulars, commanded by General Perez. Molino del Rey is commanded by General Leon and held by the Mina battalion, commanded by Colonel Balderos, the Union and the La Patria from Oaxaca and mostly National Guard from Queretaro. The force is further bolstered by about 10,000 men

under Santa Anna who are deployed between the two posts.

The enemy's left wing stands at Molino del Rey and its right wing terminates at Casa de Mata. Its weakest point is in the center. Worth selects 500 troops to assault and the command is given to Major Wright (8th Infantry). He is supported by Huger's battery. John Garland's brigade makes the right wing and it is supported by Drum's battery. The right wing is to assault the objective, Molino del Rey, and prevent the Mexicans from getting support from Chapultepec. The 2nd Brigade, led by Colonel McIntosh, is supported by Duncan's battery on its left. George Cadwalader's brigade is placed in reserve.

At 3:00 A.M., several columns move

out and form for the attack. At dawn, the assault begins. Huger's battery on a ridge commences fire on Molino del Rey. Wright bolts forward with his column. He is able to push the infantry and artillerymen back. The Americans also captured the field battery. Then suddenly, the Mexicans regroup and retake the ground after delivering a master stroke of devastation. Eleven of fourteen officers are killed during the assault. The Mexicans, however, are not to maintain their short-lived victory.

Captain Edmund Kirby Smith (later Confederate general) of Cadwalader's brigade sweeps into action. Smith's troops pound the Mexicans back in a rout. Casa de Mata and Molino del Rey on the right are both left totally isolated. Garland's brigade is able to assault and capture Molino del Rey, but on the left, Casa de Mata is a fortified citadel that contains bastions and ditches.

The charge against the Casa de Mata is initiated by the column led by McIntosh. It encounters resistance which fires from concealed positions and rivets the column. Colonel Scott, Colonel James S. McIntosh and Waite are among the first to fall. The other troops are stunned and withdraw to Duncan's battery. A Mexican column of cavalry comes from the right of their entrenchments and strikes the beleaguered column. Duncan's battery reacts immediately. It pounds the Mexican cavalry, which causes them to retreat. Sumner's dragoons then attack the confused line and it routs them. The battery then resumes fire upon the Casa de Mata, which causes the infantry to retire. Shortly there-

after, the fortifications are evacuated.

About one-fourth of General Worth's corps are killed or wounded. The official return of the troops engaged shows that 58 officers and 729 privates are either killed or wounded. Mexico suffers approximately 2,000 more casualties and 800 captured. U.S. Capt. Robert Anderson and Lt. U.S. Grant are among the first to enter Molino del Rey. (Anderson would later surrender Fort Sumter to the Confederacy, and Grant would accept the surrender of Robert E. Lee at Appomattox Court House to end the Civil War.) The U.S. 5th Infantry participates at this battle. Major Scott, Captain Merrill and Lt. Strong are among the American losses.

General Scott captures Molino del Rey and its supporting buildings. The objectives are more than he had thought, but it is not from being unprepared. During the first day of the attack, Captain Mason is sent on a reconnaissance mission that fails to detect the strong fortifications. Subsequent to the battle, General Scott sends out Captain Robert E. Lee, along with Lieutenants Pierre Beauregard, Stevens and Tower on a reconnaissance mission to determine whether Mexico City could be entered from another causeway to permit the Americans to avoid Chapultepec. The mission focuses on the southern gates, the Piedad, Nino Perdido and the Pasco de la Viga.

Captain Lewis Addison Armistead is brevetted as major for his gallantry at Molino Del Rey. Also, Pierre Gustave Toutant Beauregard serves on General Scott's staff. Beauregard is brevetted twice for gallantry during the war. Lt. Colonel Paul Octave Hebert (later Confederate general) participates at this battle. He also participates at the battles of Contreras, Churubusco, Molino del Rey, Chapultepec and Mexico City. Hebert is brevetted colonel for his gallantry. William Duncan Smith (later Confederate general) sustains a severe wound in this action. Also, William Henry Talbot Walker (later Confederate general) participates and is wounded in the back at this battle.

Robert Anderson is wounded in this action. Frederick Tracy Dent, John Gray Foster, and Lieutenant Charles Smith Hamilton are seriously wounded. All will later be Union generals. Lieutenant William Hays (later Union general) participates at this battle where he is wounded; he also participates at Contreras and Churubusco. Francis Engle Patterson (later Union general), the son of General Robert Patterson, serves as second lieutenant of the 1st Artillery and participates at this battle. Fitz John Porter (later Union general) participates. He is brevetted captain for his gallantry at Molino del Rey. At Chapultepec, he also participates and is brevetted major. Captain Henry Prince, 4th Infantry Regiment, participates at this battle. He is so severely wounded that he is disabled for about three years, but he will later become a Union general.

September 11   In Mexico, General Scott convenes a council of war. His generals and engineers attend. Scott discerns that he will assault Mexico City from the west, but initially only General Twiggs agrees with him. Scott's engineers remain interested in the city's southern approaches. Nevertheless, the attack is scheduled and it is to be from the west.

Chapultepec is a castle atop a large hill. It is also being used as the Mexican Military Academy. General Scott orders General John Quitman to have his division join with that of General Pillow at the southern gates of the Mexico City. He also informs both generals to then join him at Tacubaya, about two miles distant. At the time, Scott is with General Worth's division. In the meantime, the brigade of Riley with Captain Taylor's and Edward Steptoe's batteries is to remain in front of the gates to threaten and deceive the Mexicans by firing at them. General Twiggs, with the other brigade, General Persifor Smith's, is to remain at San Angel in the rear until the morning of the 13th. The maneuver works impeccably and when the Mexicans figure it out, it is too late.

In related activity, the battery of Captain Drum (4th Artillery) commences fire on Chapultepec. He is supported by Lieutenant Hagner (3rd Artillery), who is in command at battery No. 2. Both batteries are protected by General Quitman's division. On the opposite side are Battery No. 3, commanded by Captain Brooks and Lieutenant S. S. Anderson, and Battery No. 4, commanded by Lieutenant Stone (Ordnance). These batteries were constructed by Captain Robert E. Lee and Captain Huger with assistance of the corps and artillery officers.

September 12 United States artillery commanded by Captain Huger begins bombarding the castle of Chapultepec during the pre-dawn hours. The battle continues until dark, when firing halts to preserve ammunition. On the following morning, the guns resume firing at the castle. The Americans discover that the Mexican troops remain on the outside of the castle. Nevertheless, the guns focus on the castle and by so doing, they keep the garrison at a minimum.

September 13 THE BATTLE OF CHA-PULTEPEC The United States artillery begins its attack on Chapultepec, which according to the Mexican records is defended by about 1,000 troops commanded by Mexican General Nicholas

Bravo. An assault at 8 A.M. follows a cessation of the bombardment. Mexico City itself stands on an elevated piece of ground and it is saddled with a ditch that serves for drainage as well as military defense. Chapultepec is also where the military college is located. It must be taken before the city can be entered. General Worth is directed to keep his division in reserve, close to the foundry from where he can support General Pillow and Brigadier General Persifor Smith.

Generals Gideon Pillow and John Quitman, in position since the 11th, receive an aide-de-camp, sent from General Scott, alerting both that the attack is to be launched. With the batteries firing at the castle, both columns advance. Pillow maneuvers

Storming of Molino del Rey (Frost, *The History of Mexico and Its Wars*).

General William Jenkins Worth (Frost,
***The History of Mexico and Its Wars*).**

to the west side of the city, but his troops are compelled to move on open ground. Mexican sharpshooters are in place but are quickly taken out. At about the same time, General Pillow gets a serious wound to the ankle. Command of Pillow's division reverts to General George Cadwalader due to the absence of General Franklin Pierce, who was wounded at Contreas on (August 19).

The slope which holds the college has to be seized before the castle can be taken. General Pillow's brigade attacks from the west, while Quitman's brigade, which includes the 4th Division and U.S. Marines, comes in from the southeast. Quitman's unit encounters trouble when it is halted by a brigade that is entrenched at the intersection with the road that enters the city from the east. Quitman's brigade attacks the hill from the

south with about 120 Marines and soldiers. Heavy fighting ensues. Marine Captain George Terrett leads about 36 Marines who pursue the Mexicans while they retreat to the city. The Marines speed up the chase as they approach the San Cosme Gate causeway under an extremely heavy fire. The Marines are joined in pursuit by Lieutenant Ulysses S. Grant, who is leading about 20 infantrymen. Together, the two detachments move toward the city's San Cosme Gate.

Lieutenant John Simms, USMC, and Lieutenant Charles Henderson (son of the commandant) assault the gate, but it is too strongly defended. Instead, Lieutenant Simms and Lieutenant Jabez Rich, along with seven other Marines, attack the gate from the left side. Henderson, who is wounded in his leg, attack it from the front. The gate is seized before dark by both parties at a cost of six casualties.

In the meantime, the other part of the storming party continues to ascend the steep hill. Mexican riflemen and cannon are only part of the problem. The slope is full of rocks, chasms and mines. However, the Americans ascend so quickly that the Mexicans are driven from their positions. The Mexicans have no time to light even a solitary mine. To do so would have also blown up their fellow soldiers. The Americans gain the ditch as well as the walls. The Americans bring up ladders and scale the walls. Those who are the first to climb are the first to fall. Nevertheless, the troops continue to ascend until finally they gain the castle of Chapultepec.

After the San Cosme Gate is taken, Quitman's division, supported by Marines, maneuvers toward the Belen causeway while coming under heavy fire. The Mexicans defend the gate and halt the advance. The gate falls by afternoon. By about noon the next day, General Quitman and General Worth are readying an attack against the entrances to Monterrey; however, General Santa Anna had retreated.

General Quitman's troops speed through the streets and into the Grand Plaza. They take the Mexican National Plaza, where the Halls of Montezuma had earlier stood. When General Scott comes into the city of Monterrey, he discovers that the Marines are posted to guard the palace.

American troops, including United States Marines, capture the castle by 9:30 A.M. ("From the Halls of Montezuma," words in the Marine Corps hymn, refer to this Battle of Chapultepec.) About 90 percent of the Marine officers and non-commissioned officers who participate in the Battle of Monterrey are killed. General Quitman's staff is devastated. He loses every member of his staff during the fighting at the Belen Gate. Mansfield Lovell (later Confederate general) is wounded. Generals Pillow, Twiggs and Shields are wounded. Adley Hogan Gladden (later Confederate general) is also wounded at this battle. Major Earl Van Dorn (later Confederate general) is wounded while at the Belen Gate. The Mexicans lose General Bravo as a prisoner of war. General Juan A. Perez is killed. Santa Anna brands General Terres as a traitor and relieves him of command. In addition, he makes Terres the scape-goat for the miserable defeat at Mexico City. Also, James Jay Archer (later Confederate general) is brevetted major for his gallantry at this battle. The U.S. Mounted Rifle Regiment, which fights as infantry at this battle, receives praise from General Winfield Scott: "Brave Rifles! Veterans! You have been baptized in fire and blood and have come out steel." The compliment coming from the commanding general becomes the motto of the regiment. Captain Bibb Crittenden (brother of Union general Thomas Leonidas Crittenden), who served with the regiment, later becomes a Confederate general. James Longstreet (later Confederate general) is wounded in the leg while carrying his regimental colors (8th U.S. Infantry). William Wing Loring (later Confederate general) loses one of his arms. Also, Mansfield Lovell (later Confederate general) participates at this battle; he is brevetted for gallantry. William Whann Mackall (later Confederate general) is wounded. He also participate in action at Monterrey, Contreras and Churubusco. At Churubusco he is brevetted major. Second Lieutenant Earl Van Dorn (later Confederate general) is wounded at this battle. Cadmus Marcellus Wilcox takes part in this battle and at Mexico City.

Ambrose Everett Burnside (later Union general) is assigned to garrison duty at Mexico City. Second Lieutenant Edward Richard Sprigg Canby (later Union general) receives several brevet promotions, including lieutenant colonel, for his gallantry at the Belen Gate. Captain Silas Casey, 2nd Infantry, participates at this battle; he is brevetted major and lieutenant colonel for his gallantry. Lieutenant James Barnet Fry (later Union general), who graduated from West Point this year, is sent to the war zone. He is assigned garrison duty at Mexico City. Subsequent to the U.S. occupation of the city, Fry is transferred to West Point where he becomes adjutant. Also, Lieutenant Colonel John White Geary (later Union general), 2nd Pennsylvania Regiment, participates at this battle. His regiment is the first to enter Mexico City and accordingly, General Quitman appoints Geary as commander of the Citadel. Lieutenant George Washington Getty, an artillery officer, participates in General Scott's army as it makes its way to Mexico City. He participates at the battles of Contreras and at Churubusco.

Joseph Abel Haskin (later Union general) loses his left arm in this action. Second Lieutenant John Porter Hatch (later Union general) participates at this battle. Jasper Adalmorn (later Union general) is wounded in this action. Innis Newton Palmer (later Union general) is also wounded; he receives the brevet of captain for his gallantry. In addition, he participates at the battles of Cerro Gordo, Contreras and Churubusco. Gabriel Rene Paul (later Union general) participates; he is brevetted major and later, upon his return to St. Louis, the citizens present him with a sword. Thomas Edward Greenfield Ransom's (later Union general) father, Colonel Truman B. Ransom, is killed at this battle while leading his regiment (9th U.S. Regiment). Lieutenant Jesse Lee Reno (later Union general) participates

at this battle and at Cerro Gordo; he is brevetted as first lieutenant and captain for his gallantry. Lieutenant Frederick Steele, 2nd Infantry (later Union general), participates at this action and is brevetted captain for his gallantry at Contreras and Chapultepec. His company also participates at the capture of Mexico City.

September 13 American General John Quitman approaches the Belen Gate of Mexico City, while General Worth encroaches upon the San Cosme gate. By early evening, both positions are secured at a cost of 800 American casualties.

In other activity, twenty-nine American deserters are placed in wagons with ropes around their necks facing Chapultepec. As the American flag rises unfurled into the breeze, the wagons move, hanging all deserters.

September 13–14 The U.S. Army, under the command of General Winfield Scott, advances and marches victoriously into Mexico City. U.S. Grant remarks afterward: "Credit is due to the troops, it is true, but the plans and strategy were the General's." Also, John Breckinridge Grayson arrives as captain of the artillery. He later becomes the chief commissariat for Major General Scott. Grayson participates at the battles of Vera Cruz, Cerro Gordo, Contreras, Churubusco, Molino del Rey, Chapultepec and Mexico City. He is promoted to lieutenant colonel for his actions at Chapultepec. Lieutenant Samuel Bell Maxey (later Confederate general) participates at this battle. He also participates at Cerro Gordo, Contreras, Churubusco, and Molino del Rey. Lieutenant Maxey

U.S. troops enter Mexico City (Frost, *The History of Mexico and Its Wars*).

is brevetted first lieutenant for his valor and is put in command of one of five companies chosen to form a city police guard in Mexico City. Ethan Allen Hitchcock serves as inspector general during the campaign to seize Mexico City; he is brevetted colonel and brigadier general for his services. Lieutenant Isaac Ingalls Stevens is severely wounded at Mexico City; he is brevetted captain and major for his gallantry.

September 14 to October 12   In Mexico, General Winfield Scott departs from Puebla on August 10 but he

Opposite: General Ethan Allen Hitchcock (Frost, *The History of Mexico and Its Wars*).

leaves about 1,800 soldiers who are sick under the command of brevet Colonel Thomas Childs, 1st U.S. Artillery. Childs' garrison is composed of about 247 men of the 1st Pennsylvania Volunteers, a company of the 2nd and 4th U.S. Artillery Regiments, and one company of the 3rd Dragoons, commanded by Captain Lemuel Ford.

Colonel Childs establishes his defenses at several locations in the town, Fort Loreto and Guadalupe, a church bolstered by a ditch and an earthen wall. Childs also mans the Cuartel de San Jose [barracks] in the northeast sector. Childs uses the Cuartel de San Jose for his headquarters, but it is also utilized as the main hospital.

The people in the town had been getting along well with the Americans from the beginning, but once General Scott departs for Mexico City, the place changes dramatically. Mexican General Joaquin Rea is intent on riling the populace. He immediately sends his guerrillas into the city to get the people to rebel and to simultaneously shape up the garrison.

On August 12, several teamsters are attacked while on a supply mission. Two days afterward, the Americans are fortifying the three locations within the city and not a minute too soon. For the next 59 days, Puebla is under siege.

On 26 August, a large contingent of guerrillas raids an enclosure that holds animals. They escape with many mules. Pursuit is started by about 30 dragoons, who give chase. The dragoons are then overtaken by about 300 Mexican lancers who kill or capture about one-half of them.

On September 13, during the night, General Rea arrives with a few thousand troops. On the 16th, Rea demands that Childs surrender. Childs rejects the demand. Shortly afterward, a contingent of Mexican lancers attacks San Jose, but they are repulsed.

U.S. morale is raised considerably on the 22nd when the American Spy Company arrives with word that General Scott has captured Mexico City. Later that day, Santa Anna arrives with his retreating army that abandoned Mexico City.

On the 25th, Santa Anna repeats the demand for Childs to surrender, but again, he rejects the offer. The Mexicans begin constructing breastworks during the night as they slowly make their way to the fort. In the meantime, the Americans attack the Mexicans and they succeeded in countering the threat.

By early October, General Rea again assumes command of the Mexicans. On October 8, the bishop of Puebla dies at his residence and the Mexicans request a cease fire, to which Colonel Childs agrees.

On 12 October, American morale goes sky high at about 1 P.M. when General Joseph Lane's relief column enters Puebla. Upon seeing the column, the Mexicans retreat. Shortly thereafter, Puebla is restored to order and the populace reinitiates good relations with the Americans.

September 17   General Scott assesses Mexico City $150,000 for the protection afforded public property by the U.S. Army. Later in the year, the states of Mexico are assessed an additional

$3,000,000 for support of the U.S. Army while holding the country.

September 30 Marines attached to the USS *Dale*, a sloop, participate in the capture of the Mexican schooner *Magdalena* in the river at Muleje, Mexico.

October Georgia volunteers again undertake a mission guarding a supply train into Monterrey. Captain Chance directs five companies of the Georgia regiment to undertake the mission. He designates Lt. Colonel Redd (23 years old) to command the escort. The supply train includes about 1,500 pack mules and another 50 for the escort and 60 wagons. Colonel Redd takes his supper with Taylor. He states while eating that he had fought the Mexicans in Texas and that "they are a brave people and all the difference between them and us is that they can not shoot as well (never taking aim) and are not animated in patriotism." He thinks now they are learning to shoot better and are becoming united and patriotic. He does not intend to trouble General Patterson with prisoners, but will hang all Mexicans "who give battle from here to Monterrey."

Also, the 4th Kentucky Regiment is formed. William Preston (later Confederate general) is appointed lieutenant colonel of the regiment. Preston will also serve on the staff of his brother-in-law Albert S. Johnson during the Civil War. Major William Thomas Ward (later Union general) serves as a member of the 4th Kentucky; he is stationed in Mexico until he musters out the following year.

October 1 Marines attached to the USS *Dale* land at Mulege, Mexico,

and after a skirmish, they drive the Mexicans from the town.

October 5 The USS *Dale* stands offshore at Loreto, California, during one of its tours in search of enemy merchant vessels and privateers. On this day, a contingent of sailors and Marines aboard three U.S. cutters attack Loreto.

October 7 A Mexican contingent led by Captain Manuel Pineda attacks a U.S. force at Mulegé, Baja California Sur. They are defeated.

October 8 Mahlon Dickerson Manson (later Union general) is appointed captain of the 5th Indiana Volunteers. He musters out of the service on 28 July 1848.

October 9 Spies that General Joseph Lane sent out the previous day return and inform him that Santa Anna and his army is at Huamantla, about 25 miles from Puebla. Captain Samuel Walker, commanding Lane's vanguard, arrives at the town and spots about 2,000 Mexican lancers. Walker leads his rangers and drives into the city to scatter the Mexicans; however, Santa Anna leads a counterattack that succeeds in halting the rangers. Walker is mortally wounded during the counterattack. The rangers attempt to maintain their hold on the place. Some of the rangers find refuge in the local church. Shortly thereafter, the remainder of General Lane's force arrives and succeeds in pushing the Mexicans from the town. Captain Samuel Peter Portman (later Union general) participates at this battle; he is brevetted major for his gallantry.

General Lane, after hearing the

news regarding the death of Captain Walker, leaves his men on their own. They pillaged and burn down the town. It is the only time during the war that a U.S. force ransacks city.

General Lane fights his way into Puebla and lifts the siege in three days. In the meantime, General Rea moves to Atlixco, Mexico. Also, Captain Benjamin Alvord (later Union general) participates at this battle.

October 10   Marines attached to the USS *Portsmouth* participates in the capture of the brigantine *Argo* out of Chile in the Gulf of Mexico.

October 19   **In Mexico,** General Joseph Lane's brigade departs from Puebla at 11 A.M. They move against Atlixco, the temporary seat of government, where General Rea had retreated from Puebla.

At about 4 P.M., the column encounters Mexican pickets. In the meantime, the cavalry is off examining a hacienda along the route. Consequently, the column is halted. The Mexican pickets initiate an attack, but the cavalry had returned. It charges and the Mexicans retreat. After running about a mile and a half, the Mexicans decide to stand and fight. Then American infantry and artillery units appear on scene and the Mexicans again retreat, with the dragoons giving hot pursuit until they come upon Atlixco and spot the main body deployed in the chaparral. After concluding that the Mexicans have to be dislodged, the dragoons charge and the Mexicans raise only small resistance as they again flee. Suddenly, the infantry and artillery units catch up with the cavalry. When

they appear, the entire Mexican force retreats.

The dragoons gave pursuit for a while, but the heat of the day combined with the day's skirmishes had exhausted the cavalry's horses. The cavalry halts pursuit. Meanwhile, the remainder of General Lane's force arrives at Atlixco. He decided that it would be too dangerous to enter the town in darkness. Lane deploys his artillery in the heights that dominate Atlixco, then orders them to commence fire. After about 45 minutes, the bombardment ceases. Colonel Brough and Major Lally are directed to enter the town with great caution. By that time, the resistance is suppressed and the guerrillas are fleeing.

The town council was waiting patiently for General Lane. Once he arrives, they request that their town might be saved, which it is. On the following morning, Lane directs that the town be searched for arms and ammunition. General Rea takes two pieces of artillery with him when he flees, but pieces that are discovered are destroyed. Afterward, General Joseph Lane returns to Puebla. Lane's losses during the struggle at Atlixco amount to one.

October 20   Marines attached to the USS *Portsmouth* and the USS *Congress* participate in the capture of Graymas, California.

October 31   The USS *Libertad*, a schooner, bombards the town of Punta Sombrero. Its shore batteries are hit and knocked out of action.

November 1   Marines participate in the expedition to Todos Santos. The force returns to San Jose on the 7th and it encounters no opposition.

November 7 Marines receive orders to garrison San Jose, California.

November 11 Marines attached to the USS *Cyane*, a sloop, USS *Congress*, a frigate, and the USS *Independence*, a razee, are landed at Mazatan, Mexico. They capture the town.

November 16–17 Mexicans numbering about 300, commanded by General Pineda, attack La Paz, which is garrisoned by Companies A and B of the 1st New York Volunteer Regiment. The defenders pile logs around their barracks and repel the assault. Pineda determines that he is unable to defeat the Americans, withdraws his force on the 17th and moves to La Laguna, about five or six miles distant. The Americans sustain one man killed during the assault. The Mexicans sustain about five killed and an unknown number of wounded.

November 17 Marines supported by seamen attached to the USS *Dale*, a sloop, repel an attack against Guaymas, Mexico.

November 19–21 U.S. Marines attached to several ships, including the USS *Congress*, are guarding San Jose, California, when they are suddenly assaulted by a force of Mexicans. The Marines sustain the attacks until the 21st without losing the ground. The town is fortified, and combined American troops, although besieged until February 15, 1848, and are compelled to fight off several more attempts by the Mexicans. The Americans retain the city.

November 20–21 BATTLE OF SAN JOSE DEL CABO The Americans who have occupied the town are attacked by the Mexicans and Indians. The Americans are able to easily repel the assault.

November 24 AFFAIR AT THE PASS OF GALAXARA General Joseph Lane, while en route to Puebla, has posted part of Captain Roberts' rifle company as vanguard. His rear guard is Louisiana cavalry under Captain Lewis. As the column goes through the Pass of Galaxara about five miles from Matamoros, the train is interrupted by obstacles and it becomes quite extended. Suddenly the Mexicans appear at the front. Meanwhile, the artillery and a small train containing four wagons containing property seized from Mexicans falls way back in the rear.

In the meantime, Lane orders Colonel Hays to speed to the point and support Roberts against the enemy. About 200 Mexican lancers are discovered, then attacked and repelled. The force numbering about 35 troops pursues the Mexicans; however, after reaching a point about halfway up a hill, the Mexicans try to rally. After turning to the front to charge, they again break and flee. Colonel Hays gives pursuit, but once they get to the crest of the mountain they discover another force of about 500 men commanded by General Rea.

The Texans are not armed with sabers and they had expended their ammunition. Colonel Hays orders his troops to withdraw to their original positions, while being pursued by the Mexicans. Once they fall back and get additional ammunition, they repulse the Mexicans. The Texans hold until the artillery under Lieutenant Fields arrives, along with cavalry under Captain Lewis.

Once the artillery arrives, it is immediately trained on the enemy, which is in fast retreat over the mountain. For the next several hours, the Mexicans continue to harass the column, but do not engage the Americans. The Americans sustain two killed and two others wounded. Captain Benjamin Stone Roberts (later Union general) participates in this action.

November 27 to December 8   In Mexico, La Paz, held by units of the 1st New York Regiment, comes under another attack by about 500 soldiers, but it fails. The enemy implements a siege that lasts until 8 December. The Americans sustain no deaths and an undetermined number of wounded. The Mexican-Indian force sustains about 36 killed. The wounded are undetermined.

November 28   The remaining soldiers of the Mormon battalion are traveling from Santa Fe, New Mexico, for California on October 19. On this day, they cross the Continental Divide. As they proceed up the San Pedro River in Arizona, a herd of wild cattle attacks the party. Some of the bulls are killed. Two of the troops are wounded. Afterward, the column resumes its march to Tucson, where the Mexican garrison abandons its positions. No fighting occurs.

November 29 WHITMAN MASSACRE In 1836, Doctor Marcus and his wife, Narcissa Whitman, established the Whitman Mission at Walla Walla,

Washington. Its purpose is to convert the Cayuse Indians to Christianity. Also known as the Waiilatpu Mission, it is located along the Oregon Trail. Progress is slow because the Cayuse do not enjoy farming and continue in their nomadic ways. As time passes, immigrants continued to come into the region and as they multiply, tension increases between them and the Cayuse Indians. During this year (1847), a measles epidemic breaks out. It spreads from the wagon train into the Cayuse villages. The Cayuse become impatient with the Whitmans. They believe the couple is poisoning them. On this date, they attack the couple's home. They kill twelve settlers and the Whitmans, and destroy nearly all of the buildings. After causing the death and destruction, the Cayuse Indians keep 53 women and children for ransom.

During the following year, a force of about 500 militia, led by Cornelius Gilliam with the support of the U.S. Army, advances against the Cayuse Indians. They demand the surrender of the warriors responsible for the massacre.

December   The 5th Tennessee Volunteer Regiment is formed. Captain John Crawford Vaughn (later Confederate general) serves with the regiment for the duration.

December 7   A sentry on duty at Fort Moore (Los Angeles) fails to receive a response from a horse or cow that is passing the fort. The sentry calls the entire garrison to arms, but in the confusion of the moment, one of the troops drops a lighted fuse into an ammunition chest. The guard house is destroyed and a few troops are killed.

December 16   The Mormon battalion advances toward Tucson, Arizona, and it is prepared to engage the Mexicans; however, the Mexicans, under Captain Antonio Comaduron, abandon the city. The Mormons enter the city without opposition.

In other activity, Lieutenant Colonel Congreve Jackson departs from Valverde, New Mexico, for El Paso with 200 additional men.

December 18   In Arizona, Colonel P. St. G. Cooke writes to Don Manuel Gandara, governor of Sonora:

> CAMP AT TUCSON, SONORA, Dec. 18, 1846. Your Excellency — The undersigned, marching in command of a Battalion of United States infantry from New Mexico to California, has found it convenient for the passage of his wagon train to cross the frontier of Sonora. Having passed within fifteen miles of Fronteras, I have found it necessary to take this presidio in my route to the Gila. Be assured I did not come as an enemy of the people whom you represent; they have received only kindness at my hands.... Meanwhile, I make a wagon road from the streams of the Atlantic to the Pacific Ocean, through the valuable plains and mountains, rich with minerals, of Sonora. This, I trust, will prove useful to the citizens of either republic, who, if not more closely, may unite in the pursuits of a highly beneficial commerce. With sentiments of esteem and respect, I am your Excellency's most obedient servant, P. ST. G. COOKE, Lieut. Col. of United States Forces.

December 23–24   The Mormon battalion makes camp in Arizona at a village of the Maricopa Indians who are led by their chief, Don Jose Messio.

1848

Lieutenant James Murrell Shackelford (later Union general) enlists in Company L, 4th Kentucky volunteers; however, he does not see any action during the war.

January 2   Nicholas P. Trist is no longer authorized to negotiate peace with Mexico but he continues to do so. The successful negotiations are signaled on February 2n by Mexico and Trist.

January 7   The quartermaster of the Mormon battalion in Arizona takes a measurement of the provisions. He determines only four days' allowance remains. After the battalion encamps, the mules swim to the opposite bank of the river to obtain food. It consists of flag-grass and willows.

January 9   Commodore Robert Stockton's force, which includes Marines, engages the Californians in the Battle of La Mesa at present-day Vernon, California. Stockton's force, including Marines, is traveling on foot but are able to defeat the Californians, who are mounted. The Californians initiate a charge and try to outflank the Americans, but to no avail. They are forced to withdraw and regroup at Pasadena. The Californians are exhausted and give Stockton's force the city of Los Angeles. The Californians sustain 15 dead and about 25 wounded during the fight. Mexican General Flores returns to Mexico.

January 9–10 The Mormon battalion crosses the Colorado River and enters California.

January 12 Captain Rufus Ingalls (later Union general) is appointed assistant quartermaster. Ingalls has participated in action in the New Mexico Territory, where he is brevetted for gallantry while fighting as a member of mounted rifles and dragoons.

January 17 Colonel Cooke, commander of the Mormon battalion, writes in a letter on the day's activities: "I went through their companies this morning; they were eating their last four ounces of flour; of sugar and coffee, there has been none for some weeks."

January 19 During the Taos rebellion in New Mexico, Governor Charles Bent is killed and scalped. The remainder of the family is unhurt. They escape to the house next door. Charles Bent had married Maria Ignacia Jaramillo, who was born in Taos, New Mexico. Later, Kit Carson marries Maria's younger sister Josefa Jaramillo.

January 21–23 The beleaguered Mormon battalion arrives at Warner's Ranchero, the first house they encounter since their arrival in California. They encamp there for several days. On the 23rd, Colonel Cooke decides to advance to join with General Stephen Kearny.

January 22 Marines, part of the garrison at San Jose, California, are besieged by Mexican forces. The siege lasts until 15 February and all attacks are repelled.

January 22 to February 14 Siege of San Jose del Cabo **In Mexico**, a force of about 300 Anishinabe soldiers, bolstered by Yaqui Indians, attack San Jose del Cabo. Initially, they are able to capture some parts of the town, then suddenly, an American warship arrives to bolster the Americans. Reinforcements are landed and the enemy is compelled to lift the siege.

January 23 Commodore Shubrick arrives in Monterey, California.

January 24 Following the murder of New Mexico Governor Charles Bent on the 19th, American traders in the Mora valley are killed. A company of U.S. troops based at Las Vegas, New Mexico, attack the town of Mora. The Mexicans repel the assault; however, the Americans return about one week later and bring artillery with them. The defenders of Mora are compelled to abandon the place. Afterward, the U.S. force from Las Vegas attacks the town of Mora. The assault is repulsed, but a week later, the Americans return with artillery and commence a barrage which forces Mora's valiant defenders to abandon the town. The American troops then proceed to destroy the town.

In other activity, American John Marshall discovers gold in the vicinity of present-day Sacramento. This initiates the California Gold Rush.

January 29 The Mormon battalion arrives within sight of San Diego, California.

January 30 Marines attached to the USS *Dale* are landed at Cochon, Mexico. The town is captured.

January 31 The United States Army, having acted upon charges of General Kearny, conclude a court-martial of Captain John C. Frémont. He is found guilty of several charges, including mutiny and disobeying orders. Frémont is dismissed from the service, but intervention from President Polk changes the situation. Polk agrees with most of the charges but does away with charge of mutiny and restores Frémont to active duty. Subsequently, Frémont resigns.

February 1 The Mormon battalion departs from San Diego, California, and moves to San Luis Rey. It arrives on the 4th.

February 2 The United States and Mexico sign the Treaty of Guadalupe Hidalgo. This treaty cedes Texas, California, vast portions of Arizona and New Mexico to the United States. Portions of Colorado, Wyoming, Nevada and Utah are also annexed. America in return will pay Mexico 15 million dollars, plus an additional 3.25 million for the Rio Grande claims.

February 13 to March 15 U.S. Marines attached to the USS *Cyane* are debarked in the vicinity of Bocachicacampa, Mexico, where they initiate a skirmish with the defenders and quickly seize the town. The Marines and sailors embark on the *Cyane* and in two days will debark again to fight their way through Mexican lines to successfully lift the siege of San Jose, California. There are a couple of additional skirmishes between the Americans and Mexicans but by August 1848, all American troops are gone from Mexico.

February 15 A contingent of Marines and seamen attached to the USS *Cyane* are landed. They fight their way through the Mexican forces to lift the siege of San Jose. In other activity, Marines and seamen attached to the USS *Dale* are land at Cochon, Mexico. The town is again captured. It was seized on 30 January 1848. Elsewhere, Company B, Mormon battalion, is ordered to San Diego to garrison it.

March General Santa Anna departs from Mexico for Jamaica, where he is exiled.

March 9–16 BATTLE OF SANTA CRUZ DE ROSALES General Sterling Price moves into Chihuahua subsequent to the Treaty of Guadalupe Hidalgo having been signed. He demands that the town surrender, but General Trias declines. Noting his refusal to surrender, General Price initiates a siege. However, he also waits for reinforcements. On 16 March, Price attacks and takes the town. Second Lieutenant John Adams (later Confederate general), 1st Dragoons, is brevetted for gallantry and meritorious conduct at this battle.

March 14 Major H. S. Turner arrives at San Luis Rey. He is carrying documents for Colonel Cooke that proclaim himself as "Commander-in-chief of the naval forces." In the same circular, he proclaims General Kearny as "Brigadier General and Governor of California." General Kearny, as governor, issues a proclamation. It "absolved all the inhabitants of California from any further allegiance to the Republic of Mexico." His proclamation also says they might consider themselves as "citizens of the United States, as henceforth Americans and Californians would be one people."

March 15   Colonel Cooke issues orders No. 3:

> Captain Hunter in command of Company B, Mormon Battalion, will march this morning for San Diego. Arrived there, his company will constitute the garison for the protection of the town, and he will take charge of all the defenses of the place. (2) Brevet Lieutenant Stoneman, 1st Dragoons, will march from San Diego with his detatchment of Company C, 1st Dragoons, for this post, on the 17th inst. (3) 2nd Lieutenant Clift will proceed without delay to San Diego. He is appointed to receive there such ordnance as shall be turned over to him by officers of the navy. Lieutenant Clift will perform the duties of assistant commissary of subsistence, and assist the quartermaster at San Diego, and receive such subsistence and other property as will be turned over to him by Major Swords, quartermaster, U.S. A.

April 9   Marines and seamen attached to the sloop USS *Dale* land at Guaymas, Mexico. They capture the town and on their return to the ship, they engage the enemy.

May 8–9   Colonel Cooke dispatches a special detachment, composed of 20 battalion soldiers under Lt. Samuel Thompson, Co. C, to patrol the area near the Rancho de Feliz north of Los Angeles for Indians who are raiding the area. They later encounter the Indians and a heated skirmish erupts. Nathaniel Jones describes the skirmish: "On the 9th, at the mouth of the canyon, we separated, eight of us went up on the mountain to cut off their escape in that way. We attacked them in the head of the canyon. We killed six of them. How many there were in the first place I do not know, but there were some escaped certain. We returned to camp just before night. There were two men wounded, one in the face and one in the thigh, though not dangerous."

May 9   General Kearny arrives at Los Angeles from Monterey. A 21-gun salute is given to him. While speaking to an officer of the Mormon battalion, he says: "Bonaparte crossed the Alps, but these men have crossed a Continent."

May 25   The Mexican Congress ratifies the Treaty of Guadalupe.

May 29   Wisconsin is admitted to the Union as the 30th state.

May 30   Lieutenant Martin Luther Smith (later Confederate general), topographical engineers, is brevetted first lieutenant for his meritorious conduct while making surveys in enemy territory.

June 12   U.S. occupation troops march out of Mexico City. The last American troops leave Mexico from Vera Cruz on 1 August 1848.

July 4   President Polk proclaims the ratification of the Treaty of Guadalupe.

July 9 In California, at Fort Moore, the Californians make use of a local celebration to convince the garrison to depart from the fort. On the following day, a bullfight is held, but the battalion remains in the fort. The Californians also hold a ball and the garrison is invited to attend, but they decline. Mexican General Pico attends the festivities; however, the ruse fails.

August 2 The last of the U.S. forces depart from Mexico at Vera Cruz.

August 14 The United States establishes the Oregon Territory. President Polk signs the bill which admits Oregon as a territory but it does not authorize slavery. Oregon becomes a free territory. The bill was authorized by the Senate on the previous day.

March 3 The Minnesota Territory is organized by the United States.

Henry Sibley (later Union general) who participates in the organization becomes its first governor in 1858 when Minnesota becomes the 32nd state.

March 4 General Zachary Taylor is inaugurated as the 12th U.S. president.

June 3 The Cayuse revolt continues. An American force, including army and militia, has been used to suppress it. On this day, five warriors of the Cayuse tribe, after having been tried and convicted, are hanged. The ongoing revolt does not cease. It continues until 1855 when the Cayuse are finally defeated. They are placed on a reservation with the Umatilla Indians and their lands are confiscated. The white immigrants settle on their lands. *See also,* **November 29** [1847] WHITMAN MASSACRE.

Bibliography

Abbott, John S.C., William Garnett, W.W. Birsall, and Fletcher Johnson. *Beacon Lights of American History*. Philadelphia: Crescent, 1896.

Abbott, Samuel. *The Dramatic Story of Old Glory*. New York: Boni and Liverright, 1919.

Adams, James Truslow. *The Epic of America*. Boston: Little, Brown, 1932.

Allen, William B. *A History of Kentucky*. Louisville: Bradley and Gilbert, 1872.

American Military History: A History of the U.S. Army Colonial Times Through the 1980s. Revised 89. Washington, D.C.: Government Printing Office, 1969.

American Military History (Army Historical Series). Office of the Chief Military History, United States Army. Washington, D.C.: U.S. Government Printing Office, 1969.

Andreas, A. T. *History of Chicago*. Chicago: A. T. Andreas, Publisher, 1884.

Andrews, E. Benjamin. *History of the United States*. New York: Scribner's, 1905.

Bancroft, Hubert Howe. *History of Arizona and New Mexico*. San Francisco: History Company, 1889.

Barnes' History of the United States. New York: A. S. Barnes, 1871–1880.

Belford, Robert James. *A History of the United States*. New York: World, 1888.

Bishop, Farnham. *Our First War in Mexico*. New York: Charles Scribner's Sons, 1916.

Brackett, Albert G. *History of the United States Cavalry*. New York: Harper, 1865.

Brief History of the United States. New York and Chicago: A. S. Barnes, 1871–1880.

Brooks, N. C. *A Complete History of the Mexican War*. Philadelphia: Grigg, Elliot. Baltimore: Hutchinson and Seebold, 1849.

The Builders of a Nation: A History of the United States. New York: Stanley-Bradley, 1892.

Collum, Richard S. *History of the United States Marine Corps*. Philadelphia: L. R. Hamerly, 1890, 1903.

A Complete History of the Mexican War. Baltimore: Hutchinson and Seebold, 1883.

Condon, William H. *Life of Major General James Shields*. Chicago: Press of the Blakely Printing Co., 1900.

Connecticut as a Colony and as a State, Vol. III. Hartford: Publishing Society of the State, 1904.

Connelly, William Elsey. *History of Kentucky*, Vol. 5. Chicago and New York: American Historical Society, 1922.

Cox, James. *My Native Land*. St. Louis: Blair, 1895.

Dawson, Henry B. *Battle of the United States by Sea and Land*, Vol. II. New York: Johnson Fry, 1857.

Dillon, John B. *A History of Indiana*. Indianapolis: Bingham and Doughty, 1859.

Dimitri, John. *Lessons in the History of Louisiana*. New York, Chicago and New Orleans: A. S. Barnes, 1877.

Ellsworth, Captain Harry A. *One Hundred Eighty Landings of U.S. Marines, 1800–1934*. Washington, D.C.: Historical Section, United States Marines Corps, 1934.

Farmer, Silas. *The History of Detroit and Michigan*. Detroit: Silas Farmer, 1884.

Frost, John. *The American Generals*. Hartford: Case Tiffany, 1850.

Frost, John. The History of Mexico and Its Wars. New Orleans: Armand Hawkins, 1882.

Frost, John. *The Mexican War and Its Warriors*. New Haven and Philadelphia: H. Mansfield, 1850.

Frost, John. *Pictorial History of Mexico and the Mexican War*. Philadelphia: Charles Desilver; Claxton, Remsen and Haffelfinger; J. B. Lippincott. Boston: Nichols and Hall, 1871.

Frost, John. *Remarkable Events in the History of America*, Vol. II. Philadelphia: J. and J. L. Gihon, 1852.

Fry, J. Reese. *Life of General Zachary Taylor*. Philadelphia: Gregg, Elliott, 1848.

Goodrich, S. G. *A Pictorial History of the United States*. Philadelphia: J. H. Butler, 1874.

Grant, Ulysses S. *Personal Memoirs of U. S. Grant*. New York: Charles L. Webster, 1886.

Halsey, Francis W. *Great Epochs in American History*, Vol. 7. Funk and Wagnalls, 1912.

Hannings, Bud. *Portraits of the Stars and Stripes*, Vol. 1. Glenside, PA: Seniram.

Hawthorne, Julian. *The History of the United States, 1492–1910*. New York: P. F. Collier, 1910.

Headley, J.T. *The Lives of Winfield Scott and Andrew Jackson*. New York: Charles Scribner, 1852.

A Historical Souvenir of El Dorado County, California. Oakland, CA: Paolo Sioli, 1883.

History of Pottawattamie County, Iowa. Chicago: O.L. Baskin, 1883.

Jenkins, John S. History of the War Between the United States and Mexico. Aubern: Derby, Miller & Co., 1849.

Johnson, Frank W. *A History of Texas and Texans*, Vol. 1. Chicago and New York: American Historical Society, 1916.

Ladd, Horatio O. *History of the War with Mexico*. New York: Dodd, Mead, 1883.

Late Mexican War. New York: 1850.

The Life and Public Service of General Zachary Taylor. Boston and New York: Houghton Mifflin, 1922.

Mabie, Hamilton Wright. *A New History of the United States*. Philadelphia: U.S. International Publishing, 1898.

Mansfield, Edward D. *The Life of General Winfield Scott*. New York: A. S. Barnes, 1852.

Mansfield, Edward D. *The Mexican War: A History of its Origin*. New York: A. S. Barnes; Cincinnati: H. W. Derby, 1851.

McElroy, Robert McNutt. *The Winning of the Far West*. New York: Knickerbocker, 1914.

The Mexican War and its Heroes. Philadelphia: Grigg, Elliot, 1849.

The Military Services of Lt. General Winfield Scott. New York: N.C. Miller, 1862.

Miller, Francis Trevelyan. *America, Land That We Love*. New York: Search Light, 1915.

Miller, William M., and John H. Johnson. *Chronology of the United States Marine Corps, 1775–1934.* Washington, D.C.: Historical Branch, G-3 Division Headquarters, U.S. Marine Corps, 1970.

Morton, J. Sterling. *Illustrated History of Nebraska,* Vol. II. Lincoln: Jacob North, 1907.

Muzzey, David Saville. *An American History.* Boston, New York, Chicago, London: Ginn, 1920.

Neeser, Robert W. *Historical and Chronological History of the United States Navy, 1775–1907.* New York: Macmillan, 1919.

Neff, Jacob K. *The Army and Navy of America.* Lancaster, PA: John H. Pearsol, 1853.

Owen, Charles H. *The Justice of the Mexican War.* New York: G. P. Putnam's Sons: The Knickerbocker Press, 1908.

Perry, Oran. *Indiana in the Mexican War.* Indianapolis: Wm. B. Burford, State Printing and Binding, 1908.

Porter, Admiral David. *Memoir of Commodore David Porter.* Albany: J. Munsell, 1875.

Powell, William H. *Officers of the Army and Navy.* Philadelphia: L. R. Hamersly, 1893.

Quisenberry, Anderson Chenault. *General Zachary Taylor and the Mexican War.* Frankfort: Kentucky State Historical Society, 1911.

Rives, George Lockhart. *The United States and Mexico, 1821–1848,* Vol. II. New York: Charles Scribner's Sons, 1913.

Robarts, William Hugh. *Mexican War Veterans.* Washington, D.C.: Brentanos, 1887.

Roscoe, Theodore. *This Is Your Navy.* Annapolis, MD: Naval Institute Press, 1950.

Scott, Winfield. *Memoirs of Lt. General Winfield Scott.* New York: Sheldon, 1864.

Semmes, Raphael. *Service Afloat and Ashore During the Mexican War.* Cincinnati: William H. Moore, 1851.

Shea, John Gilmary. *A Child's History of the United States.* New York: Hess and Davitt, 1872.

Shoemaker, Floyd C. *The Missouri Historical Review,* Vol. 8. The State Historical Society, 1919.

Siefring, Thomas A. *History of the Marines.* Secaucus, NJ: Bison, Chartwell, 1979.

A Sketch of the Life and Character of Gen. Taylor. New York: S. French, 1847.

A Sketch of the Life of Com. Robert F. Stockton. New York: Derby and Jackson, 1856.

Smith, Isaac. *Reminisces of a Campaign in Mexico.* Indianapolis: Chapman and Spann, 1848.

Spears, John R. *The History of Our Navy, 1775–1897,* Vol. 1. New York: Charles Scribner's, 1897.

Speer, John. *Life of Gen. James H. Lane.* Garden City, Kansas: John Speer, 1896.

Spencer, J.A. *Complete History of the United States of America.* Benson J. Lossing. Philadelphia: William T. Amies, 1878.

Stephenson, Nathaniel W. *Texas and the Mexican War.* New Haven: Yale University Press, 1921.

Stevens, Walter B. *Centennial History of Missouri,* Vol. II. St. Louis, Chicago: S. J. Clarke, 1921.

Strother, D.H. *Illustrated Life of General Winfield Scott.* New York: A.S. Barnes, 1847.

Stubbs, Mary Lee, and Stanley Russell Connor. *Armor-Cavalry, Part 1: Regular Army and Army Reserve.* Washington, D.C.: Office of the Chief of

Military History United States Army, 1969.

Thorpe, T. B. *Our Army at Monterey.* Philadelphia: Carey and Hart, 1848.

Tomes, Robert. *Battles of America by Sea and Land*, Vol. 2. New York: James S. Virtue, 1878.

Victor, O. J. *Winfield Scott, Commander-in-Chief: Life and Military Civic Services.* New York: Eadle, 1861.

Warner, Ezra J. *Generals in Blue.* Baton Rouge: Louisiana State University Press, 1964.

Warner, Ezra J. *Generals in Gray.* Baton Rouge: Louisiana State University Press, 1959.

Wilcox, Cadmus M. *History of the Mexican War.* Washington, D.C.: Church News Publishing Co., 1892.

Wood, Clement. *A Complete History of the United States.* Cleveland: World, 1935, 1941.

Index

194

Index

E
404
„H36
2014